PRAGUE

PRAGUE
FIN DE SIÈCLE

Petr Wittlich

EVERGREEN

EVERGREEN is an imprint of Benedikt Taschen Verlag GmbH

© for this edition: 1999 Benedikt Taschen Verlag GmbH
Hohenzollernring 53, D–50672 Köln

original French edition published by Flammarion
© Flammarion, Paris, 1992
under the title "Prague fin de siècle"
Photographs by Jan Malý

English translation: Maev de la Guardia
Cover design: Claudia Frey, Cologne

Printed in Portugal
ISBN 3–8228–6530–3

Contents

Introduction

To say that Prague is at the heart of Europe is not merely stating an obvious geographical fact. Set right at the centre of the European continent, the city has been the point of convergence, and the melting pot, of an immense variety of religious, philosophical, artistic and social currents flowing in from all points of the compass. It has been a crossroads on many occasions in its history; at some times it has benefited, at others it has suffered.

Under the reign of the emperor Charles IV in the fourteenth century, Prague became "a second Rome" and subsequently the cradle of the pre-Reformation Hussite heresy. Two centuries later, under Rudolph II, Prague had become the southern capital of Mannerism, and was the city where Kepler made his brilliant calculations based on the discoveries of Copernicus, as well as the magical city of alchemists, humanists and adventurers. It was the source of the mysterious Jewish Golem legends, the site of confrontation between the hegemonic ambitions of Protestantism and newly revived Catholicism, and the birthplace of the Thirty Years' War that was to devastate Europe. And three centuries later, it was where the most terrible war of modern times erupted.

The Czech nation that over a thousand years ago founded Prague – also called the "head of the kingdom" – has always considered the city the natural centre of the country. This is where government and decision-making bodies were centralized, and it was at the city gates that the kingdom lost its sovereignty after being defeated at the Battle of the White Mountain in 1620. Bohemia, whose population consisted of a chequered mosaic of different ethnic origins congregated along the course of the Danube, became firmly absorbed into the Hapsburg Empire. It was not until the nineteenth century that the Czechs, carried along by the democratic and nationalist currents that were sweeping over the whole of Europe, reasserted themselves as a people; Prague became the centre of a nationalist struggle that was to culminate in independence in 1918.

National culture played a pivotal role from the beginning of this rebirth of Czech identity, especially as political censorship increasingly relaxed. In the initial

Jan Preisler, *The Lady and the Knight,* 1905. Oil on canvas, 74 x 100 cm. Prague, National Gallery (Národní Galeri).

stages this consisted mainly of reviving the Czech language and rallying the elite to its support; then, in the second half of the nineteenth century, the consolidation of the power of Czech society – essentially of an economic order – came to be reflected in music, the plastic arts and architecture. The Prague National Theatre, a magnificent edifice built by public subscription, became the symbol of this cultural renascence; after being destroyed by fire shortly after its inauguration in 1881, it was very quickly rebuilt and richly decorated. The city, which had been administered by Czechs since 1860, was studded with great monuments and prestigious cultural institutions. These included the Rudolfinum, which housed a large concert hall and a gallery where art exhibitions were held from 1883 onward, and the National Museum, whose majestic architecture closed the perspective of the famous Wenceslas Square in 1890. These monumental Neo-Renaissance buildings by the architects Josef Zítek and Josef Schulz were the embodiment of Prague's new national dimension.

The force behind these developments found its fullest expression in the plan for the reconstruction of the city centre, which was drawn up in the 1880s and was finally approved and executed in the early years of the twentieth century. This reconstruction, though criticized for its brutal treatment of Prague's historical heritage, was characterized by the vitality of the modern era and was necessary for the healthy growth of the city. This determination to rebuild enabled a new decorative style to emerge and flourish, and eventually to symbolize the transformation of the whole environment of Prague. The architecture of that period reads like an anthology of the upheavals taking place in Prague society, whose growth was rooted in social and economic change and was reflected above all in its political and cultural development.

Czech nationalism intensified rapidly during the second half of the nineteenth century, bringing in its wake a particularly strong reaction from the German population in Prague. Here, nationalist conflicts were for a long time veiled under what was referred to as "regional patriotism", whose partisans in Bohemia came essentially from an aristocracy that wielded enormous influence in cultural matters. However, in the 1860s, unlike the Hungarians, the Czechs were unable to obtain a "legislative arrangement" between the Kingdom of Bohemia and Austria. This accelerated centrifugal forces among the various ethnic units that made up the Hapsburg monarchy. At this point it was the bourgeois political parties that acted as the mainspring behind the movement.

For a long time Bohemia was represented within the Empire by the "Old Czech" party under the leadership of František Ladislav Rieger, a lawyer who enjoyed tremendous popularity for his talent as a speaker and for the role he played as the representative of the Czech nation at the constituent assembly meeting that was convened in Kroměříž in 1848. The party aspired to establish a new footing for the Czechs and for the Kingdom of Bohemia within the framework of the constitutional monarchy, but its efforts were not well received in Vienna, which viewed the pursuit of Slav identity with suspicion. The Old Czechs' ineffectiveness paved the way for the emergence of a far more radical opposition, embodied in the "Young Czechs", who were determined to obtain satisfaction for their nationalist demands. After defeating the Old Czech representatives in 1890, they went on to total victory in the Empire Council elections the following year.[1]

At the same time as the Young Czechs were gaining ground, a historical and literary polemic was raging in Prague. This had arisen in 1886, when two university professors, Jan Gebauer and Tomáš Masaryk, intellectuals belonging to the "realist" tendency, published an article in the periodical *Atheneum* in which they made a devastating attack on the authenticity of two respected historical texts, the *Rukopis Královédvorský* (Manuscript of Králové Dvur) and the *Rukopis Zelenohorshý* (Manuscript of Zelená Hora). These works, which until then had been considered masterpieces of early medieval Czech poetry, were shown to be forgeries made at the beginning of the nineteenth century with a view to satisfying both Romantic minds steeped in Ossianic ballads and the needs of the "patriotic" cause. During the course of the nineteenth century these texts had become an integral part of the ideological repertoire of Czech art. In 1881, the crowning event marking the inauguration of the new Palacký bridge, one of the most prestigious constructions undertaken in Prague, was a sculpture competition in which participants such as Josef Václav Myslbek were still working under the inspiration of these manuscripts. The bitter debate stirred up by Gebauer and Masaryk's publication lent greater strength to a new critical trend leaning toward the pur-

The French balloons at the Prague jubilee exhibition, 1891.

down in negotiation of the "Vienna Articles" regarding power-sharing arrangements among the various nationalities, the German liberals refused to take part. This meant that the exhibition, which was inspired by Slav solidarity and French Republican ideas, focused on the promotion of the economic, cultural and especially industrial achievements of the Czech nation alone. It is easy to understand that Franz Josef attended the exhibition with little enthusiasm. After having postponed the event several times, he immediately counterbalanced his visit (one of the last the Emperor ever made to Prague) by another one to the town of Liberec, whose sympathies lay with the Germans.

All these events show how the increase in national sentiment was transforming the Czech political landscape. Seen from present-day perspectives, these developments seem to have followed a tortuous path marked by a succession of acute crises and periods of relative calm. One crisis broke out after the parliament's rejection of the "Vienna Articles" in 1893; from then onward it was essentially students and working-class youth, far more radically inclined since the Jubilee Exhibition, who adopted a militant stance on the Czech question. When demonstrations took an anti-dynastic turn in September 1893, a state of siege was proclaimed in and around Prague, and in February of the following year sixty-eight young radicals, known under the collective name of Omladina (Youth), were given sentences of up to eight years in prison in order to dissuade others contemplating revolutionary action. Among them was the poet and journalist Stanislav Kostka Neumann, who was later to become an anarchist and a "Satanist".

During the 1890s, the Young Czechs, who now represented the absolute political majority, considered themselves the true spokesmen of the "united" Czech nation. They were liberal democrats who were in favour of extending the right to vote, and found themselves for a time at the head of the liberal movement throughout the whole of Austria. As they grew into a powerful political party, however, their radicalism moderated to the point where, under the authority of the pragmatic Josef Kaizl, they left the opposition and began negotiations with the Austrian prime minister, Kazimierz Badeni. These negotiations led to a decree guaranteeing parity of the Czech and German languages within the administration of the Kingdom of Bohemia beginning in 1897. But the decree met with vigorous opposition

suit of truth, and which refused to adhere to the Romantic national mythology propounded by the Old Czechs.

The Young Czechs' proposal to create a Greater Prague on the model of Greater Vienna, a proposal advanced in the inaugural speech of the new Empire Council, also exemplified the renewal of Czech thinking and action. This idea of unifying the centre of Prague with the expanding suburbs was to be thwarted by the categoric veto of the Austrian administration right up to the end of the monarchy.

Also indicative of the increasing political influence of the Young Czechs was the great Jubilee Exhibition held in 1891, which commemorated the centenary of the exhibition organized to celebrate the coronation of King Leopold II. This exhibition was originally intended to reflect a purely local patriotism, involving Czechs and Germans alike, but in 1890, after the break-from German nationalists in the parliament as well as among the population at large, and it was revoked. The situation deteriorated abruptly. Nationalist hysteria reached its peak in 1897 when, after several incidents of brawling in the parliament, during which knives were drawn, a pro-German demonstration in Vienna forced Badeni to resign. Violence immediately broke out in Prague, leading to three deaths, and a state of siege was once again proclaimed.

These events reflected the extreme political and social fragility of the Austro-Hungarian Empire, which was exacerbated by the intervention of yet a third party in the friction between Czechs and Germans: the central authority of the Austrian monarchy. It was in the latter's interest to mollify the nationalists' altercations, but its efforts at compromise inevitably brought the monarchy into conflict with both sides. Its role as arbiter was all the more precarious as the current government was dominated by a German conservative majority; the monarchy's inability to gain the confidence of either of the two factions doomed its policy to failure.

Nevertheless, among the high officials in the central authority, some, more aware than others of the true nature of the situation, made an attempt to break the deadlock. They avoided aggravating the nationalist conflict and gave priority to economic and cultural matters. Ernest von Koerber, prime minister from 1900 to 1904, was one of these men. He succeeded in counteracting Czech opposition by a judicious application of funding, especially for cleaning up the Prague city centre. Convinced that the social climate could be improved by a new cultural policy with a more cosmopolitan, universal outlook, Koerber took the approach of a "modern-day" statesman. This involved, among other things, support for the artists who rallied to the Vienna Secession (as Carl Schorske has pointed out), although the limitations of this particular idea were quickly made apparent with the scandal created by Gustav Klimt's murals for the University of Vienna. The Vienna Secession had far less success in painting than in architecture and the applied arts, where it was supported by the Viennese professor of architecture, Otto Wagner.

The Czechs benefited from the prime minister's cultural offensive, and in 1901 Prague saw the foundation of its Modern Art Gallery, while the Prague School of Applied Arts received Koerber's support for its partici-

pation in the Universal Exposition in Paris (1900) and the World's Fair in St. Louis (1904). During the same period, two eminent representatives of Czech culture, the composer Antonín Dvořák and the poet Jaroslav Vrchlický, were appointed members of the Chamber of Lords in Vienna. It was also under Koerber's government that the emperor Franz Josef made his next-to-last visit to Prague.

Koerber's pragmatism was also a response to the public's weariness with the sterile debates being pursued in parliament. In some areas participation in the 1901 elections failed to reach even fifty per cent. This lack of interest reflected the extreme diversity of the population of the Empire and the fact that behind the nationalist conflicts that stood at centre stage there lay a society for whom this was not the most important political debate. Certain large groups were either excluded from this issue, or excluded themselves. The working class, who were under-represented in the parliament, shared the Social Democrats' lack of interest in the nationalist conflicts, which they dismissed as "historical bric-a-brac", and during the 1890s even the intelligentsia distanced themselves from these quarrels. The concept of a "national party" as the sole representative of a nation began to lose its meaning, as a plethora of new political parties with a largely professional base emerged around 1900, changing the lineaments of "national" political life.

The radical fervour that had gripped intellectuals in the early 1890s soon abated. Their main spokesmen declared themselves dissatisfied with traditional politicking, and began to search for a different, less hidebound and more idealistic approach. In 1894 Tomáš Masaryk, a university professor at that time, published his highly influential *The Czech Question*. Here he analysed the political crisis, which he attributed to the errors of the liberals in power, criticizing them for their relativism and excessive pragmatism, which fostered a spirit of dilettantism and superficial eclecticism. Masaryk, who had already broken with the Young Czechs, felt that it was high time to give serious thought to "Czech specificity" and the nation's mission within Europe.

Masaryk was one of the turn-of-the-century moralists who denounced the evils of capitalist "materialism"

Stained-glass window, post-1900. Prague New Town (Náplavní 7).

and called attention to the decadence of modern civilization. He had been an avid reader of Max Nordau, the best known of such thinkers, and had particularly appreciated one of his works published in 1883, *Die konventionellen Lügen der Kulturmenschheit* (The conventional lies of our civilization). However, Masaryk focused his attention less on the analysis of contemporary society than on the remedies necessary to cure its evils, and hence went further than Nordau and his concept of solidarity. Masaryk's main concern was with the individual, whom he urged to seek out his own identity through introspection. He criticized the idea of social evolutionism and expressed the desire that people, and especially nations, be able to weather the twists and turns of history and eventually rediscover their own essential identity which, in his opinion, remained unaltered. According to Masaryk, each nation had a different role to play in "the universal plan of Providence", and attempting to imitate others would only prevent a nation from fulfilling its own true vocation. He was convinced that the Czech nation could find its vocation by embodying the "humanist ideal": the alliance between man and Faith. This had already been demonstrated to some extent during the Reformation, with the Czech Brethren's rejection of violence and their insistence on the power of the spoken word. Masaryk felt that this path still lay open, as long as the Czech soul remained free from corruption by amoral liberalism. He saw man's pursuit of moral law as a difficult unremitting spiritual and cultural task, opposed to violent revolution. This meant that he refused not only to bend before the blind forces of destiny, but also to seek accommodation with the "demands of the times". In his view, evolution itself was the offshoot of human will and thinking. Development depended on the character of the individual. Masaryk's outlook was not pessimistic with regard to his contemporary world: progress was possible if mind held sway over matter; the ethics of this world could be improved through man's determination and effort.

Although *The Czech Question* met with an unfavourable reception from politicians, the book was a great success among the Czech intelligentsia. The writer Josef Svatopluk Machar called Masaryk's thinking a "true Czech philosophy", and the young literary critic František Xaver Šalda, soon to become the key figure in modern Czech culture, was highly enthusiastic about

František Xaver Šalda in the 1890s.

Masaryk's ideas, which were to guide him throughout his life: "[His is] the creation of a new moral culture, the discovery of a new style of life in a time when all that was great and rooted in the past is dead, and has been replaced by nothing new. Even persons of quality have become antiquarians who exhibit styles of olden times in museum showcases, rearranging them and dusting them off – and it is they who should be inventing and creating a new mode, when the masses are living a styleless existence in a grey world without beauty or joy."[2] Young Šalda's enthusiasm, along with Masaryk's lofty moral thinking, signalled a rejection of latter-day historicism* and the birth of a new decorative style in the plastic arts.

---

* Historicism should be understood as the awareness of a national identity, and its reinforcement by the use of the country's heroes, legendary figures, military achievements and mythical history to explore and appropriate its shared past. This approach is distinct from that of historical eclecticism, which was based on references to the past and adoption of forms borrowed from it, but without involving any national consciousness.

In Bohemia it is traditional to underline the moral aspect of culture (the aesthetician Miroslav Tyrš had this in mind when he founded Sokol, the Czech national association for physical culture, on the same principle as the Greek *kalokagathia*). During the 1890s, the representatives of the younger generation rose up in protest against the total abandonment of moral considerations in cultural and political activity. Their convictions were summarized in the *Czech Modernist Manifesto,* many of whose ideas were borrowed from Šalda. They rejected the Young Czechs' populism and stereotyped discourse, and bitterly criticized the violence of both Czech and German nationalism. They raised the issue of the working classes and demanded access to cultural and social life for women, as well as universal suffrage. In a rejection of fleetingly fashionable ideas ("Realism the day before yesterday, yesterday Naturalism, today Symbolism and Decadence, tomorrow Satanism and Occultism"), the idea of true modernism was to cultivate the individual as a whole, real entity, rather than dealing with an "abstract mass". "We want truth in art, not the truth that photographs things from the outside, but the honest inner truth that can only be known to its bearer – the individual person."[3]

The manifesto was signed by Šalda and a number of young politicians, by the literary critic F. V Krejčí, and by writers and poets like the naturalists Josef Svatopluk Machar, Vilém Mrštík and J. K. Šlejhar, the lyrical poet Antonín Sova, and Symbolists such as Otakar Březina. However, these men did not constitute a homogeneous group, for their only common denominator was their moral enthusiasm for the principles involved, and they all went on to follow their own separate paths.

In the early 1890s, the young Czech literary generation nonetheless rallied together around a common theme … criticism of the previous generation, associated with the prestigious periodical *Lumír,* and in particular, with the poet Jaroslav Vrchlický, its most brilliant representative. Vrchlický was a prolific author (his works include some 270 cycles of epic and lyrical poetry and numerous translations, mainly from Latin literature), whose rich post-Romantic imagination and mastery of language earned him admiration little short of idolatry – to which his vanity made him easy prey. In addition to his teaching activities, Vrchlický assumed a number of important functions and was awarded many official honors. His notorious lack of sensitivity to new

František Kupka, cover of *Pêle-Mêle*, a collection of poems by J. S. Machar, Prague, 1903.

poetry, and indeed to the younger generation in general, made him in their eyes the representative of the empty rhetoric, canting historicism, dilettantism and eclecticism that they were attacking in the name of artistic truth – even though this meant ignoring his very real merits, including his status as the first to "open the windows onto Europe".

This conflict grew increasingly acrimonious and eventually touched on a sensitive issue, that of moral principles. The polemic actually had been sparked in 1893 by *Lumír,* when it parodied the poetry of Jiří Karásek and Otakar Březina, considered by the periodical's editor, Josef Václav Sládek, as the poetry of souls

St. Adalbert's Church, 1904–1905. Libeň, Rudé armády. Arch.: Matěj Blecha.

envenomed by spleen, the weed of melancholy that poisons all Czech youth.[4] From then on the question of Decadent art was firmly on the agenda.

Czech decadent literature was undoubtedly inspired by Western European, and especially French, literary efforts. But it was also bound up with one of the fundamental questions raised earlier, in the 1880s: Could great modern literature, and modern poetry in particular, be created in the Czech language? The Czechs, who were constantly under pressure from the comparison of their nation's cultural level with that of the Germans, sought models elsewhere, particularly in France. This led to their acquiring and assimilating so great a know-

ledge of French literature that some of them, like the poet Jaromír Borecký, became outstanding experts on the subject. Vrchlický himself, as the author of a series of portraits of French poets (*Profiles of French Poets,* 1887) and a number of translations collected into an anthology (*French Modern Poets,* 1894), was one of their major references. He had translated Charles Baudelaire, Paul Verlaine, Arthur Rimbaud and Stéphane Mallarmé, and was the first to make the French school of decadent poetry known to the young generation. However, Vrchlický's attitude to foreign literature was stamped with the all-embracing encyclopedic approach characteristic of his work as a whole. For him, the poetry produced by other nations provided a vast body of cultural material to be exploited at will within a framework of historicism and with an accent on the Parnassian virtuosity of the verse. He nonetheless deserves credit for having opened new horizons that made it possible to introduce greater flexibility into Czech poetical language.

The young poets' Oedipal-conflict relationship with Vrchlický did not prevent them from being confronted with problems of their own. And they were not simple ones, either. The challenged authenticity of the Královédvorský and Zelenohorský manuscripts had shaken the very foundations of the classical Czech repertoire, rooted in national mythology. Even German writers had been influenced by the powerful Romanticism of its thematic content; but the absolute insistence on truth by the young generation of Czechs meant that as far as they were concerned, that world was now closed to them. They also rejected official Czech historical eclecticism. In 1896 Arnošt Procházka, a representative of Czech decadent art, described the young generation's new direction in an article written for the *Almanach Secese* (Secession Almanach), edited by the young Neumann. According to Procházka, the older generation raised their children to view their contemporaries as decadent by slanting their nationalistic teaching to depict the nation's distant past as radiant, and the present day as weak, dingy and wretched: "We walk with our minds and eyes turned toward the past. [...] So take a man with a subtle mind, a sensitive heart and a noble, delicate, vulnerable soul, a man searching to fulfill a need for what is great, burning and alive, for a source of jubilation, and you will find here every reason for him to feel decadent, a child of times gone by. If this man is an artist, a poet, he will find his way to his true country, the land of dreams; he will take refuge in his vision, and experience in his imagination what reality denies him. He will seek satisfaction in the life of the spirit, and will celebrate all that is great, magnificent, extraordinary, exclusive, unique and refined. In pursuit of his own soul, he will exist with and through it, attaching not the slightest importance to the masses, the common people, fat bourgeois, guides, messiahs and genteel doctors: he will live only through his ideal."[5]

This was written at a time when Czech decadent art was becoming institutionalized. Two years earlier, in 1894, Procházka and the poet Jiří Karásek ze Lvovic had

Apartment building, 1903–1904. Prague Old Town (U Prašné brány, 1–3). Arch.: Bedřich Bendelmayer.

founded the famous *Moderní revue* (Modern Review), which made a considerable effort to introduce both decadent and symbolist authors from other countries into Czech cultural life – not only French authors, but Scandinavian, Italian and English as well. At the same time, Stanisław Przybyszewski, a German-speaking Pole living in Berlin, who had very close ties to the group associated with the review, further enriched some of the Czech decadents' ideas with his concept of "psychological naturalism".

Following a period of incubation around 1890, Czech decadent art entered a second phase marked by the appearence of the *Moderní revue*. Many of the writers who were involved in the first phase of the decadent movement, including the playwright Jaroslav Kvapil, came out afterward in opposition to it. Šalda himself, who as a writer and then influential literary critic had defended decadent art during its early years, now began to revise his position. The question of individualism was the touchstone of this evolution. In April 1895, Šalda ventured a favourable evaluation of the decadent spirit, viewing it ("in the footsteps of Bourget and Nietzsche") as the culmination of active individualism, the expression of a new individual, who was born of the old cultural ethos, but escaped from it by creating a new, autonomous one, a new life. In Šalda's view, the accusation that the spirit of decadence thrived on sickness and suffering was inappropriate. It belonged to an outdated concept of literature as a biological function of social organization, whereas Šalda felt that literature's function was primarily "cerebral". He held that the artist was "a creator, an individual, a genius, one of the high-minded chosen few, who is not merely an adjunct or offshoot of the common multitude, not an emanation or a function of it, but on the contrary, someone who uses the multitude as his material and gives shape to it. The multitude is the intermediary, the wave that transmits life and disseminates it."[6] These are the terms in which Šalda made the distinction between active individualism and egotism in decadent art. Nonetheless, he was aware that it could harbor the danger of egotism: "Decadent literature spreads perfumes too dark and heady, its exuberant blood-flowers breathe suffocating air. It dissipates the most precious strengths of that public who is sensitive to the subtleties of the soul: individualism and character, inner strength, clarity of introspection and unwavering, vigorous determination."[7] Decadent art, for Šalda, was "too much an art". In other words, its intoxicating power could overwhelm active individualism.

No such assessment could possibly have been acceptable to true decadents like Karásek and Procházka, and they refused to be associated with the *Czech Modernist Manifesto* for this reason. In their view, individualism was fundamentally opposed to the demands of democratic collectivism. The work of the poet Karel Hlaváček best expressed this aristocratic esteem for the place of individual creativity in modern society, with its emphasis on the artist's exceptional character. Hlaváček, indis-

putably the most talented representative of this tendency in Czech decadent literature, died an early death from tuberculosis in 1898.[8] Notwithstanding, his critics' irony and intransigence did not prevent him from creating what Miloš Marten, one of his successors in the *Moderní revue* group, called a poetic style that generated "a new outgrowth of lyrical inspiration". The strange musicality of his poems was often produced by the monotonous repetition of words, with shifts of meaning suggested by rhythmic changes. But until the advent of the Czech Surrealists in the 1930s, there was little understanding of this extraordinary echolalia, which plunged the imagination into the depths of the unconscious.

Not all of the other decadent artists around *Moderní revue* possessed such a delicate and intense poetic sensibility. This lack was often compensated for by the use of strange accessories and mysterious effects, and sometimes also the violation of sexual taboos. They took over the historicism which Procházka criticized in the *Almanach Secese* in their own way, by totally reversing it: their heroes, who were frequently from old families and often suffering from some kind of mental disturbance, wandered like ghosts in the dim twilight atmosphere of an old decaying city. Although never mentioned by name, this city was obviously Prague, victim of centuries of tragic history, whose patina of historical wear thus echoed the sad destiny of the writers' protagonists. To a critic like Šalda, these works were a patent indication that Czech decadent art inclined toward the kind of dilettantism that looked no further than history, "which knows and copies ten dead styles but never manages to find the eleventh, its own, new, personal style, and possesses no world outlook of its own. [...]"[9]

The split that emerged at the beginning of the 1890s reached its height at the end of the decade, at the same time as a spate of ruthlessly acrimonious personal conflicts. These polemics are of interest today, in that they show the evolution within young Czech literature that led to the formation of two different artistic approaches, each of which exerted an influence on Czech culture until the turn of the century. The conception represented by *Moderní revue* was exclusive, based on a categorical refusal to contemplate any kind of accommodation with vulgar reality. Where such an accommodation did occur in certain decadent works, it invariably involved the suffering and ruin of an exceptional individual.

The opposing concept, with Šalda its most eloquent spokesman, stressed the positive aspect of the encounter between art and reality. This encounter was considered to be a passionate duel in which the victorious party would be the one that presented the world with the union of form and content. Šalda formulated this concept in 1890, in his first major article entitled "Synthetism in the New Art", written in response to those who qualified his work as "decadent".[10] Its starting point was a criticism of Naturalism and of the attempt, especially by Zola, to provide an exact description of social reality. Šalda believed that, given the diversity of human perception, this was impossible. He felt it was far more important to examine the new mood in modern poetry, which was characterized by an almost mystical attraction to the unknown. Science, with its analytical reasoning, had turned in on itself and was concerned solely with appearances, not the essence of things. This explained why a spiritual reaction had sprung up in art, infused with a strange, anxious concern for the soul – its sense of mystery, its preoccupation with the destiny of the individual and of the world at large, its meditation on the sorrowful present, its vision of a better future – as well as for the symbolization of pure ideas. With regard to the latter, Šalda pointed out that the aim was not Symbolism, but Synthetism. Henceforth, the Symbolism only recently advocated by modern French poetry and its most illustrious exponent, Mallarmé, gave way to Synthetism, the theory of which Šalda attempted to explain, quoting the "estopsychology" expounded by Émile Hennequin, Charles Morice, Camille Mauclair and Rene Ghil. He viewed Symbolism as what Kant called the "hypotyposis" of pure ideas, and Synthetism as "concrete symbolism", or the intuitive expression of the inner union of sensation and essence. This explains why Synthetism ran counter to any kind of formalism. Its style was evocative because it revealed the very process of artistic creation.

Šalda did not think of Synthetism as a programme or a school of literature, but rather as a goal to encourage the creative writer to concentrate his strength, in order to, as Goethe had already dreamed of doing, "penetrate and embrace the One and All". Even if the ultimate aim of Šalda's exposition of Synthetism was

František Bilek, *Portrait of Otakar Březina*, 1905. Black-and-white chalk drawing. Jaroměříce, O. Březina Museum.

not clear, it nevertheless offered writers the opportunity of joining ranks in a common purpose. In this sense, Synthetism enjoyed great success, not only as a literary approach, but as a universal concept of culture. In the early years of the twentieth century, Šalda wrote a number of important articles on the new style in the plastic and applied arts, in which he was again to refer to the synthetic approach and to reconfirm its validity.

However, the response that Synthetism elicited from Otakar Březina, the greatest Czech poet of the 1890s, was enough to prove its capacity for creative inspiration. Březina's particular place on the Czech literary scene can in some measure be explained by his self-imposed isolation (he lived in the countryside and never became involved in the various polemics raging in Prague's intellectual and artistic circles), but it was still more attributable to the nature of his work, which was rooted in the deep conviction that life on earth was no more than the pale reflection of a cosmic, spiritual reality.

Whether as individuals or as a whole, true enlightenment could only be reached, he believed, through an inner awareness of this higher spiritual universe. Because of this conviction, Březina was invariably considered a mystic, and he was often quoted by the members of the Katoliká Moderna (Modern Catholics) association. Březina refused the offer to join their magazine *Nový život* (New Life) on the grounds that although he was familiar with medieval mystical thinking, his own views, independent of any dogma, also drew inspiration from the results of the modern exact sciences, and his work was concerned only with the esoteric foundations

of religion. In fact, Březina, a great reader of Baudelaire and Schopenhauer, did not consider himself a believer in the true sense of the word.[11]

Březina's early poetic vision also embraced the splenetic melancholy with which the human condition burdens the artist (by virtue of which he was published by the *Moderní revue* press). However, his third book of poetry, *Polar Winds* (1897), in which his poetic universe acquired a maturity in terms of a unity of ideas, metaphors and rhythms, was marked by an optimistic,

FACING PAGE: Apartment building, 1904–1906. Prague Old Town (Na Příkopě 7). Arch.: Jiří Justich and Matěj Blecha.

ABOVE: Detail of the facade.

LEFT: Hotel Central, 1899–1901, detail of the facade. Prague New Town (Hybernská 10). Arch.: Friedrich Ohmann.

Melantrich Street, post-1900. Prague Old Town.

the sculptor František Bílek, discovered in Březina's hymns the fulfilment of his own conception of Christian duty: to follow the example of Christ as the human incarnation of God. Bílek, whom we shall examine in greater detail later, is a good example of the new upsurge in thought and imagination that took place during the 1890s, first in literature and subsequently in the plastic arts: a determined search for objectivation, for embodiment through sight and touch, and a desire to create a new cultural universe. Curious though it may seem, this determination, which was accompanied by an imagination freed of the constraints of ideological and political commitment and the compromises of earlier days, was expressed in concrete terms in real life. Certain images translating this new "modern" frame of mind, suggested by the language of the poets and conveyed by plastic and architectural works, had a direct impact on the environment of the time. In slightly simplified terms, it became apparent that after the 1890s the predominating influence of literature, and especially poetry, was superseded by that of other arts: not only architecture and the plastic arts, but also theatre and music, which had a more marked, more "palpable" cultural influence on life. These were the circumstances that led to the emergence of the "new style" in all cultural spheres: in the arts and in decoration, in books, posters, murals, and in the architecture of monuments and housing. There was a vast expansion of artistic production, reaching significant proportions after 1900, and it gave full expression to every aspect, both positive and negative, of the new cultural ideas.

The initial consequence of this cultural flowering was the transformation of Prague in the Art Nouveau style, which is still clearly visible today. But the consequence of most importance was the establishment of a general trend in cultural and intellectual life that was closely interrelated with the modern "Czech question". At the beginning of the twentieth century, Czech culture created an alternative to nationalist politics. Albeit in a modified, assimilated form, Masaryk's "ideals for mankind" had taken root. With the increasing influence of culture in daily life, militant nationalism gradually faded almost completely away in the face of the desire to ensure active Czech participation in the construction of the modern world in Europe. That the Austrian monarchy failed to adopt these ideas itself, and made no attempt to put them into effect within its

sentimental euphoria, expressed in visions of a cosmic fraternity of mankind. In fact, Březina's "mystic flame" had less to do with abstract philosophy than with the continual development of his imagination. Each of his poems provided a new illustration of spiritual loftiness, with imagery that employed an interplay of language, colour and music to produce a marvellous synesthetic effect. Such imaginative sophistication could never win a large-scale following, and in this respect Březina occupied a unique place in Czech Symbolism comparable to that of Mallarmé in the French movement.[12]

Březina's spiritual symbolism gained fame through the proselytism of a few fervent admirers. One of them, own spheres of activity, is another matter. The fact remains that in the cultural realm conditions were now far more conducive to mutual understanding between nations.

In the nineteenth century the Czechs had been severely traumatized by an oppression that was not only physical, but also ideological. They sought support for their resistance from a number of sources, and the first answer to their appeal came from the Slav community, even though it was still suffering the consequences of Tsarist Russian policies. In 1908 a Slav Congress was held in Prague to commemorate a similar event organized during the 1848 Revolution. The debate centred on the theme of "political Neo-Slavism", which was a component of the "positive politics" imposed within the Young Czech party by its current chairman, Karel Kramář. The idea of a political alliance between the various Slav ethnic groups within the Austro-Hungarian framework ("Austro-Slavism") culminated in the

creation of an organization known as Slav Unity, consisting of representatives of the bourgeois Bohemian parties and of the Slav peoples of the south and the Ukraine. However, this policy conflicted with that of the central government, which preferred to keep a neutral parliament, and it met with opposition from the aristocracy, which had been leading Austria in the direction of a violent settlement of the Balkan question ever since the annexation of Bosnia and Herzegovina in 1908.

A great many Czech artists were inspired by "Neo-Slavism". This was a concept inherited from the Romanticism and mythology of the nineteenth century, as represented by people like Mikoláš Aleš, a popular painter of the National Theatre generation, whose "Secession" was the first instance of the appreciation of folk-inspired naive imagination. Neo-Slavism was also nourished by the themes recurrent in decorative painting at the turn of the century, especially in the

Auguste Rodin with a group of Czech artists at the inauguration of his exhibition in Prague, 1902.

Villa, 1899. Bubenc (Slavíckova 9). Arch.: Gustav Papež.

FACING PAGE

TOP: Doorway decoration, 1908. Vinohrady (Kladská 3).

BOTTOM: Frýda house, 1909–1910. Vršovice (Moskevska 4).
Arch.: Osvald Polívka

LEFT: Detail of the decoration;

RIGHT: Detail of the facade.

work of Alfons Mucha and the series of large canvases that were to make up his "Slav Epic".

However, the Czech intelligentsia's desire to adopt new artistic concepts meant that they paid special attention to the West, particularly France. As the antithesis of the rigid monarchy, France exercised a powerful attraction on the Czech national radicals and liberal democrats, to the point where Rodin's visit to Prague for his 1902 exhibition, which was theoretically a cultural event, took on political overtones and developed into a "national" affair. The sculptor's defiance of social and moral taboos had unusual consequences on the Czech political scene, but that was the way that new ideas and artistic innovations penetrated Czech consciousness and galvanized it into action. The more the Czechs knew about French culture, the more they understood its universalism. They familiarized themselves with the French debates between Naturalism and Symbolism, pessimism and optimism, and with the arguments regarding Decadence and the new Synthetism (which corresponded to the political concept of social "solidarity"), all of which were related to the question of a new style as well as, at a later stage, of Neo-Classicism. Their universalistic concept of culture enabled these Czechs to break out of narrow nationalism and to participate actively and innovatively in the advanced Parisian artistic trends such as Cubism.

This new permeability to European culture also consolidated new exchanges within the Austro-Hungarian intellectual and artistic world. Modern Czech artists were able to appreciate Viennese art, which had been the object of sharp prejudice during the nineteenth century, when a Czech critic like Miroslav Tyrš could condemn Hans Makart as an example of an unhealthy Decadence. Now, the Viennese Secession met with a ready response from Prague, particularly in architecture and the applied arts, thanks mainly to Czech architects who had spent time in the cosmopolitan studio of Otto Wagner, and who had been in contact with German students there. In painting and sculpture, on the other hand, the decorative style of Klimt's work met with opposition from the Czechs, who tended to focus their attention on France.

A new consensus with German artists and writers also took shape within this universalistic conception of culture; Jan Kotěra acclaimed the work of the architect Josef Zasche as an example of modernism, and the

young generation that emerged around 1907 (the year when universal suffrage was established in Austria-Hungary) in the avant-garde group Osma (The Eight) organized joint exhibitions by Czech and German painters. However, these positive examples should not conceal the strong ongoing nationalist rivalry, which occasionally found violent expression in the streets. A state of emergency was again imposed in Prague for a short period in 1908, and this time the modern artists tended to set a good example, even at the risk of antagonizing their public. This was in fact what happened during the controversy that arose in Prague in 1912–1913 over the politically sensitive competition for the monument honoring Jan Žižka ze Trocnov, the national Hussite hero.

The city of Prague itself, where the two communities had lived side by side for a very long time, contributed to calming nationalist rivalries. Rainer Maria Rilke, a shining light of modern poetry, was born and grew up there, and his first collection of work expressed a strong attachment to the strange historical veneer generated by this long cohabitation, as well as a certain affinity with the Czech national renascence. Rilke nevertheless left Prague in 1896. Other German writers did likewise: Gustav Meyrink, the author of *The Golem*, left in 1906, and Franz Werfel in 1912. But the greatest of them all, Franz Kafka, wrote in 1902: "Prague never lets you go. This little mother has claws."[13] He stayed. Kafka never described the magical atmosphere of old Prague in the romantic vein of the Czech decadents, but the psychological climate of the city at the turn of the century powerfully influenced the unique atmosphere he created in *The Trial* and his other works. Kafka's sensitivity to the tension and the emotions concealed beneath the greyness of daily life was all the keener because he was Jewish and aware of belonging to a people who, despite their age-old presence in Prague, had always been confined to the role of observer in local conflicts. In Kafka, observation attained the perfection of vision in a crystal ball. Although his novels and stories appear to be devoid of historical references, they provide an extremely accurate and objective assessment of life in Prague at the beginning of the twentieth century.

Czech ideas about culture were clearly taking a more modernizing approach, but there was no single programme as such. Literature and literary criticism, whose

development during the 1890s has already been outlined, drew their inspiration from a concept of modernity that, despite efforts to establish a synthesis, each school developed along its own lines. It was the elaboration of programmes and the emergence of dissensions that set the tempo of the rather cyclical patterns in Czech culture at the turn of the century.

During the 1890s the general climate of Czech culture was still considerably influenced by a historicism characterized by a syncretic relationship to the culture of bygone days, a predilection for stylistic refinement and a richness of poetical language and decorative form. At the same time as Western thinking and art gradually gained ground in Prague, the problematics of Decadence and Symbolism also came to the fore. Toward the close of the century the new international decorative style, particularly Belgian and French Art Nouveau, fostered the creation of a Czech counterpart. This materialized not only in architecture – which took the lion's share because of the renovation of the centre of Prague – but also in music and especially literature, where it was responsible for a renewal of poetic language.

The beginning of the twentieth century saw the emergence of new and more vigorous artistic concepts. Reinforced by the echoes coming from other world cultural centres, and given impetus by the reception accorded to artists such as Rodin, whose work emphasized the notion of a modern artistic spirituality, these new concepts enabled artists to establish a more subjective relationship between the material and the spiritual. This was the point of departure for the subsequent regeneration of the concept of "national art", in the sense of the glorification of the race, its history and its most eminent figures. The Czech cultural authorities had difficulty confining this vitalistic concept to the framework of national mythology, which explains an important evolution in Czech culture that occurred around 1910. While the synthetic and decadent programmes of the 1890s were still being pursued, the new generation, inspired by the avant-garde concept of Cubism, suddenly set off in a new direction.

All this cultural activity in Prague, which played a crucial role in Czech society, showed the extent to which it was stimulated by the turn-of-the-century environment. It was also seen as reflecting the consciousness of Czech society, a role already fulfilled by music, which was considered to have universal value by outstanding individuals such as Arthur Schopenhauer. Soon this role was also fulfilled by architecture, the plastic and visual arts (particularly theatre, which drew large audiences to both classic and variety performances), and by literature. In every sphere, word and image responded to each other in a mutually enriching way by means of the evocative power generated by a shared "matrix" common to all art forms.

Modern artists felt obliged to take a stand against the deluge of dilettantism that had appeared alongside historical eclecticism. They did so in what was perhaps a reductive manner, not entirely untainted by a certain "primitivism", with the aim of creating a "new style". This desire for purification and a return to the original role and purpose of art were an integral part of the programme. On this score there arose a conflict between, on the one hand, the hard-line decadents and symbolists, who rejected nature and emphasized the importance of the ideal and individuality in art, and, on the other, the vitalists and upholders of the unity of art and life and "art for all", who attributed great importance to nature. This divergence of views lay at the origin of the diversity and flexibility of the "new art", which provided a more favourable terrain for the development of modernism.

While the naturalists and the impressionists were primarily concerned with an objective vision of nature through the sensory stimulation of the eye, the symbolists gave greater weight to the "inner eye" of imagination and fantasy. Nonetheless, these different trends found a common denominator in the decorative style of the time, whose rhythms were a strange combination of symmetry and asymmetry, naturalism and abstraction, the entelechies of natural growth and the psychic force-lines popularized by hypnosis, which were the subject of study by the "new psychology". This spiritual movement, which found expression in ornamentation and geometrization, reflected reality as

Insurance building, Prague, 1903–1905. Prague New Town (Národní trída 7) Arch.: Osvald Polívka. Period photograph.

much as it influenced it, and was undoubtedly the most interesting aspect of the new style, in that it was the nucleus of a modern culture in the process of gestation.

The whole of European civilization was affected by this evolution at the turn of the century. Everyone expressed it in their own way and with their own particular style, depending on where they were. I shall now try to describe in greater detail how this movement developed in Prague.

The 1890s

On the threshold to modernity

The importance of the World Expositions of art, science and culture in the second half of the nineteenth century cannot be underestimated. Organized in the great metropolises of Europe and the United States, the first of these was held in London in 1851. Such events, which were manifestations of national pride in every field, propounded one of liberalism's favourite theses: that progress, and technical progress in particular, was best served by example. In this context, art was conscripted into the service of politics and big industry and found itself propelled out of its usual sanctuaries – museums, art galleries, concert halls and theatres – into the profane eye of the public. Works of art became subject to favourable or unfavourable reaction by a general public whose opinion, often swayed by the press, was not always well informed; whether they were illustrious professors or pupils at the start of their careers, artists could not remain indifferent to the views of the public at large.

The most important aspect of these exhibitions, however, was that they revealed trends in contemporary taste, especially in architecture and the decorative arts, and one can see in them the beginnings of a major reform movement that, with the international Art Nouveau style, was to reach its height at the end of the century.

During the 1890s, Prague was literally obsessed by exhibitions of this kind. First was the jubilee Exhibition of Countries of the Kingdom of Bohemia, which was held in 1891 on a vast site provided by the municipality at the edge of a park near the city – the former royal hunting grounds of Bubeneč. The exhibition occupied 140 buildings, most of them fanciful pavilions erected for the glory of a wide-ranging variety of business enterprises. Each of these demonstrated the high level of Bohemian industrial achievements, and because of their industrial performance, these enterprises had come to be known as the "locomotive" of the Austro-Hungarian empire. Promotion of industrial products went hand in hand with a wide range of public attractions, which drew over two million visitors that year. Among the most successful was a display by the Prague dirigible

FACING PAGE AND ABOVE: Palace of Industry, 1891. Holešovice. Arch.: Bedřich Münzberger.

PRECEDING DOUBLE PAGE: Hotel Evropa, second-floor café, 1903–1905. Prague New Town (Wenceslas Square 25–27). Arch.: Bedřich Bendelmayer and Alois Dryák.

balloon training centre, in which French aviators were invited to take part. There was also an illuminated fountain installed by the Prague industrialist-inventor František Křižík (who designed Prague's first electric tramway); at night visitors were enchanted by jets of water leaping in sprays of colored light over one hundred feet into the darkness.

The greatest triumph was undoubtedly the Palace of Industry, built as the heart of the exhibition. Its dimensions were impressive: 680 feet long, covering a surface of nearly 140,000 square feet. Its gigantic scale had been made possible by new construction techniques whereby traditional masonry was replaced by huge iron arches and glass walls. Although the use of iron as the main material was part of a highly modern concept of architecture at the time, the style in which it was used still bore historical reminiscences – the design of the arches reflected the inspiration of the Gothic groin vault.

The Palace comprised a central section formed by eight supporting arches 82 feet high, set at 125-foot intervals. These rested on four corner-pylons covered with masonry and decorated in an imaginative ornamental style. Above this base rose an open spiral staircase surmounted by the Bohemian crown of King Wenceslas. An appearance of lightness and fragility emphasized the building's mobility: the initial project actually provided for movable wings on each side of the central section to enable the exhibition space to be modified as required.

The architect Bedřich Münzberger was responsible for the overall conception of the building, but it was František Prášil, the chief engineer at the Prague ironworks, who executed the five-hundred-ton central construction. Münzberger had originally envisaged a traditional masonry building for the jubilee exhibition, but with the agreement of the executive committee he subsequently modified the plans in order, in his own words, "to represent modern times in the very materials used in the central building, and also to use the metal construction to obtain greater space, thereby facilitating the arrangement of the objects to be displayed."[1]

The alteration of the project was undoubtedly inspired by the "glass palaces" featured in previous international exhibitions, especially the metal structures at the Universal Exposition in Paris in 1889. Motivations of a practical as well as an ideological nature underlay these modern monuments. In France, both the Hall of Machines designed by Victor Contamin and Ferdinand Dutert and the Eiffel Tower were meant to symbolize the Republican government's scientific and industrial policy, which was measured in terms of the volume of iron production. This urge for representation inspired the Czechs, who were intent on advertising Bohemia's high degree of development within the empire. The small-scale replica of the Eiffel Tower built on Petřín Hill is another indication of French influence.

From then on, modern Czech architecture was governed by one imperative: it had to be functional and contemporary. At the time, the use of iron and glass was considered the most vivid expression of modernity by theoreticians like Prague's Hubert Gordon Schauer, who had already written about this in *Národní listy* in 1890, when the jubilee exhibition was in preparation. The practical advantages of these materials were assessed – glass, for example, permitted maximum lighting for the objects exhibited – and so were their aesthetic virtues: "The glass palace astounds everyone with its lightness, elegance and daring."[2] The most remarkable feature was the work of the glassmakers. It was the first time this type of ornamentation, whose imagery harmonized with the structure itself, was used, and for which rolled glass, produced in Czechoslovakia, was employed.[3] The luminosity of the space had an immediate impact on the public, especially among the younger generation.

For the visitors to the Palace of Industry, these new concepts of space and decoration were appropriate to exhibitions, but elsewhere they remained the exception rather than the rule. Comparisons were not often made with the monumental architecture of public buildings, despite Schauer's provocative criticism of the buildings on Vienna's Rinstrasse, which he attacked vigorously for their eclecticism and lack of vitality.[4] Nevertheless, the Palace remained permanently in the Prague Exhibitions Park, and was employed later to house other major events such as the 1895 Ethnographic Exhibition and the 1898 Architecture and Engineering Exhibition, both of which significantly influenced the younger generation.

The Palace's architecture is not entirely devoid of historical influences, as can be seen in the decoration of the pylons and on the traditional pediment over the main door of the building's entrance. At that time, modernism in architecture was seen as a technical rather than an aesthetic matter, and the presence of ornamentation went unquestioned.

Historicism still dominated thought and taste at the end of the nineteenth century, and all forms of cultural imagination tended to bear both its stamp, and, contradictorily, that of the notion of progress. This paradox of a leap into the future going hand in hand with an obligation to respect history explains the perseverance

The Hanau Pavilion, 1891. Prague (Letenské sady). Arch.: Otto Hieser.

Hanuš Schwaiger, *Saint George*, 1892. Fresco, Průhonice Castle.

Vojtěch Hynais, study for *Judgment of Paris*, 1892. Oil on canvas, 58 x 100 cm. Prague, National Gallery.

of outdated styles in architecture. However, the historical references, although initially clearly defined, gradually blurred as architecture acquired increased freedom and as public access to art became more and more democratic; eventually a general tendency toward eclecticism took hold.

Thus, in the course of the nineteenth century, historicism in art and architecture underwent a certain evolution. The initial period of romantic historicism with its highly coloured patriotic visions of the nation's heroic past was followed by one of "scientific" historicism. After 1850, positivist thinking demanded the archeological study of historical monuments, which often led to renovation work of dubious artistic merit, and encouraged architects to adopt a more systematic approach, seeking their inspiration for new buildings in dictionaries of historical styles. By 1900, historicism in art had entered a third phase, in which some aspects of the earlier romanticism re-emerged and were combined with the eclectic historical models that had been imposed by conservative curators, restorers and publishers during the previous, second period.

This wealth of accumulated knowledge gave rise to the sort of saturation found in late historicism, where a particularly apposite detail often stirred a strong emotional reaction and commanded greater impact than the rest of the work. These kinds of works, by such architects as Josef Zítek in Prague (the National Theatre, the Rudolfinum), drew inspiration from the classics.

Following this came a period during which monumentality gave way to a preference for intimacy and a richness of visual effects, though still confined by the demands of social representation. Some of the small-scale buildings put up for the jubilee exhibition were typical of this "autumn" phase of historicism – for instance, the Principality of Hanatt's pavilion by Otto Heiser, which still exists today. This pavilion was intended to promote the principality's metalwork products, and was designed as an amalgam of decorative mouldings, principally ironwork and lights manufactured in Bohemia. Its style was something between late Renaissance and Baroque, and its mannerism could be seen as an expression of the decadence of historicism. Despite its rampant eclecticism, the building possesses a charm of its own that is enhanced today by its setting in a romantic park.

The picturesque element that was characteristic of contemporary art-lovers' tastes found greater freedom of expression in privately commissioned work. Count Sylva Taroucca, for example, had Jiří Stibral modify his castle in Průhonice, near Prague, in a picturesque manner that involved the creation of an English-style landscaped park that emphasized the neo-romantic look of the place. The painter Hanuš Schwaiger executed a large *Saint George* scene in the courtyard of this castle.

The example of Hanuš Schwaiger is valuable for an understanding of the particular characteristics of late historicism and its development in the direction of Art Nouveau. Born into a cosmopolitan family, he was considered a black sheep because of his desire to become an artist. His teacher in Vienna, Hans Makart, appreciated the originality of his pupil's personality as well as that of his art. He bought Schwaiger's first *Pied Piper of Hammelin,* based on a Nordic folk tale that always fascinated the artist, and which he painted in several versions. The legend of the mysterious flute-player who delivered a rodent-infested town of the pests until the day he was betrayed by the townsfolk, whereupon he made off with all their children, wonderfully symbolized the difficult relationships that existed at the end of the century between artists and middle-class society. In some versions of the painting, Schwaiger managed to depict the tale in a novel manner, by reducing the image to its essential lines and surfaces, and using color as the emotionally dominant chord. Furthermore, the musical nature of his subject led him to render the mysterious sound of the flute by plastic means. With this synthetic use of life, color and form, Schwaiger became the forerunner of the Art Nouveau style.

Schwaiger's favorite genre was the grotesque, which combined naturalism and fantasy. This was already apparent in his *Anabaptists* (1889), representing the siege of the town of Münster in 1534 by a radical sect of the Protestant Reformation that had established a communist theocracy there. Here, Schwaiger's view of history was less concerned with the powerful, famous traditional heroes than with the secondary, somewhat caricatural figures, who symbolized a "second" historical force, one which was present in destruction, fanaticism and desperate rebellion. In a similar manner, Schwaiger brought naturalism and fantasy together in a series of pictures that were inspired by the humble milieu of the common people, which he knew well, having spent almost the entire decade of the 1890s in a gamekeeper's cottage in the Hostýn hills of the Moravian Beskid Mountains. In these works he often depicted encounters between Man and fairy-like characters such as gnomes, water sprites and will-o'-the-wisps. Though these images are humorous, they nonetheless express a definite philosophy, centred on the mythology of the forces of nature that exist outside civilization and its boundaries.

Schwaiger's independence, which earned him great respect, went hand in hand with genuinely innovative work. The cover he did in 1885 for the *Album of Wiesner's Tales* has to be considered the first Czech attempt to bring a fresh approach to the art of illustration, through a combination of the poster genre and a non-descriptive conception. Grotesque and fairy-like figures link the lettering, the images and ornamental stolons in a single, rhythmic entity that, although still unsystematic, already prefigured Art Nouveau style.

In 1887, Schwaiger exhibited some of these works in the Ruch Gallery in Prague, thereafter influencing a younger generation who particularly appreciated his freedom of action. "No one was less easily led than he, and he followed his own inclinations freely."[5] Miloš Jiránek later commented that in Schwaiger's case the man was always greater than the painter, and his artistic activity was only the complementary expression of his world view.

Yet Schwaiger was not to become really well known or appreciated until after 1900 – the official Bohemian art scene in the 1890s was dominated by others. The 1891 jubilee exhibition provided a huge retrospective covering the previous century of Czech plastic art, and it was precisely works from the most recent period that aroused the greatest public interest. This was confirmed by Karel B. Mádl's account of the retrospective in his book commemorating the exhibition. Mádl was second only to Tyrš as the most active and committed of the art critics, who championed the new names in Czech painting and sculpture.[6] In the painting section, the two pictures that drew particular attention were *The Murder in the House* by Jakub Schikaneder and *The Construction of the Wall of Hunger in Prague under Charles IV,* by Emanuel Dítě – two works that corresponded closely to the taste of both painters and public. Dítě, who began his work in the early 1880s while studying in Munich, here renewed ties with the fash-

Hanuš Schwaiger, project design for title-page of the *Album of Wiesner's Tales*, 1885. India ink and watercolor, 24.5 x 17.3 cm. Prague, National Gallery.

ionable historicist genre and brought it up to date with allusions to current social issues and the economic crisis which were affecting Central Europe. Schikaneder's *The Murder,* which was based on a true incident, underscored the trend toward individual social drama. To the public, who viewed the sordid image of a dead woman lying in a small suburban courtyard as the dramatic illustration of a suicide, the title of the painting was misleading. Mádl, however, valued this ambiguity: the public should not be content to take a title at face value, but should analyse and evaluate it in terms of the work's pictorial aspects.

While Mádl respected the public's interest in these works, he also searched the exhibition for other first-class material. He was enthusiastic about the work of Vojtěch Hynais, particularly a sketch for his famous curtain for the Prague National Theatre, made in 1883 to replace Ženíšek's original, which had burned. Hynais was born into a Czech family living in Vienna, and, while attending the Academy of Painting, had frequented the studio of Anselm Feuerbach. A grant enabled him to visit Venice, where he was dazzled by Tiepolo's handling of light, akin to the illusionistic tendency prevalent in French academic painting at the time. He went to live in Paris in 1878, and there gained the esteem of Paul Baudry, who secured his admission to the School of Fine Arts, as a pupil of Jean-Louis Gérôme. Hynais did not return to Prague until 1880, when he took part in the competition for the decoration of the staircase, salon and boudoir of the royal box at the National Theatre. The allegories of Spring, Summer and Autumn that he produced for the occasion won immediate admiration: whereas most of the local artists, although excellent draughtsmen, had a problem with colour, Hynais demonstrated a purely pictorial lightness of touch and inventiveness learnt from his teachers in France.

The situation turned out to be rather more delicate with regard to the stage curtain, which he envisaged as an allegorical *tableau vivant* in the naturalist spirit, to illustrate the national subscription fund launched for the construction of the theatre. This completely baffled the commissioning body, whose horizons were confined to traditional idealism and who were especially doubtful about the predominantly grey and pink colours inspired by late Italian Baroque. After a series of legal complications and a court case that Hynais won, the curtain was finally hung on the sole responsibility of the artist in order to avoid postponing the imminent opening of the theatre season. In the event, the work was very well received by the public, who admired the elegance of the figures and the modern use of colour. Its acceptance represented the triumph of the now unanimous taste for French contemporary art. Indeed, the National Theatre stage curtain was really Prague's first major initiative in the application of a neo-baroque concept to a decorative picture, and announced the Art Nouveau style.

At the jubilee exhibition retrospective show Hynais also exhibited a large painting entitled *Truth*, which he intended to be emblematic of his approach. It depicts a beautiful naked woman emerging from a well, with a mirror in her hand. The painter's model was Suzanne

Valadon, and the well was one that stood in the little courtyard of his new studio in Montmartre.[7] With this work, in which no detail is omitted – not even the garter-marks, which were to draw criticism from a member of the Vienna commission when he applied for a grant to enable him to finish his *Judgment of Paris* – Hynais emerged as a fervent adept of photographic accuracy. Despite negative reactions, his *Truth* won him the Czech Academy of Arts and Sciences Award, with a prize of one thousand gold ducats.

Hynais' fame during this period had grown to such an extent that in 1893 he was appointed professor at the Prague School of Fine Arts, together with Václav Brožík, another Czech celebrity living in Paris, who specialized in large-scale canvases on historical subjects. However, whereas Brožík's visits to the school were few and far between, Hynais moved back to Prague, where the teachers formed a guard of honour to receive him.

Hynais' influence on Czech painting really began with his *Judgment of Paris*, on which he worked in Paris from 1889 to 1893. He was well aware that what he had accomplished in this picture was something totally new. He exhibited the painting in Paris, and sent only the preliminary studies to Prague – deliberately so, it would seem, for these went even farther out on a limb. They showed a new way of perceiving the nude in natural surroundings, in part through the introduction of the technique of "green tints" on skin, which was widely imitated later on. For young Czech painters, this technique became a means of establishing closer links between human figures and nature, one of the basic tenets of Art Nouveau. With this work, Hynais opened the gates to modern art and Impressionism in Bohemia, although, paradoxically, he later came into conflict with their supporters. In 1898 the large picture he showed at the Union of Fine Arts Exhibition in the Rudolfinum had already met with reservations, and Jan Preisler's *Spring* was composed as a reaction to Hynais' themes and technique. Hynais' work, therefore, greatly stimulated his compatriots and his influence even extended to poster art, a medium in which he distinguished himself as much at the jubilee exhibition and the Ethnographical Exhibition as in the field of commercial advertising.

Hynais' hospitality turned his Paris studio into a refuge for Czech artists who had come to spend some time in the world metropolis of art; numerous innovations and a considerable amount of information reached Bohemia via this route. This was how, for example, the sculptor Josef Václav Myslbek, probably the greatest artist of the National Theatre generation, came to owe so much to Hynais. Myslbek's letters to Hynais in Paris bombarded him with questions and requests for photographs of recent French works and other information.

Myslbek visited Paris in 1878, at a time when there was a growing demand for sculpture in France: the French were building public monuments as a means of soothing the traumatic effects of defeat by the Germans. The particular mood of this new pathos, invented by French sculptors to match the circumstances, was expressed perfectly in monumental form, and it so captivated Myslbek that he became its spokesman in Bohemia. This was not a matter of mere imitation, however; the French tragic element found an echo in Myslbek's work because it reflected a similar reaction to the fate of his own people. Myslbek was also fascinated by the technical skill of French sculptors, especially in the rendering of drapery, a technique in which he himself excelled. His favorite theme – the relationship between the body and idealized drapery – was related to a certain extent to the relationship between the body and nature that Hynais had established through the use of coloured light. In both cases, the result was a new poetization of the art object, very characteristic of the 1890s.

Myslbek had become known since the 1870s thanks to his work on a number of monuments in honour of the Hussite national hero Jan Žižka ze Trocnov, which reflected the renascence of both Czech nationalism and the monument form. Later, his contact with French sculpture helped Myslbek perfect his gift for monumental sculpture in this field. The seriousness of his *Dedication,* a sculpture representing a man in a Roman toga with his hands placed on his chest in an altruistic pose, which he made for the attic level of the Vienna parliament, earned him both the admiration of his colleagues and a solid reputation abroad. Its content seemed to express the attitude of the Old Czechs and their desire to realize Palacký's idea of the Austrian State – that is, a moral commitment between the two sides, an idea which was vetoed by Vienna.

Like the Old Czechs on the political front, Myslbek's monumentalism also went through a crisis in the early 1890s. This is visible in his work *Music*, a sculp-

Josef Václav Myslbek, *Music*, second casting, 1892–1894. Bronze, 108 cm. Prague, National Gallery.

ture for which he made several models between 1892 and 1894. His choice of subject clearly indicates his passion for what he considered the greatest of the arts. "Music – the soul – springtime – flowers", he wrote in his notebooks as a sort of programme, which, applied to the sketches, reveals the striking magnitude of an inner conflict. Myslbek initially hesitated between two different ideas for the statue. The first was of literary inspiration, representing a feminine personification of Music, and a tree, here mythicized as the first musical instrument. The tree, symbolizing the relationship between art and nature, bore a set of strings, and the names of great musicians, including Czechs, were inscribed on its trunk. In the second version of the project, the allegorical figure held an ancient string instrument, the small lyre-like Czech *varyto,* and represented "the kiss of consecration" in a way that imbued the action with profound significance.

Sketches for the allegory of *Music* with the tree correspond to themes favoured by the neo-romantic Czech poet, Julius Zeyer, and they occupy a unique place not only in Myslbek's work, but in Czech plastic arts of the 1890s as a whole. Their delicate fragility, achieved through a strong development of line in space, freed them from monumental pathos and reinforced the lyrical quality of their form. The second of the sketches was a more personal vision in which Myslbek introduced drapery that he lightened by the use of hatching, and where the figure's attitude and closed eyes suggested a kind of ecstasy. It foreshadowed the later development of the Czech Secession, which took this sensitivity to greater lengths and expressed it above all in decoration. It is possible that the sculptor drew his inspiration for this version from the decorative sculptures of his contemporaries. Not only could he have learned about them from Hynais – who appreciated the importance of decorative art (he himself painted vases for the Sèvres porcelain manufacturers) – but Myslbek also taught sculpture at the School of Applied Arts in Prague at the time. Whatever the case, these sketches

showed that Myslbek had not been unaffected by Hynais' studies for the *Judgment of Paris,* even though he only drew on them loosely in his work as a sculptor.

This invasion of a new pictorialism into the hitherto unyielding world of Myslbek's work was perhaps related to doubts he had begun to feel about his work. This questioning became apparent in the notes he made for *Music,* where he complained of a contradiction between the "supernatural invisibility" of music that is accessible to everyone "in God and in joy", and the inaccessible "materiality" of plastic art whose means of expression are more limited.[8]

This crisis reached its peak in the autumn of 1894. In attempting to comply with a request from the Grants Committee to lighten the model's drapery (which had been approved earlier), Myslbek made even more severe changes in his programme. He then designed *Swansong,* depicting a reclining female nude listening to the song of a dying swan. The artist made every possible effort to obtain permission to carry out this radically innovative idea, but in vain. *Swansong* was the furthest Myslbek ever went in his relationship with modern currents in poetry and the plastic art. The statue stood halfway between Neo-Romanticism and Symbolism, and dealt with a theme that was common in modern poetry and the plastic arts at the time. Its illusionist quality was characteristic of decadent lyricism, inas-

Josef Václav Myslbek, *Swansong,* 1894. Bronze, h.: 38 cm. Prague, National Gallery.

much as it expressed the idea of death as a passage or a transition, and related it to art.[9]

In the end, Myslbek used a standing figure for his *Music*, clasping the *varyto* and embracing it with a kiss of initiation. But he only completed it ten years later, giving his work solid plastic forms stamped with a lyricism inspired by the idol of his youth, Josef Mánes. Thus, in the iconography of the 1890s, *Swansong* remained no more than a study, one of the incarnations of poetic imagery, which sought a solution to the problem of allegory.

In 1895, Jan Preisler, a young graduate of the school where Myslbek taught, produced a new illustration in charcoal on the themes of Music and Song for the album *Allegorien und Embleme*, published by the Viennese firm Gerlach und Schenk. In counterpoint to the central scene, where a drunken satyr lies on his back, Preisler put Music on the left – a semi-nude female figure gazing sadly toward a distant horizon – and Song on the right. He depicted dying swans singing at the foot of cypress trees in an idealized southern sea-shore landscape, and then ornamented the whole with garlands. Although this composition was intended for the elegance of a salon, the subtle handling of charcoal instilled it with true poetic nostalgia.

For some time the "swansong" theme was the point of convergence for the major figures of two generations – one in full maturity and the other in its youth – whose common feature was their emphasis on poetry. There was, however, a marked difference between them: to Myslbek the "swansong" was very personal, a simple "sweet dream of the giant-maker", as Vrchlický charmingly put it, whereas Preisler's drawing was a project for a mural destined for public exhibition. This was where the two generations took opposite approaches. To the elder, the artist's intimate vision could be expressed only through studies and sketches, while the younger, on the contrary, projected a new sentimentality into public view. It was certainly no accident that almost all the important artists of the "1890s generation" turned out to be major illustrators, graphic artists or painters who executed decorative work for the new architecture.

These artists did not open themselves up or present their personal, intimate feelings to general scrutiny in a neutral fashion: indeed, this outward projection required authenticity, which they guarded with the greatest care. But even the great Myslbek did not escape criticism when he created his mythological groups in the 1890s for the Palacký bridge, using themes taken from *Manuscripts*. His stonecutters finished *Lumír and Song* in 1888, *Libuše and Premysl* in 1892, *Záboj and Slavoj* in 1895 and *Ctirad and Šárka* in 1897. In this series of two-figure scenes, Myslbek accentuated the monumental effect, particularly through the use of large amounts of drapery. But the younger artists disapproved. At the very time when Mádl's monograph on Myslbek appeared, they roundly criticized these sculptural groups as being inferior in quality to the original sketches with which the sculptor had won the competition. The sketches, they claimed, still displayed the richness of the "pollen of expressiveness and of the soul", contrary to the purely formal virtuosity of the final version.[10]

Something far more fundamental lay behind this agitation: it was the very concept of the nature of art and its influence on society that was in the process of change. Until then, imposing monuments or large, pretentious paintings displayed at annual art exhibitions had sufficed, but now a certain omnipresence of art seemed to be demanded. Art was gradually being transformed from a luxury into an everyday necessity. Inevitably, it lost many of its precious qualities in the process, and often verged on kitsch, but it nevertheless enabled increasing numbers of artists to realize their dreams and make a living from their work. Less importance was attached to representation, and there was a trend toward art that was more personal, even though it was immediately circulated to the widest public possible via modern means of reproduction.

The first result of this deep change in society was an upheaval in values. The destabilization was clearly apparent in the vacillations observed in urban architecture, which were to end only with the advent of Art Nouveau. Until that point, the rich palette of historicism enabled architects to work in a variety of modes. This diversity grew out of the confrontation of widely divergent tastes that resulted from a breakdown of traditional social class barriers and the rural exodus toward the large cities. In Prague, there was an unprecedented wave of construction, especially of tall buildings; the construction industry had never seen better times, and with the invention of high pressure water piping it became possible to construct higher edifices.

Josef Václav Myslbek, *Záboj and Slavoj*, 1892–1895. Vyšehrad.

These new circumstances created a demand for the replacement of traditional building materials by other materials that would be less costly, without looking "cheap". Architects discovered two solutions: the facades of ordinary residential buildings could be either decorated with stucco or painted. Both methods were relatively inexpensive and easy to adapt to budgetary requirements.

Thus decorative work on building exteriors became the daily bread of young painters and sculptors graduating from the School of Fine Arts and, to an even greater extent, those from the School of Applied Arts. Work of this kind was also offered within the building programmes undertaken by major institutions, as a token of support for national artists. Generally, wealthy private citizens, mostly merchants, contractors and hotel and restaurant owners, took the lead. As a result both of their support and of the influence of the decorative

aesthetics promoted by the great trade fair exhibitions, "painted buildings" came very much into fashion in Prague in the 1890s.

The early days of "painted buildings" still witnessed a search for historical motivation, and in this spirit the architect Antonín Wiehl pioneered a style known as "Czech Renaissance" which, contrary to former styles based on the Italian Renaissance, looked to local tradition for inspiration. Wiehl's building on Wenceslas Square, finished in 1896, epitomized this new style, with a very characteristic semi-circular glass porch and asymmetrically arranged bow windows. The facade was decorated with genre paintings after sketches by Mikoláš Aleš, a painter of the National Theatre generation and pioneer of decorative facade-painting, who had already displayed his abilities in Prague and other cities. Wiehl was one of the most interesting figures in Czech late historicism. For the 1891 jubilee exhibition, for example, he proposed an entrance door which was a curious mixture of a triumphal arch motif together with bastions of popular inspiration, as well as a number of wooden pavilions in which he made free use of a variety of techniques and form to illustrate "modernism."

Nevertheless, the great master of this free mixing of styles so characteristic of late historicism remained Friedrich Ohmann, who was born in Lvov and was appointed professor of architecture at the School of Applied Arts in Prague in 1889. Later historians of modern architecture were to describe him as being "of a lively temperament, recklessly eclectic, a man of moods and wild inconstancy, and yet undeniably possessed of the soul of an artist".[11] It is clear today, however, that the apparently chaotic work of this eclectic architect was dominated by a certain polarization, significant in the development and emergence of Art Nouveau architecture. This polarity amounted to a confrontation between the Renaissance and Baroque styles, which was actually the expression of a burgeoning divergence between two entirely different concepts of art. This question was a central preoccupation in aesthetics and art history at the time.[12]

Not all the architectural undertakings of the 1890s were quite so unorthodox, but most show the gradual definition and maturation of two genres. The stronger of the two was linked to the emergence of Neo-Baroque classicism, which had already made an appearance in

FACING PAGE: Wiehl's house, 1894–1896. Prague New Town (Wenceslas Square 34).
ABOVE: Detail of the facade.

Hynais' stage curtain for the National Theatre. After decades of architecture inspired exclusively by Neo-Renaissance classicism, Neo-Baroque only came into its own in the 1890s. Created by Josef Schulz, a Court Counsellor and professor at the Prague Technical School, the National Museum on Wenceslas Square was completed in 1890. The building still bore the stamp of classicism, although its monumentality seems to arise more from an effect of illusion and exaggeration than was the case in Josef Zítek's work. Schulz was an exponent of late historicism who bowed to the city's new aesthetic demands, and in whose work the references to historical models were much fainter. This tendency was also evident in his subsequent works in Prague, among them the Museum of Decorative Arts, built between 1897 and 1901.

The Neo-Baroque style found fertile ground in Prague, a terrain already prepared by the splendid wealth of its Baroque heritage. Indeed, Prague had always been a Baroque city, which tended to facilitate the harmonious integration of the Neo-Baroque style. The Count Jan Petr Straka Academy, built between 1893 and 1895 by Theophil Hansen's pupil Václav Rostlapil on the banks of the Vltava (the Czech name for the Moldau River) at Malá Strana is an excellent example of this style.

In Prague, Ohmann at first favoured a rather "severe" Neo-Baroque style (the Palace built in 1891 for the industrialist Valtera); soon, however, he came to appreciate its freer expression. As he saw it, the Neo-Baroque concept offered advantages in the handling of large structural volumes required in a big city, such as that of the Assecurazioni Generali insurance building on Wenceslas Square, which he constructed with Osvald Polívka in 1895. Finally, in his renovation of the Karlin Variety Theatre between 1896 and 1898, he reached a stage where the historical element was no more than a springboard for his imagination to chase the ghost of past splendours.

However, Ohmann's work in Prague also included some very different buildings. These were reminiscent of the Renaissance heritage, but not the classical Renaissance type, rather the northern Renaissance, earlier propounded by Wiehl and embodied in the "painted buildings". Here the important thing was not the plastic element, but the facade, with its figurative or ornamental painting. This idea allied architecture more closely with graphic art and decorative painting of the period, at a time when the earliest manifestations of Art Nouveau were just beginning to be seen. The articulation between line and surface was soon to become the major preoccupation of creative artists working within this tendency.

In Ohmann's view, the decoration of these bourgeois buildings should express elements of intimacy and their roots in local history. One decorative element which ran counter to High Renaissance and Baroque "cosmopolitanism" was, for example, a Saint Wenceslas rendered in the late medieval spirit (the Schnirch house on the Old Town Square, in 1897). Another eclectic feature was the use of wooden bay windows freely inspired by folk architecture, featuring floral decoration, of which the two 1897 "Bohemian Eagle" houses at the fruit market and on Celetná Street, respectively, are good examples.

The Corso Café on Na příkopě Avenue, finished in 1898, presents a synthesis of all these works. The cafe

The Corso Café, 1897–1898, now destroyed. Arch.: Friedrich Ohmann.

was destroyed during the 1920s and only photographs remain, but it was reputedly the first Art Nouveau building in Prague. On closer inspection, however, it seems more like an assemblage of all the elements preceding that style: the painted facade (the mural painting was done by Arnošt Hofbauer), the Neo-Baroque stucco details (the genii around the name-board on the facade), and even "engineering" elements in the architecture (the main cornice executed as a glass and metal marquise). The café's interior was undoubtedly where the style was most coherent. Nonetheless, this work was very close to the spirit of Art Nouveau, as can be seen also in the project for the facade of the Central Hotel in Hybernská Street, dating from September of that same year, 1898, which truly belonged to that style. Ohmann had been promoted to a professorship at the Academy of Fine Arts in Vienna, and so two of his Czech pupils, Bedřich Bendelmayer and Alois Dryák, carried out the project.

The Corso displayed a very picturesque attic storey, with a pine-cone motif which seems to echo that on the new Zemská Bank building, finished in 1896, standing just opposite on the same avenue. The latter was the work of Osvald Polívka, soon to become one of Prague's most prolific architects. The Zemská Bank was very representative of Prague architecture of the 1890s, both in its canons of proportion and in its decoration. Polívka was already well known from his collaboration with Antonín Wiehl between 1892 and 1894 on the construction of the Pražská městská spořitelna (Prague City Savings Bank). A comparison between the latter and the Zemská Bank gives a clear idea of the evolution of late historicism in Czech architecture. The Savings Bank was still conceived in the spirit of Renaissance classicism, which is characterized by symmetry and a balance between vertical and horizontal masses. The Zemská Bank, on the other hand, was based on very different canons of proportion, in which verticality was the predominant movement and the tectonics of the building remained discreet. Its historical references were mannerist, with a tendency toward the picturesque, characteristic of the genre, which can be seen in the unusual decoration of its facade. The elevated base, with a mezzanine commercial area, gave the building a definite air of elegance, despite its somewhat excessive decoration.

This wealth of decoration suggests of an effort to give the greatest possible number of artists the opportunity to express themselves. The Bank did indeed pride itself on its image as a promotor of young talent. The facade displayed outstanding mosaics executed from designs by Mikoláš Aleš, as well as works by the sculptor Stanislav Sucharda, and the rather more Art Nouveau-style botanical decoration executed by Celda Klouček and Anna Boudová. A staircase made

RIGHT: The Zemská Bank. General view and detail of the attic storey, 1894–1896. Prague New Town (Na příkopě 20). Arch.: Osvald Polívka.

"The Bohemian Eagle" house, detail of the bow window, 1896–1897.
Prague Old Town (Ovocný trh 15). Arch.: Friedrich Ohmann.

The Zemská Bank, detail of the facade, showing the emblem
and lunettes.

"The Bohemian Eagle" house.

Second facade, at 30 Celetná Street.

of extremely expensive materials led toward the entrance, where there were some naturalistic works representing the different regions of Bohemia, signed by the sculpors Bohuslav Schnirch, Stanislav Sucharda, Antonín Procházka and František Hergesel. The interior was decorated with a series of paintings by Karel Vítězlav Masek, Karel Klusáček and Emil Holárek, that provide a good illustration of the current taste for *tableaux vivants*. The most important works were located near the entrance, including *Saint Wenceslas Blessing Work* and *Work, the Source of Prosperity* by Maxmilián Švabinský, a young graduate of the School of Fine Arts. While the composition of the latter paintings respected traditional symmetry, the freshness of their colours surpassed the realism usual at the time and gave a strong poetic feel to the work. The very individual use of colour was obtained, on the one hand, through Švabinský's subtle handling of the range of his palette (the harmony of dark green and white was interspersed with other tones, especially yellow), and on the other, through the decorative organization of these colours over the surface of the painting. The rich, emotionally stimulating variety of colour modulations combined with the flat, decorative design to produce compositions that contributed to the creation of a style. Thus, Švabinský's earliest work, which received well-deserved appreciation, opened up a new direction for decorative painting.

More Baroque in concept, Polívka's vivid historicism found its full expression in the architecture of another building of the Prague City Savings Bank on the Old Town Square (1898). Among the various rich exterior decorative elements of the building, Ladislav Šaloun's *Fire* and *Water* – already a symbolist sculpture – and the groups created by Bohuslav Schnirch on the attic level (*Fire Alarm* and *Extinction of the Flames*) were particularly striking (p. 121). The rear facade of the bank, giving onto Salvátorská Street, was at once more sober and closer to the burgeoning Art Nouveau style. This building, which sparked considerable con-

troversy, was constructed at a time when the whole of Prague was preparing for the Architecture and Engineering Exhibition. This exhibition was to parody the dead end in which eclectic historicism found itself, mocking it with the installation of a tavern called The Non-Sense, which reproduced the jumble of styles characteristic of the hasty construction then current in Prague.

This event stimulated a movement in favour of a new, modern type of architecture that at least would not lend itself to derision, a movement that carried all the more weight in view of the major renovation work about to be started in the centre of Prague. The debate, whose opening salvoes were fired in the periodicals *Zprávy spolku architektů a inženýrů v Království českém* (News Bulletin of the Association of Architects and Engineers of the Kingdom of Bohemia) and *Volné směry* (Free Tendencies), evinced concern for giving new Czech architecture a national character of its own, rather than imitating what was being done elsewhere in Europe under the heading of "modern architecture". The conservatives feared the influence of Otto Wagner and his Vienna school, whose urban-looking stations for Vienna's circular railway were particularly attractive. The time had come, it was thought, to decide the future of architecture and of the plastic arts as a whole. Even the older generation, who had been trained in the historical style, appeared to be aware of the need for renewal. But the youthful contingent often insisted that even if the Czech national character had to be glorified, its art could not cut itself off from the rest of the world as though by a Great Wall of China. The critic for the progressive magazine *Volné směry* wrote: "On one side, there is historicism, on the other, its negation (absolute if possible), that is, modernity, and between the two there is this kind of happy medium that some people have found, to safeguard patriotism in art. [...] All progress depends on a successful evolution of tradition and ossified formalism, with respect for the old, but desire for the new."[13] The course was set for Art Nouveau.

Prague City Savings Bank, rear facade, c. 1901. Prague Old Town (Salvátorská 6). Arch.: Osvald Polívka.

Decadence and symbolism

The nineteenth century saw the birth of a veritable cult of art that burdened artists with constraints which were not always easy to overcome. The idealized image inherited from Romanticism of the creative being inspired by genius imposed the highest demands on artists, while at the same time confronting them with a mirror in which the reflection of their pride, idealism and aspirations could not conceal the sobering reality of their everyday lives, their shortcomings and their doubts. From another angle, the distinction between art and craft created a caste of the elect, although this did not spare the chosen few from suffering a permanent and painful questioning of their own identity. They had to come to terms with their relationship to a society that was in the process of change, and whose aesthetic choices were as yet uncertain. Moreover, the direct contacts between artists and those who commissioned their work had been replaced by a new form of patronage, henceforth bound up with institutional hypocrisy or with the anonymity of a market swayed by the bombast of the art critics. However, the artists of the new era found that the greatest problem posed by individualism lay within themselves: their personal search for authenticity. It is understandable that to this end they looked for help from every possible source: from so-called traditional values, philosophical ideals, aesthetic norms, the great heroes of the world, as well as the inner heart of their own rebellion.

The second half of the nineteenth century saw a rapid growth in the discontent that ideological and social upheavals had sparked among artists. The system and nature of art instruction, which determined the hierarchy of positions and the subjective judgment of works, was challenged by new generations who began to criticize their elders and the established order. However, the right to criticize, which they exercised with passion, brought them face to face with the problem of proposing a viable alternative. Thus all artists were obliged to introduce "something new" into their field, to attract attention and distinguish themselves from their competitors in order to break out of their anonymity. The ensuing race for originality became a social fact.

Distinguishing oneself became all the more difficult because the new concept of art – as having absolute value – made it theoretically possible for any artist to achieve success.

The almost neurotic dilemma of the modern artist, caught between the universal and absolute value of art and the reality of day-to-day existence, had a determining influence on the turn-of-the-century art scene. It was particularly distressing to the more sensitive among them, who felt more keenly this contradiction that touched the very roots of the creative process. Even their most spontaneous, audacious and revolutionary reactions were counterweighted by the fundamental dictate that art possessed an essence of its own which their work needed to capture and reveal in order to answer the enigma of the universe.

Such ideality in art appeared to be threatened on two fronts, as was suggested by the two caricatures executed by Maxmilián Pirner around 1874, while he was still a student at the Prague School of Fine Arts. In one of these, entitled *The School of Fine Arts*, a group of teachers is administering a copious enema to a Pegasus suspended from a pulley; in the other, a small figure armed with a large camera and an articulated dummy is labouring up a hill. According to the young Pirner, neither empty, traditional idealism nor mechanical naturalism could solve the problem of art. Pirner was later to complete his studies in Vienna and become the great hope among young Czech artists. When the Prague School of Fine Arts was reorganized in 1887, he was called upon to teach the new genre painting class. He probably owed this appointment to the large *Demon of Love* series, whose tragic scenes were set in a contemporary context, and which had great success in Prague that same year (1887) in an exhibition at the Ruch Gallery. Pirner was not a genre painter, though, and was more interested in broad themes dealing with ideals. He was strongly influenced by Jaroslav Vrchlický, whom he admired and whose work he illustrated, and he adopted the Parnassian concept of an all-powerful Poetry that transcended national and social boundaries.

However, Pirner seemed to be expressing what was to some extent a shattered ideal. At the end of the 1880s, he painted large canvases in which he attempted to adapt his Neo-Romantic idealism to Salon painting. He entered his *Finis* for the jubilee exhibition. Its sub-

Maxmilián Pirner, *Finis*, 1887. Oil on canvas, 100 x 130 cm.
Prague, National Gallery.

Maxmilián Pirner, *Medusa*, 1891. Pastel, diam.: 59 cm.
Prague, National Gallery.

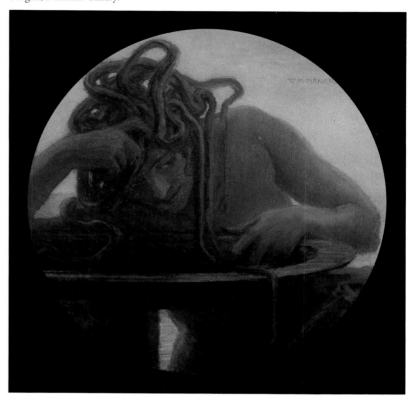

ject was the conflict between the world's two prime
powers, Life and Death, personified respectively by
a luminous image of the Muse, Poetry – a winged
figure holding a harp, resting on a terrace overlooking the sea – and a Gorgon, represented as a dark
demon clambering up to the terrace in the company
of a skeleton. On the steps to the terrace lie the
three Fates, who have been cast into sleep by Poetry
and who seem to be about to awaken as Death
approaches. Poetry, surprised, is on the verge of being
confronted by a rival far more dangerous than any
other: the End of All Things. The conception of the
painting was what people at the time liked to call
"philosophical", and it had a strangeness induced by
its disturbing colour and the composition of the three
nudes. Although these Fates remained engraved in
the imagination of Czech artists at the turn of the
century, the work was not well received by the public,
as was apparent from the critical diffidence of the usually sympathetic Karel Mádl.

In fact, Czech painting had by then already set course on the road to naturalism. Pirner, who at that point was also going through a crisis in his private life, was so disappointed that he left unfinished another large project that he had worked on between 1886 and 1893, the enormous triptych *Life, Love, Hate and Death*. The centre panel of the triptych depicts a stirring scene showing the Poet astride Pegasus, rising up to the heights where Genius awaits him with a crown of laurel. But just before the poet arrives, he is struck down by another demon, Frustra. This painting, which seems to paraphrase a Baroque altar, shows the extent to which Pirner had followed the Neo-Baroque craze that struck Bohemia in the early 1890s.

Pirner's attempts to give academic allegory a new look came up against both the new tastes of the public and the contradictions inherent in his own character. His problems intensified after Hynais arrived in Prague: the encounter between two diametrically opposed artistic concepts quickly turned into animosity. In *Green Reflections,* a pastel executed in 1895, Pirner mocks on Hynais' pictorial theory on the reflection of coloured shadows: the picture shows an ecstatic crowd observing the inside of a well – derisively named *Castalia's Source* – filled with duckweed. With this kind of spite, Pirner also sought revenge for Hynais' success with his *Truth* at the jubilee exhibition.

Pirner was a failure with the public and with the radical fringe of the younger generation. In 1899 he received the final blow from Jiránek, who held that the paintings that Pirner had submitted to the Manes Union of Artists' exhibition were outdated. "We are all too aware that this manner of philosophizing has no place in painting; we are no longer accustomed to these laboured allegories."[1] Pirner never exhibited again. He withdrew into his studio, turning it into an almost impenetrable fortress.

His work nevertheless remained topical throughout the 1890s; *Ver Sacrum* (no. 10, 2nd year), the magazine of the Vienna Secession, an association of which Pirner was a regular member, devoted an issue to him in 1899. Here, it was Pirner's revolt against the decadence of art that drew the greatest respect. This revolt was expressed in a number of paintings in a grotesque or more serious vein, such as *Eros and Chaos*, in which the image of a handsome, young, androgynous figure rising up from a confused mass of semi-human creatures clearly shows the Neoplatonic inspiration of Pirner's Neo-Romanticism, and his belief in the immortality of the creative soul.

If Pirner remained topical as an artist, it is because of his frustrated idealism, which was engendered by the hothouse atmosphere of decadence. Hence his strange formal ornamentalism, which acquired increasing importance in the course of the 1890s. This was first exemplified by his 1891 painting *Medusa*, where the mythological figure is portrayed looking at herself in a metal plate. The motif is certainly reminiscent of the Gorgon in *Finis*, although Medusa's terrible gaze better illustrates the legend. The composition of the head of snake-hair, which echoes her general appearance, is quite remarkable. Pirner's later alterations of the painting respected the internal logic of the original version. Traditionally, this pictorial representation of the Gorgon Medusa expresses the relationship between beauty and death, the paradoxical union between Eros and Thanatos, the conflictual link holding naturalism and idealism together.[2] *Medusa* repeats the allegorical composition of *Finis*, albeit in a very simplified manner, but without losing the principle of the conflict between beauty and terror. The painting is indeed both beautiful and terrifying. Here, the decorative element is used to enhance the strange union of opposites: it is the expression of the decadent aesthetics in which beauty invariably harbours the shadow of death.

Pirner's *Medusa* was not concerned with merely inserting ornamental elements into the scene but, in a far more interesting and spontaneous way, using its own lines to make ornament an integral part of the picture. Some of Pirner's other works from the 1890s (the sketch for the *Hippocrene* painting from the Pegasus Cycle around 1893, for example) show that these ornamental shapes originated in the chaotic forms of Neo-Baroque style. This dynamic surge of poetic imagination can be understood as the artist's rendering of a mysterious energy which is external to the material world, but nevertheless exercises considerable influence over mankind. It is true to say that Pirner never went beyond the horizons of Neo-Romanticism, and his idea of terror was restricted to the grotesque level of tales full of fairyfolk and gnomes. One wonders at the origin of this wellspring of imagination that bore him on toward a new concept of ornament. Incontestably, however, Pirner was both a precursor and an

Maxmilián Pirner, *Hippocrene,* preliminary study for the triptych *Life, Love, Hate and Death,* c. 1893. Black and white chalk, 19.5 x 31.5 cm. Prague, National Gallery.

initiator, and he had a following of younger artists who showed a growing interest in this new way of re-evaluating allegory.

Foremost among them was František Bílek, who in 1887 was already studying at the School of Fine Arts. After abandoning his original intention of becoming a painter (he was partly colour-blind), Bílek quickly proved to be an excellent illustrator. On the advice of his teacher he turned to the plastic arts, where he achieved such remarkable results that he obtained a stipend from the Chevalier de Lanna that enabled him to travel to Paris at the beginning of 1891.

Bílek's separation from the Prague art world brought about a sharp reversal of his values. A sensitive young man, who did not know French well enough to fit into his new surroundings, Bílek found himself homesick for his own country, where he had received a strongly religious family upbringing. If his later memoirs are to be believed, it was from this point onward that he devoted himself to spiritual and religious matters. He

witnessed a vision of light, and heard an inner voice asking him to proclaim God's truth.

Instead of going to the School of Fine Arts, Bílek followed the advice of the sculptor Dalou, to whom Hynais had introduced him, and went to the Colarossi Academy, a private school where his teacher, Injalbert, is said to have praised his work as faultless. The following year, therefore, Bílek decided to work on his own. In Paris, he admired the museum collections, especially the casts of medieval hermetic works displayed at the Trocadero Palace. He was very moved by this art, so distant from academic models, and whose content and form corresponded to his own search for meaning.

Unfortunately, there is no record of how Bílek reacted to contemporary art, which he certainly studied during his stay in Paris, since, as the portrait of him by the Polish painter Stanislav Wyspiański shows, he did not live an isolated life there.

During 1892, Bílek produced two sculptures in Paris from which the whole of his future work emanated.

František Bílek, *Tilling the Soil Is Punishment for Our Sins,* 1892. Plaster. Prague, Hlavního města Prahy Gallery. Period photograph.

The first of these, *Golgotha – Hill of Skulls,* depicted the Holy Virgin and John the Apostle seated at the foot of the Cross, from which the horizontal bar had been removed. Though the subject was commonplace, its treatment was not. Bílek introduced naturalist and Neo-Baroque elements of expression into his sculpture. The decorative elements, as well as an unusual way of handling materials, such as the ropes hanging from the cross and the crown of thorns made of braided barbed wire, were incontestably naturalistic, as was the manner in which the Virgin was represented. On the other hand, the stylization of the figures, especially the stooped figure of Saint John, was Neo-Baroque.

While Bílek's *Golgotha* displayed certain features of composition common to French sculpture at the time, his second "Parisian" work, *Tilling the Soil Is Punishment for Our Sins,* was truly original. A naked, ascetically emaciated Christ in a state of exhaustion is "tilling" a hard surface consisting of a number of panels covered with small inscriptions. In front of him, on an extremely reduced scale, small figures rise out of the earth and desperately try to lift up the Tablets of the Law. These figures represent the sins of Man, redeemed by the suffering of Christ. With this contrast between the large central figure and the small ones, Bílek invented an image that later was often copied by other Czech artists to express the contrast between the moral grandeur of the individual and the "smallness" of mundane material interests.

In a way, these two works complement each other. The absence of the body of Christ from *Golgotha* creates a tension that evokes the vision of *Tilling.* In the first work, sorrow is expressed by extreme stylization – Neo-Baroque, but with a deeper intent – as, for example, in the characteristic way that John's bare foot projects over the sculpture's plinth. Bílek himself justified this motif as being the fermata of the "S-line", which governs the forms of matter and is considered a "symbol of life".[3] And so a new Art Nouveau line was created, justified by the content of the work.

Bílek submitted *Golgotha* and *Tilling* to the Grants Committee; their singularity and naturalism provoked a scandal, shocking the Committee members, who had been trained in the classicism then prevalent, with its subjectivist conception of traditional themes. Some very bluntly disparaging comments from Myslbek crowned the disaster. Bílek's grant was withdrawn and he had to return to Prague in humiliation at the end of October 1892. He withdrew to his native Chýnov and spent many long years recovering from this painful experience.

In 1892 the episode was seen as a personal failure for Bílek, whereas it was in fact the first serious confrontation between two fundamentally different concepts of art. It is true that Bílek's own particular mentality prodded him to desperately harangue the Czech cultural narrow-mindedness current during the 1890s, but the artistic extremism that this attitude fostered turned out positively in the end: he became the dominant personality of the Czech Secession in the plastic arts at the turn of the century.

Pirner's example had greatly inspired Bílek; he had obviously been impressed by the evocative Fates in Pirner's *Finis,* for both the symbolic Pegasus motif and that of the prostrate figure stretching out a helpless arm, the symbol of Man's attachment to the earth, appear in several of his works (the charcoal drawing *Z Biti o Byti,* and the sculpted wood *Parable of the Great Czech Decline,* dated 1898, in which a similar figure is lying near the ruins of an idol). Bílek was even more influenced by the Neoplatonic symbolism of light, which he subsequently adopted.

Regarding the role of the artist, Bílek shared the view, widespread among the preceding generation, that the artist must be the educator of his people and lead them to higher moral ground. But because of his origins, his character and the curious circumstances of his life in Paris, he took this mission extremely seriously, with an almost messianic fervour. He sought a counterbalance to the social decadence he saw all around him, and found it in an opposing force: religion.[4] His religious mythology, elaborated into an original system, was really an artistic ideology of the fantastic, and during the 1890s the Passion of Christ was the focal point of Bílek's imagination. For him, Christ was God, but also "the Son of Man" – in other words, the symbol of humanity's tragic struggle for a higher existence. In art,

František Bílek, *The Meaning of the Word "Virgin",* 1897. Wood, 153 x 93.5 cm. Prague, National Gallery.

opposition to Myslbek, who had dominated the jubilee exhibition. *Christ Crucified* showed not only Bílek's artistic maturity but also his profound understanding of the work of art as a symbolic undertaking.

During the three years Bílek spent on this sculpture, other major works also saw the light. In 1897 he tried his hand at ceramics – a return to the tradition of his home town, Chýnov. His graphite-coloured vases, decorated with a mixture of human figures and floral motifs, were strikingly original.

Bílek drew his inspiration for developing the symbolic function of light, so important in his *Christ Crucified,* directly from the Bible. Indeed, like all heretics, he considered this the sole authoritative source of higher knowledge. For his relief sculpture, *The Meaning of the Word "Virgin",* which was originally commis-

František Bílek, *Christ is Dead ...*, 1897. India ink and flake white, 52 x 70.5 cm. Prague, National Gallery.

František Bílek, vase, c. 1900. Earthenware, h.: 19 cm. Prague, UPM (Uměleckoprůmyslové muzeum).

this gnostic concept had its initial footing in naturalism and the Neo-Baroque, which were both characteristic elements of Bílek's early work. In the autumn of 1896, he made a sketch of Christ, first the face, then the body, which even then was composed of angular forms. He continued to work on this until 1899, and made a number of preliminary clay models before completing an immense sculpture in wood. During this period, Bílek concentrated on developing the central theme of the work. His correspondence with the poet Julius Zeyer provides a step-by-step description of the procedure he followed.[5] Bílek originally envisaged his sculpture as a tortured, illusionistic image of the Passion of Christ, which was intended to have a powerful effect on the viewer. Zeyer, however, insisted that he give the face a less morbid, more divine expression, by investing it with light. This forced Bílek to go beyond expressive naturalism and model the statue in the angular form he had used earlier in 1896 in a sketch of the body. His *Christ Crucified* thus became the first great sculpture executed in a truly Art Nouveau spirit, and put him in sioned by Zdenka Braunerová, the text of the Gospel was the point of reference for his unfettered meditation on the relationship between light and darkness. In Neoplatonic fashion, light was seen as the emanation of the world's fundamental creative energy, existing outside of matter – a world "made by a slumbering brute who hid light behind clouds and his own shadow, the better to sleep".[6] To express this idea, Bílek created a composition that was highly unusual in sculpture at the time, including fragments of an open book, pictures containing human figures, candles, stars and many other symbols and small inscriptions. In this way, innumerable details were accumulated within a single plastic unit, by means of a gradation of light between the various planes of the relief.

As his symbolist vision matured, Bílek turned to materials such as wood that were appropriate vehicles for his conceptions, while enabling him to work with limited means. Bílek's sculpture reflected a contemporary trend toward a revival of the romantic vision of nature as the objective origin of human existence. He began to link Man with the tree, the Old Testament symbol of life, which is stretching toward the Light, an idea first expressed in his drawings. In 1899, a preliminary drawing entitled *Mother!* presented the fantastic vision of a nocturnal landscape dimly lit by a rising moon; against this, part of a tree trunk, bathed in light, takes on the form of a human face with the closed eyes of a sleepwalker. High in the sky overhead shines a hazy star for which the soul of the tree seems to yearn. The drawing is set in a sculpted frame carved with a dreamlike figure with arms outstretched, while alongside, stars and a sinuous line form a pathway. Anthropomorphism is used here to express the mysterious metamorphosis of matter into a spiritual substance with cosmic dimensions.

According to Bílek, in this way Man too is subsumed under the fundamental cosmic law that infuses and unifies material and spiritual reality. This idea was expressed in a more didactic fashion in a large charcoal drawing dating from the following year, *The Place of Harmony and Reconciliation*. In this work, after a "cruel struggle for life", a pair of pilgrims are singing as they reach an avenue lined with trees that are turning into people, forming a cathedral vault with their uplifted hands. A luminous hand appears there, full of "Grace and Truth". Bílek also used the tree, symbol of Man's

František Bílek, *Mother!*, 1899. Charcoal. 139 x 83 cm. Prague, National Gallery.

union with Nature, in his portraits, including those of his parents sculpted in the wooden beams of the picturesque studio-home he built for himself in Chýnov.

Bílek's works from the end of the 1890s came after his break with the Modern Catholics, and reflected his personal search for a symbolist concept based on ancient religious symbols. This unorthodox emphasis on a personal spiritual vision reminded his contemporaries of William Blake. He paid little attention to art being created in the style of the times, and was against

Viennese ornamentalism. Nevertheless, his work is marked by shapes that are characteristic of Art Nouveau and are closer to the "springs of life" of Blake – who was at the origin of the English Modernist movement – than to the ornamentalism then in fashion.

In 1899, desiring to establish a more coherent body of ideas, Bílek created a series of about twenty-six drawings on loose sheets, assembled as a treatise under the title *Number and Reading of the Human Body through Letters.* Its basic thesis – that man was part of the cosmos – echoed evolutionary and cyclical theories. Life was seen as a process of continuous growth that reached a peak, declined, and then began anew. For Bílek, this dynamic concept originated in the gnostic belief in the possibility of freeing mind from matter, a belief offered by the natural world but constantly thwarted by the "nature" of man. His treatise also featured a speculation of Pythagorean inspiration, according to which the symbolic body of man was divided by mystical numbers, from the highest unity down to the bottom seven.

To further develop his symbolist vision, Bílek conferred with several poets belonging to the same movement. During the last five years of the century, his closest confidant was Julius Zeyer, whose tact and constant encouragement were instrumental in the creative liberation of Bílek's anguish. When Zeyer suddenly died at the beginning of 1901, Bílek honoured his memory with a work inspired by the earlier preliminary drawing, *Mother!* His representation of the poet escaping from the waves of a tempest was incomparably superior to monumental art of the time; this personal innovation led Bílek into monumental sculpture.

In 1900, a competition held in Prague for the design of a monument to the national martyr Jan Hus was won by Ladislav Šaloun. His project was an attempt to go beyond the limits of the conventional allegorical arrangement then in favour in naturalist *tableaux vivants.* The suffering Hus, wearing a heretic's cap, is standing at the stake, flanked by an emotional group of Hussite "Fighters for God" and another distraught gathering of people exiled during the period following the defeat at White Mountain. Two other projects attracted attention, one by the sculptor Stanislav Sucharda and another by the architect Jan Kotěra. Both of these represented a gigantic, solitary Jan Hus, accompanied only by some small figures on the pedestal. Although reminiscent of Bílek's *Tilling,* it is more likely that the motif was inspired by an 1880 drawing by Mikoláš Aleš, portraying the great national painter Josef Mánes as a giant holding a lighted candle as he crossed the Old Town Square in Prague, surrounded by small figures representing members of the narrowminded *petite bourgeoisie.* These different works concurred in expressing the opposition between the lofty moral worth of an exceptional individual and the passivity of the common mass.

Whether they were depicting Christ or the great historical figures – particularly Hus, the Czech archetype of the Secessionist revolted by humanity's decadence – these artists perceived the tragic dimension in their subjects. While these works hearkened back to a historical ideal, they also represented the problems faced by the individual in that epoch. The dual scale applied to the figures reflects this idea, but it also presents a new approach to the structure of monuments, and raises the question of whether it is appropriate to use a monument as a vehicle for moral comment.

Bílek did not take part in the competition, but he did work on a depiction of Hus nonetheless. *The Tree That, Struck by Lightning, Burned for Centuries,* a wood sculpture made in 1901, presents the arched figure of Hus rising out of the rocky ground like a great tree, his eyes closed mystically and his hair swirling like flames. The symbolic use of light in Bílek's earlier works here acquires a pathos that emphasises not Hus's defeat, but on the contrary, the force of a belief in truth founded on cosmic law. Hus is thus abstracted from history and placed in a universal, impersonal world in which he appears as a hero. This positive portrayal, celebrating the victory of the individual's inner force, allows it to transcend the traditional pessimistic Czech vision, and replaces naturalism by synthetic form. It is interesting to note that this vision, so unique when first used, was later embodied in a monument over thirty feet high erected in Kolín-on-Elbe just before the First World War.

Bílek's exceptional position in Czech art at the end of the 1890s was not solely attributable to his religious imagination. In fact, given the mood of pessimism prevalent at the time, religious themes were a source of inspiration for many other artists, including the painter Felix Jenewein. Jenewein's works achieved a grandiose monumentality that focused on the expressiveness of large figures that were treated almost as sculptures and

Felix Jenewein, *Judas*, 1896. Gouache, 36.4 x 51.3 cm. Brno, Moravská Gallery.

occupied the entire foreground (*Judas*, 1896). Colour remained merely as an enlivening adjunct. This kind of composition was obviously influenced by the art of stained glass, which was greatly appreciated at the time. In *The Plague* (1900), a parable of an epidemic in the Middle Ages, Jenewein departed from conventional themes and attempted to create a "universal" ballad on the apocalypse inexorably awaiting humankind. However, here he came up against the intransigence of young critics, the severest of whom was Arnošt Procházka, who criticized the work's philosophical and psychological inconsistencies.[7]

Procházka's judgement is interesting, if only because it was pronounced by an important representative of the Czech decadent literary trend associated with *Moderní revue*. Although Procházka and Jiří Karásek ze Lvovic, who founded the group in 1894, refused to be identified as decadent and sought the collaboration of "all modernists", their biting criticism and scepticism regarding the Czech cultural situation eventually obliged them to clarify their position and accept the label. Procházka nevertheless believed that decadent art did not express decline, but an awareness of moral decay that called on artists to defy the hypocritical conventions of society That he saw this decay as permanent, or even considered Bílek's "white-hot spiritual visions" as "a symbol

of infinite, immutable universal suffering" is symptomatic. His pessimism did not prevent him from demanding that artists have no scruples in showing the darkest side of social and private life. Procházka believed that this dark element was concentrated in the relationship between men and women, and he liked to deal with this subject through mythological comparisons. The French authors who emerged from the naturalist trend impressed him by the cynicism with which they exposed mercantile logic, and by their openness in describing sexuality. But Procházka did not know, any more than they did, the real reasons underlying the moral crisis of modern society. Above all, he was fascinated by the decadent concept of the *femme fatale* as the root of all evil.

This was the angle from which he approached literary and pictorial work in his criticism for *Moderní revue*. He had a particular affinity with the artists recommended by Joris-Karl Huysmans or by Przybyszewski and the engravers, who added poetic commentary to literary works. This led him to write essays on Félix Vallotton, Odilon Redon, James Ensor, Aubrey Beardsley and Henry de Groux, and to reproduce works by Félicien Rops and Edvard Munch. His magazine brought before the Czech public a number of artists who had become well known by the turn of the cen-

tury. Significantly, Procházka set up a publishing house as an adjunct to the magazine. Already in its earliest publications, which included Otakar Březina's *The Mysterious Distances,* it was remarkable for the originality of its taste, both literary and typographical. For financial reasons, Procházka published his books as small fascicules in an elongated format, with the title printed in very simple type. The resulting ascetic look was precisely what produced the impression of novelty: until then the idea of "fine books" had implied heavy, lavishly decorated bindings with traditional ornamentation. Sober elegance and affordable prices were the trademark of this new cultural concept, which met with a favourable reception, particularly from its targeted public, the Czech intelligentsia.

In addition to the simple lettering *Moderní revue* used for the titles of its book covers, new graphic elements linked to Art Nouveau ornamentalism made their appearance in the books. The young Stanislav Kostka Neumann was among the first to use this style in a collection of poems of 1896, *The Proud and Passionate Apostrophes.* Neumann was an amateur illustrator, as were many writers in the nineteenth century, not the least of them Victor Hugo; such a passion for drawing, unhindered by the demands of professionalism, was a means of letting the imagination take flight by allowing a free exchange between word and image. Neumann left the *Moderní revue* group within a very short time, but transferred his concern for drawing to *Nový kult* (New Cult), his anarchist magazine, for which he drew a series of abstract decorative designs recalling the work of the Belgian artist Henry Van de Velde. *Moderní revue* later took on its first "in-house" graphic artist, another poet-illustrator, Karel Hlaváček. He worked on graphics for the *Moderní revue* throughout its third year. It was during this period, between his return from military service after contracting tuberculosis in the autumn of 1896 and his death from the disease in the summer of 1898, that he produced most of his rather limited graphic output. It comprised illustrations for a collection of Procházka's works called *The*

Sorrows of the Soul, engravings for magazines, the graphic design for the title of the Krakow periodical *Zycie,* projects for the covers and frontispieces of his own anthologies, *In the Early Hours* and *The Vindictive Cantilena,* a small number of other engravings and a few, small, unbordered drawings *in margine.* This was not the coherent ouput of a professional illustrator or engraver, and for a long time it was considered a minor part of his overall oeuvre – as was his poetic work, for that matter, even though today it is seen as the most significant manifestation of Czech decadent art.

Hlaváček's tragic fate, together with his broad concept of the work of an artist, contributed to the ascendancy of decadent art in the *Moderní revue* circle. Both his life and his work were riddled with contradictions. Although he came from a modest working-class background, Hlaváček aspired to the most elitist values. He pushed his experience to the limit, and there found an exaltation that he dared to express in words and images. In a letter to Stanislav Przybyszewski, Hlaváček spoke in very frank terms about this source of his creation: "The feeling of something brutal, terrifying and dreadful – that is what I was trying to convey. Something beyond our knowledge, from which we want to escape and to which we are condemned to be slaves. Yes, you are right: to me everything looks frightening, I see monsters everywhere, it's in me, it's physiological, for I love Fear. I love Fear for Fear's sake. I often deliberately linger in Prague after dark so as to be able to walk in the blackness of the night for two hours on my way home, across long, deserted stretches of the suburbs, past the brick factories whose furnaces are used as shelter by Prague's vagrants. I have a heart defect, and my most pleasurable sensation is the feeling of horrifying, orgiastic fear that thrills through my whole being with the sudden pain of an attack, and that mad anticipation of the moment when everything might snap. [...] With fear, I mortify my body and revive my soul. Forgive me for revealing my intimate feelings here, but it is necessary to do so if I am to discuss my drawings.

"So I conceived *The Exile* as someone banished from the sexual paradise. You can see how the dreadful thirst for the lost paradisiacal purity of Sex has already turned his mouth into the mucous tissue of female genital organs gaping in convulsion. Ah, Mr. Przybyszewski, I did the whole drawing in a single breath, and drew it in an absolutely realistic way, but then I was overcome

Karel Hlaváček, *The Exile*, 1897. Charcoal and coloured chalk, 26.5 x 24.3 cm. Prague, Památník národního písemnictví.

with such repulsion and horror at my work that I had to get rid of it. Then I redid the whole thing in a stylized fashion, if only because of the public prosecutor.

"The same thing happened with *The Execution of the Soul*. Here my intention was to express the psyche's terrible hatred for all things material. Material reality strangles sexual reality with its brutal, hairy hands. Here, too, the hideous fingers were transformed into horrible penises, which I also had to stylize. [...]"[8]

As this letter shows, Hlaváček interpreted Art Nouveau stylization as a way to legitimate images that in essence were private and shocking. Key to the problem

was sexuality, a social taboo that the *Moderní revue* group addressed with great zeal. Hlaváček tried to deal with this issue by replacing traditional allegorical contrivances with modern symbols. To some extent, he saw this in terms similar to psychoanalysis (which appeared at about the same time) – as the expression of an individual's unconscious dealing with its traumas, essentially of sexual origin, through dreams and fantasies. In the initial, uncensored phase, these fantasies were expressed through new and varied forms, of which the satirical-grotesque style was the most obvious example. Hlaváček's caricature of an intellectual with the body of

Karel Hlaváček, *The Ghost*, 1897. Pastel, 32.5 x 48 cm. Prague, Památník národního písemnictví.

a flea and the ears of a bat (*Metamorphosis*, 1897) is one of a number in this genre.

Hlaváček's experimentation was especially interesting when it included symbols that related directly to his personal obsessions, but were at the same time part of the symbolist repertoire. One of these motifs, which recurred frequently in his work, was the Moon. On the project for the cover of *In the Early Hours,* a huge moon is rising behind a rock-like shape with a naked woman leaning against it and playing with a large snake. An ornamental version of the cover shows a nude man, the poet, lying in the open and watching the rising moon.

The Ghost (1897) presents another, more original motif: a woman and the moon bound together. Here, the outline of the moon appears like a halo behind the head of the woman, whose face is hidden by flowing black hair. All that can be seen of her body is the arms, as though she were a ghost emerging from the moon's shell. (The ghost is reminiscent of Munch's variations on the theme of the vampire. The two artists no doubt shared this symbolic concept of woman linked to the moon, the personification of a dark force at once demoniacal and dangerous, yet fascinating.)

The lunar shell is often repeated in Hlaváček's

drawings, such as *The Pilgrim Woman* – which was reproduced in *Moderní revue* – in which it rests on the earth to form both a pathway and a magic circle. The moon is also a constant feature in his designs for wallpaper, where it predominates over plant and animal forms.

The moon motif shows how deeply Hlaváček's work was influenced by symbolist poetry and how, in his drawings, it provided a unifying link between form and content. It is interesting to note that here his intuition did not contradict the old symbolic tradition in art, in which the circle could also represent a dream image.[9] Hlaváček, however, tended toward the exclusive predominance of the symbol in the visual field, which reflected his desire to abolish the frontiers between the outer world and the inner world, to the advantage of the psychic universe.

In this respect, the imaginary in Hlaváček is as rich as it is strange. It implied a fundamental re-evaluation of contemporary Neo-Romantic imagination. A comparison of Schwaiger's gnomes and fairy figures with Hlaváček's demons reveals a displacement from the amusingly picturesque toward a distinctly more personal expression that touches on a variety of social taboos. True, the stylization and ornamentation of the crudest images represent a certain censorship, but they also constitute the Trojan horse whereby these images infiltrate the viewer's mind and address his most intimate thoughts. Hlaváček therefore managed to create an alliance between the new formal stylization and its dynamic and symbolic significance – an alliance that proved highly stimulating to the development of modern art.

Hlaváček was also the author of biting criticism and essays on plastic art in which, like Procházka and Karásek, he encouraged the lay-man to become familiar with modern forms of expression. The three men launched pitiless attacks on the annual exhibitions organized at the Rudolfinum in Prague by the Fine Arts Association. This was an Utraquist association founded in 1835 by the members of the aristocratic Society of Patriotic Art Lovers, which also ran the School of Fine Arts in Prague. The numerous works shown at its Salons were of very variable quality, and especially suited to a public with lowbrow taste. The *Moderní revue* radicals, as well as the Czech art community in general, especially its younger members, vehemently criticized these exhibitions for their lack of coherence and contemporary relevance – the odd modern work strayed in only by chance and native Czech artists were greatly underrepresented.

Discontent was already being voiced in the 1880s with traditional art institutions, whose standards were considered too low, and particularly with the teaching at the School of Fine Arts. Young artists went abroad for their training, above all to Munich, which for a long time was particularly attractive because of the Piloty school. During the first half of the 1880s a small colony of young Czech painters and sculptors formed in Munich and founded an association which they named after the famous seventeenth-century Czech painter, Škréta. This organization of Bohemian students drew up the first manifesto of the Czech Secession, which took the form of an open letter of admiration to Mikoláš Aleš, whose illustrations for *Manuscripts* had been scathingly condemned by the classicist-leaning *Nádrodní listy* critics in Prague. The young Czech artists considered Aleš to be the prototype of the pure artist, misunderstood by national political figures. The letter was accompanied by an eloquent drawing by Luděk Marold – who had just been expelled from the School of Fine Arts – representing a young girl mockingly breaking the crutch on which a reactionary is supporting himself.

Most of these insolent young people had already gone back to Prague when Pirner and the landscape painter Julius Mařák were appointed teachers there in 1887. In the same year they created another student association, this time named after the great national Romantic, Josef Mánes, which was to become the main association of Czech artists. Reaching that point turned out to be no easy matter for the new association. It quickly established links with the progressive student movement and with Omladina (Youth), but its early bohemianism, which went hand in hand with a somewhat vague concept of art, lingered on in its functioning and discourse. Only in the first half of the 1890s did it really begin to gain influence, partly thanks to the arrival of new members.

During the Škréta period, the young painters published two collections of their manuscripts in Munich: *Paleta* (Palette), which featured a collection of their studies and drawings, and *Špachtle* (Spatula), which had a satirical bent and focused especially on caricature.

In 1894, the Mánes Union of Artists published *The Palette Letters,* a selection of the best drawings from *Paleta. Moderní revue* reviewed – not unkindly – the Mánes Union's first venture into publishing, in which historicism and folklore predominated: "Attractive on the whole, but executed only in well-known, conventional genres. What happened to the new trends in modern painting? Has Bohemia gone back to sleep again?"[10]

In 1896 the young plastic artists launched a more ambitious undertaking: inspired by the Munich periodical *Jugend,* they began to publish their own magazine, *Volné směry* (Free Tendencies). This publication, together with the independent Mánes Union exhibitions that followed,[11] was the vehicle for the younger generation's entry into the Czech cultural arena where, under fire from the critics, it realigned and sharpened its thinking and quickly reached maturity.

The fundamental question arose: could the concept of Secession be applied to the Mánes Union? Curiously enough, the spokesmen for the Mánes Union refused to associate their attitude with the kind of categorical

rejection of the degradation of art made by the Vienna Secession. They protested against the exhibitions organized at the Rudolfinum, but saw their own modernity as "a simple step forward in the natural evolution of [their] art" – as stated in the group manifesto published in the March 1898 issue of *Volné směry,* marking the occasion of the association's first exhibition.

To the young plastic artists, who were trying to distance themselves from bohemianism and to prove the solid grounding of their efforts, the questions of technique and form were vitally important. They developed these topics in a manifesto in March 1898: "Many are those who still believe that in order to find pleasure in art it is not enough to solve a simple problem of colour or find a decorative solution. On the other hand, there are many who consider that an idea poorly expressed artistically is defensible, and may even be qualified as a work of art. There is a tendency to forget that, just as there are what can be called literary ideas and musical ideas, there also exist purely pictorial ideas, and that these are also worthwhile. There are a great many impressions that are absolutely impossible to ex-

Karel Hlaváček, *Demon,* 1897. India ink, 5 x 11.4 cm. Prague, Památník národního písemnictví.

Arnošt Hofbauer, poster for the 2nd exhibition of the Mánes Union of Artists, held at the Topič Salon, 1898. Color lithograph, 110 x 84 cm. Prague, UPM.

ist from the painter's eyes and enables him to give true expression to his individuality and to transcend the limitations of matter".[13]

Applying this programme presupposed clarifying the relationship between drawing and colour. In 1896, the young artists of the Mánes Union still displayed a preference for drawing. *Radikální listy* published a comment praising their enthusiasm in printing a three-volume album of the work of Mikoláš Aleš, the Union's honorary president, but which also contended that work on paper was, by itself, no longer adequate for the scope of modern painting, which required "full reproduction of subtle shades of colour to convey the feelings that reflect the individual personality and subjectivity of the artist's soul". To which the Mánes Union replied: "On the contrary, for us, conveying our inner self, our moods and feelings, through such a simple medium as drawing has an artistic value at least as great as, if not greater, than painting."[14]

Such faith in drawing stemmed from the excellent quality of the training they had received in this discipline in schools in Prague. Pirner and Hynais, but also František Ženíšek, were eminent illustrators, and their pupils benefited greatly from their teaching. In addition, drawing enabled the young artists to react more swiftly to new trends from abroad.

At the root of the evolution of new figurative Czech painting are two artists who, although from different schools, had complementary modes of expression. Maxmilián Švabinský, one of Pirner's pupils, started off in the direction of poetic idealism, incontestably inspired by the English Pre-Raphaelites and, more immediately, by their French admirers in the early 1890s. Švabinský's 1896 *Communion of Souls*, which is more sensitively expressed in the preliminary pen drawing than in the final oils, takes up the very popular motif of a motionless figure day-dreaming in the midst of a landscape. This work reflects the view that melancholy is the most creative human emotion, a notion that appeared as far back as the eighteenth century, and was developed by the Romantics. The work still retained a great many Neo-Romantic elements, such as the fanciful apparition of the Muse dressed in a white

plain in words, but than can be captured on canvas by a brush or sung in mysterious melodies. And who is to say that this or that particular impression or idea is the least valid?"[12]

This point of view was no doubt justifiable and compatible with the original symbolist principles, as expressed, for example, in Mallarmé's description of how meaning burst forth from an evocative poem. In this respect the path of modern art was already laid out, even though Czech plastic artists at first linked the notion of form to the direct study of nature, which "removes the spectacles of the philosopher or the moral-

Maxmilián Švabinský, *Communion of Souls*, 1896. Oil on canvas, 65.5 x 45.5 cm. Prague, National Gallery.

garment, who approaches the young artist and soothes his burning brow. Or the similarly idealized southern landscape, with dark cypresses whose shapes, like flames swept by the wind, combine sadness and ecstasy. Švabinský's penchant for English painting is again obvious in his study for the drawing *Joy-Joy* (1899), representing lovers floating through the air; this is, so to speak, a "quotation" of the right-hand part of Dante Gabriel Rossetti's *Paolo and Francesca da Rimini* triptych.

Similarly, in the triptych *The Wind and the Breeze*, the first important work by Jan Preisler (a former pupil of the School of Applied Arts), the airborne figures were greatly inspired by the linearity of Edward Burne-Jones; when the English painter died in 1898, it was Preisler who wrote his obituary in *Volné směry*. From the start, however, Preisler's work also showed the influence of French sensualism. Exhibitions in Vienna and Munich had familiarized the Czechs with the work of Edmond Aman-Jean, Henri Martin, Henri Le Sidaner and other "painters of the soul", who stripped the English model of its linear graphism or gave it the more picturesque interpretation typical of the French approach, with its nuances of poetry and colour, as expressed by the poetry of Paul Verlaine. *The Kiss*, executed in 1895, already belonged to this genre: in a garden, at night, flowers exude a perfume suggested by colours that, though painted in sfumato, are blazing.

This confluence of English idealism and French sensuality was the starting point for the development of the qualities specific to the new Czech modern "school". In the center of *Autumn*, a triptych painted by Preisler in 1897 for Gerlach's edition of *Allegories*, a melancholic woman is standing in the middle of a field of meadow-saffron. Her mantle is fluttering in the wind, and a flight of white swans with outstretched necks and wings forms a graceful arc. The field extends far into the dark horizon of a forest, and the female figure stands next to a grove of young trees, whose linear branches and slender trunks give the painting a marked element of stylization. This work expressing the sad but serene harmony of late autumn greatly inspired artists at the time, and came to symbolize the mood of an entire generation. Preisler's work ever more closely reflected this new mood as he moved beyond the naturalist concept, giving it greater density through the use of elaborate symbolism, and thus incorporated the values of

Jan Preisler, *Autumn*. Illustration for *Allegories*, published by Gerlach, Vienna, 1897.

Art Nouveau. *Autumn* began as an allegorical personification, but by means of two spatial orientations – lengthwise, with the wind sweeping the flight of the swans, and in depth, with the receding landscape – Preisler succeeded in expressing in purely plastic terms a consciousness of the inexorable passage of time and of the emptiness surrounding the static figure. In accomplishing this, he also succeeded in making allegory the symbol of the new conception of the world.

This development reaffirmed the personal style that Preisler had evolved. In 1896 he had already achieved splendid success with *Easter,* a triptych in charcoal, whose central panel depicted a young pig farmer sitting under a leafless tree in a twilit early spring landscape. In an attitude of melancholy, he is listening to the Easter bells, which are being rung by angels in the left-hand part of the triptych, while at the same time he is also gazing with the wide-open eyes of a seer at the mysterious image of Christ on the cross that appears on the right side, like an ancient fresco. The plastic effect of this association is negated by the painting itself, which focuses on the ghostliness of the vision and heightens the aesthetic essence of the picture, thus achieving a synthesis of sensory stimulations. This effect is due largely to the realistic landscape, which is a freely executed rendering of the countryside around Preisler's home in the Bohemian town of Beroun. By using the theme of a human figure set in a landscape, Preisler was able to establish a link between an idealized vision and a reality that was intimately and emotionally familiar, and hence to invent a pictorial structure that was stimulating and entirely in keeping with the spirit of the times.

Landscape was an emotional mirror that held a fundamental significance for young Czech painters, just as it did for many contemporary Czech lyrical poets. Thus it was no accident that the first exhibition by the Mánes Union, held in 1898, was dominated by landscape artists. The rise of Czech landscape art had been confirmed in 1887 with the appointment of Julius Mařák as a professor at the School of Fine Arts. The pupils in his landscape classes recalled with gratitude the dedication and pedagogical talents of this Neo-Romantic, whose open-air summer courses became legendary. Mařák bequeathed them the concept of "mood", which – though not without friction – became the watchword of young painting in the 1890s. In the first issue of Volné směry, the great poet and art critic Jan Neruda, who belonged to the previous generation, alluded to the young artists with a sigh: "All mood, no thought." Yet what he considered as lacking was seen by these youths as the fundamental principle of their artistic sensibility. The painter František Kaván gave an explanation of the word "mood" in an essay on Mařák. For Kaván, it was the most important concept of all, going far beyond mere sensory perception, for it enabled the artist to creatively express his most intimate world. It was the state that gave birth to "extraordinary collections of earthly signs in the soul", together with a loftiness and sense of wonder that expand our awareness of our own existence. The content of the impression depended on the individual, on "a strong conception of the world as a unity" where themes, actions, shapes and colors came together in a harmonious balance.[15]

As a concept, "mood" was also of interest to art theoreticians. In 1899 Alois Riegl, a key figure in the Viennese school of art history, published an article under the title "Mood: the Content of Modern Art", in Graphische Künste, a periodical that was also read by the Czech modernists. Using a contemporary landscape as an example, he gave a very broad definition of "mood" as a notion that conveyed the new conception of the world and that attempted to establish a novel harmony between rational knowledge and emotional belief. For Riegl, it was a sweeping overview that enabled an artist's "mood" to find expression.

The younger generation, however, invested this notion with a more subjective content. Mood belonged to the art of nuance and half-tones, which enthralled the symbolists at the time. Its changeability was the expression of an uninterrupted flow of emotions, which the artist endeavoured to mirror. A similar view gained strength in literature, and in its early years Volné směry, which had an influential literary section, clearly reflected the widening cultural horizons of the young painters. The poems and stories published in the magazine often introduced a mentally unstable character who calmed the chaos of his emotional life – infected with the "poison of civilization" – by contact with nature and attentiveness to its ebbs and flows. The thesis that a picture is a mirror that reflects moods tended to associate artistic expression with the state of mind of the creative individual, and therefore subordinated art to the subjectivity of the emotions. The nature of the role thus attributed to "mood" later had to be revised, but it nevertheless gave birth to an art of unprecedented influence.

The changing states of nature were particularly appealing to the sensibility of the young landscape artists. Spring and autumn, morning and evening, seasons and the transitions between them, all acquired a deeper significance in their work. Autumn, whose rich colours did not preclude the suggestion of life's melancholy end, was indisputably the favourite subject of painters in the first half of the 1890s, and, from a

Otakar Lebeda, *View over Lužnice*, 1899.
Oil, 50.5 x 66 cm.
Prague, National Gallery.

František Kaván, *Flow*, 1896. Oil on canvas,
102 x 132 cm.
Prague, National Gallery.

Antonín Slavíček, *Autumn at Veltrusy*, 1896. Oil, 66 x 50 cm.
Prague, National Gallery.

Maxmilián Švabinský, *Round Portrait*, 1897.
Oil on canvas, diam. 105.5 cm.
Prague, National Gallery.

Antonín Hudečck, *Evening Silence*, 1900. Oil on canvas, 120 x 180.5 cm.
Prague, National Gallery.

strictly pictorial standpoint, the theme also lent itself admirably to the invention of a new decorative concept.

The canvases that Antonín Slavíček painted in the park of Veltrusy Castle and the Hvězda estate are representative of this period. In some of these he used the in-depth perspective of a tree-lined avenue in autumn to create a feeling of the relentless flight of time. Or his eyes fell on a birch coppice whose apparent monotony yielded a decorative gradation of form and colour that could "sing" within the subtle nuances of a gentle, limited register. The themes of Slavíček's "mood" canvases seem to reflect a shift from what was still a Neo-Romantic and Neo-Baroque conception toward one consistent with Art Nouveau style.

Each of Slavíček's friends, who were all pupils of Mařák's, had his own particular tendency. In the beginning František Kaván was a realist painter, but his *Flow*, dating from 1896, is infused with the lyrical view of nature that was typical at that time. This led him to a greater sensitivity to atmosphere in landscape, through a discreet stylization of groups of trees and the use of symbolist motifs. Kaván also wrote "decadent" poems and maintained contacts with Hlaváček and the *Moderní revue* circle. Nevertheless, his teacher, Mařák,

criticized his interest in Symbolism, and Kaván withdrew from his class at the beginning of 1896.

In the previous autumn, the young Otakar Lebeda, one of the most promising talents in the landscape class, went with the older Kaván to southern Bohemia where he painted dark, gloomy ponds. Driven by an inner restlessness, Lebeda travelled a great deal. His work consisted mainly of melancholy canvases in which the sun rarely appeared; his colours, which were on the dark side to begin with, later became harsh and aggressive. He softened the severity of his treatment by using short strokes in the composition of the picture or by modelling the landscape with thick, heavy colour. In the two years before he committed suicide, his pictures reflected his constant struggle with the mental illness that had begun to afflict him. His vision increasingly turned from a nostalgia for twilight views – whose mistiness is reminiscent of the pastels he drew in Bechyně, where he may have been reminded of his dead friend, the sculptor František Hošek – toward the dramatic expression of the bond between man and the earth.

Antonín Hudeček's "mood" canvases, on the other hand, show much lyrical subtlety. His motifs were simple, but his technique refined. His method was a

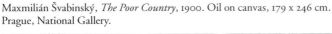

Maxmilián Švabinský, *The Poor Country*, 1900. Oil on canvas, 179 x 246 cm. Prague, National Gallery.

Jan Preisler, illustration for poems by Julius Zeyer, 1899. Charcoal, 21 x 35 cm. Plzeň, Zápodočeská Gallery.

free extension of French Pointillism that consisted of covering the picture's surface with half-tones broken by light in a mosaic of small, coloured spots. This created a flat image, excluding expressive effects while augmenting the overall intensity. *Evening Silence*, 1900, became one of the standard models of the new landscape art. Its theme, a view into the gleaming eye of a pond, recalls a similar treatment by Lebeda and underscores the common ground between this landscape genre and Symbolism: man face to face with the mystery of the earth. Yet a back view of a woman in city dress framed by trunks of saplings provides a balance expressive of a harmony bathed in melancholic serenity. This effective synthesis is one of the best examples of how important this landscape style was to modern painting.

Figurative painters were also sensitive landscape artists. One of these was Švabinský, whose perception of nature, and a new concept of woman as the personification of nature, led him beyond his initial Neo-Romanticism. In 1897, he painted *Round Portrait*, modelled on his fiancée, Ela Vejrychová, which won him an honorary diploma at the Universal Exposition in Paris. This portrait, rather conventional in appearance, is impregnated with the atmosphere of the times through its harmony of greens and purples. The depiction of the young, seated woman has an almost photographic look, which is counterbalanced by the Bacchic mood of the vine-covered trellis behind her. There is a similar inner polarity, though attenuated by a hint of melancholy, in the character of the girl herself. Ela was also the model for *The Poor Country*, a large allegorical work painted in 1900. Here the artist produced an exemplary treatment of the figure within a landscape – a theme that would be of great importance in the new Czech painting. The painter knew this open, windswept landscape intimately from his stays in the Czecho-Moravian highlands. He depicts it under a golden sun, and in a shaded part of the hill, where a demure young girl sits facing the viewer, the purple heather glistens enchantingly.

At the Mánes Union's third exhibition, *The Poor Country* showed the heights to which its members aspired and, along with Hudeček's *Evening Silence*, which was also exhibited, the painting charmed visitors and critics alike with its nobility and its modern styliza-

tion. The melancholic tone of these two pictures never-theless suggests that their harmony still harbours the psychological syndrome that characterized the end of the century. Around that time Švabinský painted a portrait of Maurice Maeterlinck, marked by a dualism (the poet in town clothes, day-dreaming, with his imagined vision set in a smaller vignette underneath the portrait) that underlines the fragility of the balance between dream and reality. In 1897, Šalda made a simi-lar analysis of Maeterlinck's play *Aglavaine et Sélysette*, which he compared to a work by Gerhart Hauptmann: "Both of these plays express modern man's fervent de-sire for a life that is purer, loftier, more intense, more cheerful and more varied. But each also expresses the weakness of man, his lack of preparation for the third realm of the Spirit, his fear, horror and dread before the transitory phase, and his anguish over his trials and failures."[16]

Next, it was Jan Preisler's work that provided the most sensitive expression of this modern spiritual tur-moil. In 1899 he made twenty drawings to illustrate Julius Zeyer's poem "Brave Young Roman Vasilich's Song of Sorrow", which, although still set in the world of ancient Russia, was a very modern treatment, in the best Neo-Romantic tradition, of the human condition. The hero leaves his country in search of happiness, but loses his soul after encountering a phantom *femme fatale* – a "dark sorrow" whom he flees, in vain, beyond the black river. The poem tells of the hero's tragic depen-dence on his own ideal image, which obstructs normal relationships with other people and leads to his doom, thus depicting the danger of narcissism as a beautiful, deadly obsession.

Illustrating this poem freely, like a musical accom-paniment, Preisler captured the very heart of Zeyer's song. The drawings trace the evolution of the charac-

Jan Preisler, *Spring,* triptych, 1900, Oil on canvas,
LEFT TO RIGHT: 112 x 70 cm; 112 x 186 cm; 112 x 70 cm.
Plzeň, Zápodočeská Gallery.

ter's dream image; the most intense of these represents
the pale features of the ghost like a mask floating in a
birch wood, while the faces of two figures melt together
into a single, androgynous form. This drawing shows a
certain similarity to the work of the Belgian symbolist
Fernand Khnopff whose impressive series of paintings
Preisler saw at the first Vienna Secession exhibition.
This influence recurs in several of Preisler's works,
including *The Memory,* a drawing for one of his melancholy poems that bears a resemblance to Khnopff's
painting, *Tenderness.* Both evince the same consterna-
tion of the modern creative artist confronted with an
unattainable ideal of beauty.

Preisler was keenly sensitive to this frustration, more
psychological than technical, as he ever more urgently
felt the need to express himself through painting. For
the first Mánes Union exhibition, he began preparing a
series of canvases called *The Cycle of the Knight Errant,*

Jan Preisler, illustration for Julius Zeyer's poem *Brave Young Roman Vasilich's Song of Sorrow*, 1899. Charcoal, 23.2 x 37.7 cm. Prague, National Gallery.

but he never finished it. When it came to executing the works, he found himself unable to resolve the conflict – also reflected in his character's progression toward an ideal image – between form and content, which Hynais' extremely popular Luminism made mandatory at the time.

Preisler only found a solution to this conflict with a commissioned work, a large triptych entitled *Spring*. Undoubtedly, his intention here was to propose a modern alternative to Hynais' *Judgment of Paris,* a long-awaited work that was eventually exhibited at the Rudolfinum in Prague in 1898, but which turned out to be a disappointment. Painting had come a long way since Hynais finished this picture, and while Preisler's *Spring* did indeed resemble *Judgment of Paris,* it transformed Hynais' painting in a very singular manner. In a valley being drawn out of its winter sleep by the wind and sun, a pubescent peasant boy sits with his head resting against the trunk of a birch tree and his hands clasped; behind him stands an idealized female nude, a red-haired, poetic, modern Venus who personifies the

blossoming of spring. On the side panels of the triptych are two other young girls, whose allegorical function is unclear, but who evocatively complete the picture's poetic atmosphere. In this painting, simplicity replaces Hynais' richness, and modesty his salon-style eroticism. The adolescent's hands, joined in a gesture of supplication, are at the centre of the composition. The three female figures in this work are modern-day goddesses, but can also be imagined as the Three Fates, who might have entered this familiar world after leaving the suffocating inferno of Pirner's Neo-Romanticism.

Preisler's *Spring* presents both an "exterior" and an "inner" vision, but there is also an interplay of two pictorial techniques at work. The centre is still painted with a Hynais-style luminosity, which reflects coloured light onto the youth's white shirt, while the wings of the triptych show no illusionistic effects; the painting is given greater density by non-descriptive colour possessing a decorative quality.

Preisler's intent is more easily understood in the light of the fact that *Spring* was commissioned by the architect Jan Kotěra to decorate the interior of the building he was erecting on Wenceslas Square, which was the first well-defined example of the Art Nouveau style in Prague. Preisler, however, did not conceive of his painting as mere decoration. Indeed, it was as a veritable manifesto that the work met with great success at the third exhibition of the Mánes Union, where it was presented with Švabinský's *The Poor Country* and Hudeček's *Evening Silence*. Mádl, one of the foremost Czech art critics, grasped the importance of *Spring*: "This is a painting with ideas that belong to the end of the nineteenth century. It is not the result of an accumulation of knowledge or borrowed metaphysics, but the offshoot of an intense inner life that is doubly sensitive to sorrow and joy and that depicts these with each stroke and each change of tone. It is worth noting, for future reference, that it was painted in 1900."[17]

In *Spring* Preisler solved a series of problems that Czech painters encountered in the 1890s. He managed to shift the conflict between naturalism and idealism, which sparked the crisis in the first place, onto new ground where it was able to bear fruit. His adolescent's universe is made up of poetic visions as well as the resonances of nature. Puberty, at once joyful and tormented, encompasses the processes of psychological development and of natural rhythms, and the point of this combination is to surmount depression and to mature emotionally. Hence, in Preisler's case, Šalda's Synthetism began to override the strongly decadent tone apparent in the illustrations for Zeyer's poem. This is proved by the painting's decorative qualities, together with its contribution to the promotion of the new decorative style, with the stated purpose of achieving a progressive change in modern man's environment. Thus there was, on the threshold to the 1900s, a manifest desire to transform the confusion of the past century into a new, positive and spiritual sense of life.

Toward a new style

Karel Chytil, the dynamic director of the Museum of Decorative Arts founded in 1885 by the Civic Chamber of Commerce and Crafts, was the first in Prague to comment on the new decorative style known as "Art Nouveau". In the Chamber's bulletin, which strove to keep the Czech creative industry well informed and to promote its commercial potential, Chytil described the new work coming out of Paris as "bizarre and fantastic, brilliant and full of charm. It shows remarkable mastery of technique and makes excellent use of its materials. Hot, creative blood runs through it, and if this sometimes goes to extremes and boils over, who can take it amiss?"[1] But could Chytil then have foreseen the overwhelming success this new style was to have in his own city?

Art Nouveau seems to have appeared first in drawing and graphic art. It could already be seen in Hynais' project for the cover of *Die Kunst für alle* in 1894. Its longitudinal positioning of the attractive woman draped in flowing garments, and of the stylized tree trunks, the placing of the two figures in a flat, decorative design, along with the use of unusual typography gave rise to numerous variations in the decorative arts of the period. Hynais used these devices (which showed how deeply he had assimilated the new taste) not only for commercial art, but in ornamental oil painting as well. The Neo-Baroque work he had begun earlier at the National Theatre was completed in 1901 with an allegory of Winter done in the Art Nouveau style. There was no slavish attachment to ornament here either, on the contrary, the picture combined a very strong sensuality, created especially by his use of colour, with a very pliant, almost elastic stylization.

The young artists, who took the whole matter more seriously, adopted more radical approaches. *The Wind and the Breeze,* a charcoal triptych by Jan Preisler that was exhibited at the Rudolfinum in 1896 and was greatly appreciated by the critics, still remains the first real example of Czech modernism.[2] Significantly, it was reproduced on the cover of the first issue of *Volné směry* and was still serving to represent the artist's work at a collective exhibition of the Mánes Union of Artists in Vienna in 1900. It is interesting to note that its composition is reminiscent of a Rodin sculpture, *Fugit amor,* particularly in the pose of the young man in the centre, who is floating aloft on his back with arms longingly outstretched toward the provocative feminine allegory

Karel Vitězslav Mašek, poster for the Architecture and Engineering Exhibition, Prague, 1898. Colour lithograph. 128 x 68 cm. Prague, UPM.

Facing page: Alfons Mucha, Project for a poster for the Architecture and Engineering Exhibition, Prague, 1898. Watercolor. 108.5 x 85 cm. Prague, National Gallery.

Jan Preisler, *The Wind and the Breeze*, triptych, 1896. Charcoal, LEFT TO RIGHT: 35 x 54, 35 x 86, 35 x 54 cm. Prague, National Gallery.

of the Wind, who is desperately trying to escape him. Preisler, however, was not as expressive as Rodin, and his approach in this work was far more decorative, rather like a project for a mural painting. The triptych's decorative style was reinforced by the use of two allegorical figures, treated in such a way that the whole composition was structured by an undulating linear arabesque. Although the repetition of the arabesque was a fundamental structural characteristic of the new decorative style, what the public really admired were the details. The allegory of the Breeze, on the left-hand side, was a popular favourite, and it was indeed consonant with the fashion that had sprung from French Intimisme of the 1890s. Preisler later attempted to reproduce this part of the work in a large painting, but finally realized that he was only pandering to a superficial vogue and abandoned it.

Promoting and disseminating the new decorative style meant that both its subject matter and especially its forms had to be made easily understandable to the public. Alfons Mucha achieved this in his 1897 one-man exhibition at the Topič Gallery in Prague. Mucha, who was not accepted at the Prague School of Fine Arts, first spent some time in the stage-decoration workshops of the Vienna theatres. Help from a patron then enabled him to study in Munich, where he became president of *Škréta,* the Czech young artists'

association there. It was in this capacity that he wrote the famous open letter to Mikoláš Aleš. In the autumn of 1887 he settled in Paris, but his hour of glory was not to come for another seven years.

During this period Mucha earned his living by doing illustrations and graphic work part-time. He frequented artists and was in contact with the most modern, and most poverty-stricken, among them. He met Paul Gauguin, who was one of the *habitués* of a cheap restaurant on the rue de la Grande Chaumiere, and when Gauguin returned penniless from his first visit to Tahiti in 1893, Mucha offered him hospitality for a while in his studio. Paul Serusier, the Nabis, the symbolists as well as the Polish, Hungarian, and Dutch synthetists, along with many other artists, were regular customers at this restaurant, and the basic concepts of a new art were forged in endless discussions there.

Mucha's undeniable gift for spectacular compositions and a taste for the fatalism of Wagner's historical dramas were already evident in his illusionistic illustrations for Xavier Marmier's *Contes de grand-mère* (Grandmother's tales) and Charles Seignobos' *Scènes et épisodes de l'Histoire de l'Allemagne* (Scenes and events from the history of Germany). By a stroke of luck, at the end of 1894 Mucha received his first commission to do a poster for Sarah Bernhardt, depicting her as Gismonde, the title role of a play by Victorien Sardou.

The poster was an instant success, and the preliminary sketch for it suggests that Mucha may have derived his inspiration from Gauguin and synthetic Cloisonism. The poster undoubtedly owed its success to the way modern graphism was used to idealize the actress, who was venerated in Paris. Indeed, Sarah Bernhardt was seen as an incarnation of "the eternal feminine", who appeared as a kind of new divinity behind the mask provided by her various roles.

Over the next few years, the contract Mucha signed in the aftermath of this success generated a series of posters that are landmarks in the history of modern graphic art. The artist used his entire range of expression in them, from a tender colour harmony for *The Lady of the Camelias* to violence in *Medea,* but the whole series was informed by a single vision that embraced all these different facets. In 1897 Mucha drew an idealized portrait of the "divine" Sarah for the magazine *La Plume,* using only the head, seen full-face, surrounded by a nimbus of ornamental work. The facial expression was sufficiently ambiguous to suggest several possible emotions. Veiled by a slight cloud of sadness, the abstractness of the line erased all trace of real expression, while at the same time its immobility evoked a kind of mystical trance.

Mucha did not find his own style with the first poster, and in 1895 he was still undecided among a number of possible courses. The following year, however, the floodgates seemed to open, and Parisian graphic art was inundated by his characteristic style, which was completely different from that of artists such as the famous Eugène Grasset or Carlos Schwabe. Mucha's prolific output included colour lithographs for decorative panels representing the four seasons, flowers, daytime scenes, stars and precious stones. He also drew magazine covers, designed catalogues, calendars, postcards, and even soapboxes. For these he created innumerable variations on the theme of a beautiful, languorous woman, usually seated, enveloped in a horseshoe-shaped nimbus and surrounded by a richly decorated frame. Strong lines were used to progressively draw the eye inside the labyrinth, a complicated ornamentation of intertwining motifs such as stolons and long, flowing tresses. Even though their use as publicity may have seemed superficial, Mucha infused them nonetheless with a symbolist idea. Orthodox symbolists viewed Mucha's commercial designs as a desecration of their concepts, but were powerless against their public appeal. Indeed, the artist himself felt that this new concept of art belonged to the world at large.

Mucha extended his formula to the decorative arts and interior design. For instance, he translated his drawing into three-dimensional terms in his designs for

Karel Vitězslav Mašek, *The Prophetess Libuše*, 1893. Oil on canvas, 193 x 193 cm. Paris, Musée d'Orsay.

the fittings and decoration for Georges Fouquet's jewelry shop in Paris, for which he also created several pieces of jewelry. One of these is the most splendid pieces of Art Nouveau jewelry ever made: a bracelet in the shape of a snake in enamelled gold, attached to a magnificent ring by slender chains. Here, too, the symbolist vision of the *femme fatale,* imagined in terms of the oriental splendour of the biblical Salome, lies behind the artist's creation. A similar labyrinthine ornamentation was applied to tapestry, but its highest development could be found in book illustration, one of the essential fields of the new decorative art movement. In Mucha's hands, Robert de Flers' symbolist variation

of an ancient Provençal legend, *Ilsea, Princess of Tripoli*, was transformed into a paradigm of the "total work". The richly decorated book was conceived as a single graphic unit incorporating a masterly combination of figurative illustration, ornamental motifs, text, titles, vignettes and decorated paper. In 1901 a shorter version of *Ilsea* was published in Prague, where it became a much-admired example of the new art of book design.

Mucha's 1897 exhibition in Prague had actually opened earlier in the Paris gallery of the magazine *La Plume,* and had also travelled through Germany, but it was the first time this entirely ornamental decorative style had been shown in Prague. Its success encouraged Czech artists to try their hand at this kind of work and helped to popularize the new modern style.

Even though he was overburdened with work in Paris, Mucha maintained a constant interest in events in his own country. He entered a design competition for the poster for the Architecture and Engineering Exhibition with a sketch depicting an allegory of Architecture as a seated girl wearing a head-dress of poppies; in her hands she holds the twin emblems of a wooden house and a Baroque church. The freshness of this design sets it apart from his Paris work, which was often excessively stylized. It was particularly appealing to the

Villa, 1901, Bubeneč (Slavíčkova 7). Arch.: Karel Vitězslav Mašek.

LEFT: Apartment building, entrance door, 1908. Josefov, (Široká 9). Arch.: Karel Vitězslav Mašek.

young members of the Mánes Union and to Hlaváček, who lauded Mucha's decorative approach, his purity of line and the harmony of his colors.

Mucha's design, however, did not win the competition; the jury preferred a project by Karel Vitězslav Mašek. Although definitely inferior from an artistic standpoint, the figures and decorative setting of the winning entry displayed a fragile artificiality more in tune with the particular form of mannerism still prevalent even in Prague architecture. Mašek, whose painted work oscillated between naturalism and the decorative style, was an interesting representative of this period of transition from the aesthetics of late historicism to modernity. While in Paris in 1893, he painted *The*

Prophetess Libuše (today in the Musée d'Orsay), in which his curious use of a kind of pseudo-Pointillism as a decorative device in the ornamentation of the figure – a mythical Czech prophetess-princess – was years ahead of a similar, extensively used style that appeared in the stucco masks and ornamentation in Prague architecture around 1900. On the other hand, Mašek's work usually consisted of illusionistic allegorical pictures with a naturalist bent, in which gradations of light were used to maximum effect. He also made decorative paintings of rustic scenes – which Hlaváček deemed "perverse" – and took an amateur interest in architecture. He designed the plans for his own picturesque villa (Prague-Bubeneč, 1901), which he considered to be a "total work of art". Its free mixture of themes, some inspired by the new cult of nature and others drawn from the historical repertoire, made for a charming interior and exterior, which included traditional motifs from folk architecture. During the competition for the Architecture and Engineering Exhibition poster, Mašek was named professor of ornamental design at the School of Applied Arts. For Mucha, Mašek's appointment aggravated his frustration with the competition result, and

Jan Preisler, poster for the 9th exhibition of the Mánes Union of Artists, "Worpswede", 1903. Colour lithograph, 80 x 118 cm. Prague, UPM.

further demonstrated that Prague was still behind the times.

The debate triggered by the competition focused greater attention on the modern poster; Hlaváček, who considered poster design a decorative art in its own right, wrote an article entitled "Streetcorners in Paris" for *Moderní revue,* in which he introduced artists like Jules Chéret, Théophile Alexandre Steinlen and Henri de Toulouse-Lautrec to the Czech public.[3] In the following months, the young artists of the Mánes Union reacted by producing posters for their opening exhibitions. Indeed, a poster competition, open only to members of the association, was organized for the first of these exhibitions and was won by Arnošt Hofbauer, who had already decorated building facades in Prague. His poster, a daring criticism of local art patrons, showed a young woman – an allegory of Art – disturbing the comfort of a hugely fat little oriental god representing Money and Mediocrity. The work's modernism lay in the stylized naturalism of the figures. Hofbauer also produced the poster for the second exhibition, depicting a schooner displaying the Mánes Union's emblem, cleaving full speed ahead through a violent sea, with a sailor on board throwing a lifebuoy to a drowning man – Hofbauer's way of extolling the role and importance of the Union. The poster was clearly inspired by Hokusai, and its Japonisme, with colour reduced to a simple harmony of rust, blue-green and white, was characteristic of the new Art Nouveau spirit. Hofbauer's cover for the third-year edition of *Volné směry,* which depicted a nude boy kneeling at the foot of a statue of the god Pan, gazing in wonder at the spirals of the Milky Way, demonstrated how the new decorative style could be combined with a symbolist theme.

The quality of Czech poster art remained at a very high level from then on, and improved even further as artists drew away from linear design and began to make greater use of surface colour. This trend was already apparent in the poster Hofbauer designed in 1899 for a poetry recital given by the actress Hana Kvapilová. The double view of the subject, who was reflected in a mirror so as to be seen from a frontal angle as well as in profile, became another richly meaningful theme in symbolist poster art.

The posters for the exhibitions of the Mánes Union were designed by first-rate artists, and had a decisive influence on future poster art, such as Preisler's work for

Vladimír Županský, poster for the Rodin exhibition, 1902.
Colour lithograph, 158 x 84 cm. Prague, UPM.

the exhibition of French painting in 1902 and for the Worpswede group's show in 1903. Vladimír Županský in 1902 produced a superb Rodin exhibition poster, which shows Rodin's statue of Balzac against a background of swirling cosmic lines. Works like these also inspired designers of commercial posters, which were of a fairly high standard at the time.

The conception of the poster as a pictorial work exploiting both the potential of the entire surface and the emotional expressiveness of colour had an immediate effect on plastic art as a whole, and graphic art in particular became the interface between the two. The way it overlapped both was apparent in the work of Vojtěch Preissig, the most important illustrator of the time. Preissig was a pupil of Friedrich Ohmann at the School of Applied Arts in Prague, where the decorative possibilities of floral designs were already being studied. His designs grew more sophisticated in Paris, where he helped Mucha in his studio and attended Émile Delaune's school of graphic art. Preissig's output during that period included works such as *Spring*, a watercolour painted in 1899 and repeated as a colour engraving in 1900, based on the union of a girl and a flower. Though the two were often associated in a single theme at the time, this work stood out for its particular style. Although Japonisme was also Preissig's basic source of inspiration, his line was far more delicate than Mucha's, to the extent of almost being absorbed by the colour and flat tones; this contrasted with the robust strength of Mucha's line, which seemed to be a concentration of the physical aspect of form. The evanescence of Preissig's line had no spiritualistic intent, but was purely lyrical and poetic. In fact, his imagination was entirely that of a painter. This approach is clear in his wallpaper designs from that period, in which the floral motif is so abstract and flat that naturalism disappears completely and the surface becomes the ground for sophisticated graphic patterns. Preissig's case clearly indicates the new decorative style's evolution within Czech art; far from being a mere passing fashion, this style was a deep-rooted phenomenon and a crucial step along the path to modernity.

The School of Applied Arts was the natural centre of the new decorative style in Prague. The school, which had been founded ten years earlier at the height of eclectic historicism, gained prestige during the first half of the 1890s by supporting new ideas that actually benefited its own fields of interest. These new ideas, which had originated in England, gradually found fertile ground, and the belief grew that the decorative arts had a role to play in the new modern style. Two facts explain the school's increasing interest in this phenomenon. First of all, in 1896 two teachers, Myslbek and Ženíšek, left to join the nationalized School of Fine

Arts, where the views were more in line with their own. This enabled the School of Applied Arts to concentrate more fully on its originally established programme. Secondly, early the following year intense preparation began for the 1900 Universal Exposition in Paris, at which the School was to hold an independent exhibition of its work in a decorated interior of the Austrian Pavilion. The same pavilion was also to house another decorated interior paid for by the Prague Chamber of Commerce and Crafts, with Czech Technical School teachers Josef Fanta and Jan Koula as artistic directors. Obviously, this confrontation provided a natural stimulus to the creativity of pupils at Applied Arts. An examination of the photographic documents of the pavilion, shows that the interiors representing Czech decorative art at the 1900 Universal Exposition were more a heterogeneous collection of objects than a stylistically coherent ensemble.[4] The construction and fittings of the Applied Arts exhibit were Ohmann's work, but despite his skill as an interior designer, the contents struck visitors as an arrangement of a few "party pieces". In the

Jan Koula, writing desk, 1900. Wood, rep cloth and embroidery, h.: 138 cm. Prague, UPM.

Josef Fanta, chair, 1900. Wood, gilt leather, bronze, h.: 68 cm. Prague, UPM.

other interior, Fanta showed more daring with his space, decorated as "a Czech intellectual's study", but he, too, was unable to develop a coherent style.

Fanta's project was based on the contrast between the ground floor, which was decorated like a home, and the study floor, the walls of which were covered with paintings in a mythological-cum-allegorical style by František Urban, Preisler and Karel Špillar, and with a ceiling of imposing wooden beams. Jan Koula designed the entrance, which he decorated with folk art motifs. The most interesting element in the area designed by Fanta was the furniture, which was outstanding in its relatively simple geometric shapes and its sober decoration. Ludvik Wurzel's maple-wood cabinet decorated with ornamental bronze plaquettes and terracotta, as well as his nest-shaped easy chair and writing desk, were plainly influenced by traditional styles, although they had shed their conventional trappings. Koula's folk-style credenza was striking for its elaborate decoration rather than its originality. In fact both designers' concepts were rooted in the earliest expressions of the reform movement that had already appeared, especially in England, some twenty or thirty years previously. They still seemed innovative in Czech circles, but were virtually out of date elsewhere.

On the whole, the interior decorated by the School of Applied Arts gave the impression of being even more heterogeneous, but it nonetheless included some works that came close to current international trends. The teachers took the lead in the School's search for a common language and had their young graduates exhibit alongside themselves, which gave rise to a more dynamic style.

Jan Kastner, who headed the wood-sculpture class, exhibited a challenging work, a large Czech altar in polychrome wood. He exploited to the full his considerable knowledge of medieval wood carving, which he modernized with an unusual combination of naturalistic relief and hieratic attitudes in the figures. Kastner's efforts to do away with traditional forms are also reflected in his furniture, such as the witty and ingenious three-legged folding chair, the back of which is decorated with the head of an American Indian and mother-of-pearl incrustation.

Another important person at the School of Applied Arts was Celda Klouček, a clay-modeling teacher with a bias toward the ornamental, who was responsible for

Arnošt Hofbauer, poster for a poetry recital by the actress Hana Kvapilová, 1899. Colour lithograph, 110 x 81 cm.
Prague, UPM.

one of the exhibition's most impressive works. This was an elaborate doorway made of limestone, which demonstrated how closely his class was involved with architecture. Some of the ceramic vases made in his workshop were also among the finest pieces in the exhibition. Klouček's influence can also be seen in the plastic qualities of the metal objects – belt-buckles and ink-wells – created by Emanuel Novák, as well as those of his own pupils, whose designs he often suggested himself. All the evidence points to Klouček as the source of Art Nouveau's infiltration into Czech decorative art.

Before joining the school, Klouček had worked with the Berlin decorator Otto Lessing. He had attended the School of Applied Arts both in Vienna and, for nearly six years, in Frankfurt. His early work showed the influence of late Italian Renaissance art and Mannerism, which can be seen in a book of his sketches published in Prague in 1893. Brilliantly versatile, however, he also worked in the Neo-Baroque tradition of rich stucco work. In 1895 Klouček abandoned historicism and, for the first time, his pupils' end-of-year work bore a clearly naturalistic stamp. He began using ceramic clay as a malleable, inexpensive material for experimenting with the stylization of natural shapes, and dropped the traditional acanthus-leaf decoration in favour of local flora. Poppies, guelder-roses, laurels, mallows, primroses and elders provided him with a highly original repertoire that was well suited to the new ceramic colours. Stalks, leaves, flowers and fruit were arranged over the surface of the object in a naturalistic manner that respected the rhythmic articulation of its decorative design.

The rounded shape of ceramic vases was conducive to the development of the new ornamental style, and offered the possibility of linking new forms and modern ideas. The symbolists had already given thought to the relationship between a vase's interior space and exterior substance, and concluded that the vase was the symbol of a new art whose visions were drawn from the depths of the unconscious.[5] A vase was made of clay – earth, in other words – hardened in fire, and the artist's imagination gave it a form that held water, the nutritive element enabling flowers to grow through air toward the sun. The symbolism of the association with natural elements was further heightened by the focus on flowers, the undisputed symbol of art in general.

Around 1900, Anna Boudová-Suchardová, a painter of flowers and decorative floral design, created a series of Art Nouveau ceramic vases. She specialized in two different types of work, one of which consisted of fairly simple vases and chalice-shaped bowls decorated with stylized motifs in the Japanese manner, executed in a harmony of the purple and green shades popular at the time. In sharp contrast, she also made rougher vases covered with a "natural" monochrome glaze whose effect was emphasized by motifs in relief. Like František Bílek's graphite vases, all of these pieces bear the characteristic stamp of their author.

The vases made by Celda Klouček and his pupils (Václav Mařan, Rudolf Hameršmíd, Václav Sidlík, František Soukup, Karel Pavlík and Robert Hájek, among others) fitted in more with the conventional craft style of the School of Applied Arts, which makes it easier to follow the evolution of Czech ornamentalism. Vases made in the initial period displayed a naturalistic surface relief; from the formal standpoint, they were inspired by prehistoric examples, and the colour work tended toward a markedly pictorial effect. During the peak of their production, between 1899 and 1904, apart from a few somewhat whimsical exceptions, the vases were generally very simple. They were tall, narrow and cone-shaped, or else low and wide, their flat and stylized decoration, which was sometimes incised in the clay, usually spread symmetrically outward from a central element. There were also some instances of evocative, asymmetrical stylization that emphasized the flatness of the decoration even further. A monochrome glaze was used, mostly green or yellow, though sometimes blue or pink. The School's ceramic vases were tall and narrow, with a symmetrical decoration of small stalks bearing fruit or flowers that formed handles on the sides. They were predominantly white, accented with small details in various colours.

From ceramics to stucco decoration was only a short step; the work of Klouček and his pupils on Art Nouveau architecture provided them with the opportunity to take it. Klouček's reliefs and friezes for the Zemská Bank in 1896 showed a pronounced naturalism, which was even more evident, though in a Neo-Baroque context, in his stucco work on the Straka Academy in that same year. Subsequently, the evolution of Art Nouveau concepts in Klouček's work featured chiefly in buildings with no great architectural character, to which his decoration made a welcome improvement. One of these was the Vohanka building in Prague, in 1898, followed two years later by the museum in Plzeň, on which Klouček collaborated with the architect Josef Škorpil. Klouček enjoyed working in a team on projects where he felt free to follow his own inspiration in the design of the facades and interiors. It was in these conditions that in 1902 he created the imposing stone facade of the Credit Bank in Prague, which was built by Matěj Blecha's company. This is incontestably Klouček's best-known work, and his talent as a sculptor is evident in the decorative reliefs – masks, branches, ornamental snakes, putti, inscriptions and especially his Mercury on the attic storey.

Art Nouveau decorative concepts gradually matured in Klouček's work. His numerous pupils promulgated his ideas so rapidly in new buildings that, in the public's mind, they became largely identified with the style itself. Naturalism and a sensitive sculptural rendering of plant and figural motifs were constant features, but the ornamental rhythm had to be adapted to large-scale works. Klouček handled this mainly through a symmetrical development of the sinuous lines of the vegetation over friezes and panels on either side of a central motif, usually a female mask. This composition took up the theme of a figure set in a natural landscape that, as mentioned earlier, was a central motif in the work of the young Czech painters. Unlike the idealized Neo-Renaissance style *mascheroni,* Klouček's Art Nouveau masks displayed a wide range of expression that well illustrated the new feeling of sensitivity.

The masks were also attractive stylistically. The frontal representation of a girl's face with a look that was at once vague and languorous, framed by ribbons, veils, or plant tendrils, allowed a delicate interplay between a basic symmetry and numerous asymmetrical naturalistic elements. In this formal mirror-effect the motif acquired a deeper significance, which Klouček perceived only intuitively. Psychological analyses of these compositions have shown that they symbolically expressed the process of individuation, in which the plastic work itself represented a complex perception of the human psyche. The symmetrical reflection of the right and left sides signified the desire to balance its conscious and unconscious elements. This analysis is corroborated by the strange expressions of Klouček's masks, whose dreaminess and sensualism are intricately combined with the ideality of the character they represent.[6]

The new decorative style basically owed its success to evocative symbols such as these, which were very much in tune with the mentality of the times. Klouček's mask motif was widely imitated in Prague, not only in Art Nouveau facades and interiors, but also in other forms of plastic art. It became the predominant motif

Prague Credit Bank, details of the facade decoration, 1902.
Prague Old Town (ulice 28 října 13). Arch.: Celda Klouček.

Prague Credit Bank, detail of the facade decoration.

Turnov Professional Training School, comb, post-1900. Silver, alabaster, Bohemian garnets, tortoise-shell. Prague, UPM.

of Art Nouveau jewelry, for example, where it developed in subtle forms and eventually was refined into a new kind of amulet. Along with the teacher Emanuel Novák, a number of talented graduates of the School of Applied Arts contributed to this trend, including František Anýž, who founded an important business in Prague, and Josef Ladislav Němec, who, after three years perfecting his art in Paris, became the figurehead of the newly created Professional School of Jewelry in Prague.

The early forms of Art Nouveau stylization, with their characteristic linearity and the use of curves, either in Mucha's style or in Klouček's peculiar plastic variation, met with immediate success and were widely adopted. This was largely due to the system of professional training that existed at the time, under which the Prague School of Applied Arts was in touch with a whole network of other professional schools. These included the schools of ceramics in Bechyně and stone-sculpting in Hořice, the Turnov school of metalwork, the school of woodwork at Chrudím, the school of art-metalwork in Hradec Králové, and many other institutions that readily propagated the Art Nouveau prin-

ciples. Their enthusiasm and high quality of teaching very quickly enabled them to train many artist-craftsmen suitable for recruitment by contractors and architects, to such a degree that Art Nouveau became established as the standard style shortly after 1900.

Mucha's *Decorative Documents,* compiled in 1902, was undoubtedly the richest of all collections of naturalist Art Nouveau drawings. Their floral motifs reveal the minuteness and subtlety of the Art Nouveau ornamentalist's observation of the specific characteristics of each plant, its proportions and the different stages of its growth, as well as the way the artist put this to use. Mucha reconstituted these plants and flowers using black and white to underline the contrast between their positive and negative forms, which imparted a linear rhythm to the repetitive floral motif. His elimination of relief from the design made it possible to achieve a continuity of the ornamental line, whose vitality was ensured by a dynamic flexibility; this line became the symbol of growth. The idea of the eternity of nature, brilliantly expressed in plastic terms, corresponded to the theory of the reincarnation of human souls and of life after death. Thus, inanimate creatures also were to be included within this fundamental concept, by interpreting their morphology in biological terms and transmuting their physical substance into fantasy forms. Thus Mucha's *Decorative Documents* became a textbook on the nature of things, in which he developed the notion of a universe permeated with a unique biological creative force that made all things homogeneous, and he proposed the new decorative style as a means of expressing this.

Art Nouveau naturalism probably owed its success to the fact that, unlike eclectic historicism, it proposed a new idea of unity that could be considered integral to modern art. However, there were problems involved in the application of this idea of unity to the field of decoration. Even in Mucha's most elaborately ornamental work there were obvious discrepancies in the strength

Anna Boudová-Suchardová, vase, 1900. Panned ceramic, h.: 14 cm. Prague, UPM.

Left: Celda Klouček's professional training school, vase, 1900. Ceramic with coloured glaze, h.: 16 cm. Prague, UPM.

Right: Václav Mařan, vase, 1900. Ceramic with coloured glaze, h.: 16 cm. Prague, UPM.

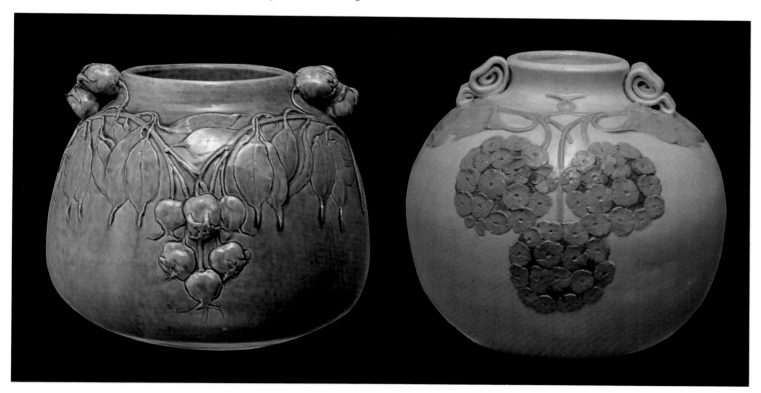

of different parts of the drawing, with the strongest lines being used to delineate the principal decorative element (usually a female figure), which was drawn within a closed outline. His flat rendering of form was translated into particularly plastic terms: only the shadowed area of the figure was concentrated in a line, and the greater the density of matter, the heavier the stroke. Klouček envisioned decorative relief in a similar way: the sculpted mass and the basic surface always had to be clearly differentiated, despite the tendency to fill up the whole surface and to establish the rhythm of the whole as a single entity.

Traditional respect for the separation between figure and background had not disappeared at this stage of Art Nouveau, even though it had opened the way for a new concept of the whole in which the interpenetration of mass and space expressed an innovative, dynamic conception of the universe. It was symptomatic that Klouček was actually a decorator, and not an architect. His approach to building was the same as that of a graphic artist to paper: his interest lay in the surface of the facade, not its construction in space. By its very nature, the technique of stucco shaped his conception of the object as a projection from the ideal surface of the facade, extending outward toward the viewer. What went on behind the facade was of no interest to him. However, the evolutive logic of this style led to the nature of the object itself losing its significance and brought up the problem of the transparency of space.

Glass-making was the decorative art of the time that by its very nature provided a positive response to this intuitive problem; this may have been one of the reasons why Art Nouveau glass enjoyed such a great success.

Bohemian glassworks already enjoyed centuries of tradition. By the end of the nineteenth century, they had become major enterprises that carefully looked after their interests in the worldwide glass-business, and their reaction to the new international decorative style was therefore totally professional. The industry's interest in this novelty began to increase in the mid-1890s, particularly after the success of Tiffany's exhibitions of his Favrile glass in Paris. In 1897, the glass manufacturers planned production in the northern Bohemian town of Liberec to meet the demand for the new coloured glass, which their experience enabled them to market at a competitive price without compromising its quality or originality.

Production of this glass already met the most exacting standards at the time of the 1900 Universal Exposition. The Harrachov Nový svět Glassworks in Krkonoše, which was famous for its engraved and painted glass, won a gold medal for a service decorated with floral motifs. Similarly successful was the Fenomén glass produced by the Widow of Jan Lötz Glassworks at Klášterský Mlýn in Southern Bohemia, which today is the most famous of the Czech glass manufacturers specializing in the Art Nouveau style.[7] This glassworks, under the management of the able Max von Spaun, specialized at the time in dense, coloured glass worked into strange, irregular shapes decorated with linear curves. This was produced using rolled and combed glass threads, and enchanting colours were obtained with layers of opalizing chemical quartz that gave the vases a shiny metallic appearance. The Palme-König Glassworks in Kostany preferred to use an extremely attractive weblike relief of strands of coloured glass on its vases.

Stanislav Kostka Neumann, praising Tiffany's coloured glass in *Moderní revue*, argued that this was a modern material which was inherently decorative by virtue of its subtle hue. Therein lay the true novelty of this glass, which "does not cast a chill into the artistic soul".[8] Specialists, however, tended instead to remark on the loss of transparency, which they considered so essential to this material. Nevertheless, at the turn of the century glass was seen as the quintessential material of artistic imagination and aesthetic fantasy.

In 1900 there were numerous indications that the general movement toward a modern style was headed for success: the intense activity in the workshops of the Prague School of Applied Art, which produced innovations in ceramics, furnishings, art metalwork and jewelry; the support for the latest poster art and other graphic techniques associated with the new concept of book design; the glass industry's eagerness to manufacture the novel products; and the tempering of young talent in painting and sculpture in the face of public scrutiny. One discipline in particular was preparing to assemble all the solo voices into a great symphony to the glory of the new "total work of art": this was architecture.

But architecture was barely emerging from the crisis of historicism at the time, and showed signs of modernity only in small-scale decorative work and projects planned for the future. It was only in 1898 that the

Emanuel Novák, candlestick, pre-1908. Molded brass, h.: 20.5 cm. Prague, UPM.

Prague public first saw the early manifestations of the Art Nouveau style in architecture, at the Architecture and Engineering Exhibition, where Alois Dryák, one of Ohmann's pupils, decorated the central hall of the Palace of Industry. It was designed in white, with colour used sparingly, and featured characteristic small pillars surmounted by the head of Hermes and lateral wall lamps concealed under stylized saplings made of plaster and cardboard. Later that same year, Dryák created the architectonic base for Sucharda's monument to Palacký, built as a wide exedra flanked by Art Nouveau pylons.

Prague still awaited the architect truly capable of forging a synthesis of the decorative disciplines and possessing a breadth of vision that would enable him to attain a higher dimension. This person was to be Jan Kotěra. He had attended Otto Wagner's special class in architecture at the Vienna School of Applied Arts from 1894 to 1897 and came to Prague in 1898 to replace Friedrich Ohmann at the School of Applied Arts. In the extraordinarily stimulating atmosphere of that international school, he became friends with the future leading lights of the Austrian Secession, Josef Maria Olbrich, Josef Hoffmann and Kolo Moser. Though his

ABOVE, LEFT: Emanuel Novák, belt-buckle, 1900. Silver, h.: 8 cm. Prague, UPM.

ABOVE, RIGHT: Josef Ladislav Němec, brooch, pre-1903. Gilt silver, chalcedony, diam.: 6 cm. Prague, UPM.

BELOW: Emanuel Novák, ink-well, pre-1908. Moulded brass, 25 cm, Prague, UPM.

ambitious early projects still bore the stamp of late historicism, from 1897 onward he made a conscious move in the direction of modern architecture.

Kotěra always retained the principles acquired from his training under Wagner, and outlined them in a 1900 article called "On Art Nouveau" published in *Volné směry*. His statement emphasized that the important thing in architectural design was not what the viewer admired most, the decoration, but instead the building's purpose and its spatial construction, which determined the decoration's expressive form. "Hence, architectural creation has two functions: first, the creation of the space, and second, its decoration. The creative conceptualization of space is truth itself, and the decoration is the expression of truth."[9]

This theoretical proposition goes straight to the heart of the "new style". The practice of late eclecticism was based on its general separation of the functional and artistic aspects of building. An erudite eclectic could dress up the same planning design in the garb of any number of historical styles. His sole consideration would be which one to adopt for a given work, and the client's desires were the decisive factor. This was the outlook that had governed architects' training until then, especially in technical teaching establishments.

Before Kotěra erupted onto the Prague scene, the debate about modernity was usually confined to discussion of the new forms of decoration. Kotěra's views, influenced by Otto Wagner (whose treatise on modern architecture was later published in Czech), eventually provoked an awareness of the wider implications of the new style, opening up a new perspective on the evolution of modern Czech architecture. He was later to be criticized from the standpoint of systematic functionalism for not having transcended the old dualism in his own practice. This criticism neglects Kotěra's belief in

OPPOSITE: Widow of Jan Lötz Glassworks, Klášterský Mlýn, vase, 1900. Blue glass, iridescent, with intertwining thread decoration, h.: 21 cm. Prague, UPM.
BELOW, LEFT: Widow of Jan Lötz Glassworks, Klášterský Mlýn, vase, post-1900. Green iridescent glass with relief decoration of interlaced threads, h.: 12 cm. Prague, UPM.
BELOW, RIGHT: Widow of Jan Lötz Glassworks, Klášterský Mlýn, vase, 1902. Colourless glass with opalescent touches, encrusted, iridescent, h.: 16.8 cm. Prague, UPM.

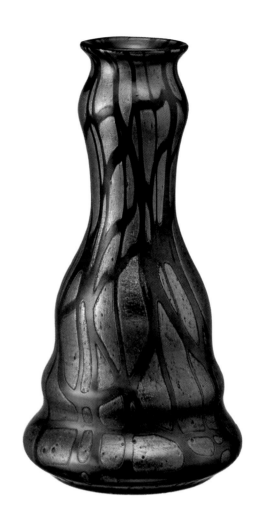

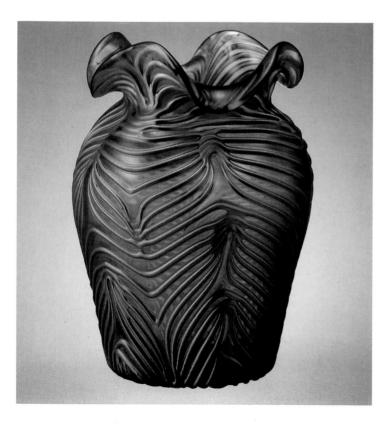

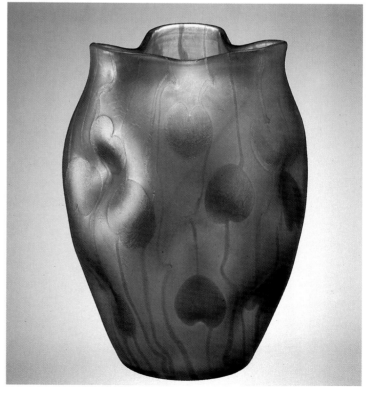

the Secession theory of the "total work of art", in which the functional and decorative aspects were seen as complementary, and the very notion of function was interpreted in a far richer sense than it was later by the proponents of functionalism.

As soon as he assumed his appointment, Kotěra began putting his concept of the residential building into practice in Prague, even though he was hampered by numerous constraints. In 1899 he designed the Peterka building on Wenceslas Square. This building consisted of shops at the ground-floor level, with apartments on the upper floors. The facade was organized in three sections: a wider central part, jutting slightly forward from the ground floor upward, and two narrower side sections, culminating in three gables on the facade. It is noteworthy that in its basic formal distribution this structure is reminiscent of Preisler's *Spring*. In the Peterka building, which was Kotěra's first major work, the balance between functional and decorative qualities was reflected in the dimensions of the windows (its ground-floor shop windows were unusual in Prague at the time), and especially in the relationship between the wall surface and the linear ornamentation on the facade. The latter's sober colour was also novel, along with its touches of gold and a few characteristic details, including the absence of framing around the windows. The building's verticality was another typical feature. A high stone base reaching from the ground floor up to the shop-front mezzanine relieved the visual bulk and considerably increased the lyrical impression of the building as a whole. The interior spaces were also conceived in a homogeneous style. The light stucco decoration of plant motifs and masks did not detract from, but instead enhanced, the serenity of the surfaces and the elegance of the doors, metalwork, light fittings and other details.

The Peterka building is a successful example of a modern "total work of art". Its poetic character is typical of Kotěra's ideas at the turn of the century, when he was building mainly for the Czech modernist intelligentsia. His family houses became the symbol of values dear to the Secession: intimate surroundings and a sense of privacy, such as that found in the family circle. Great attention was paid to the layout and fittings of interior spaces, in which economy, comfort and new sanitation requirements were taken into account.

Even in the shapes of the houses, which were set in gardens, Kotěra sought a synthesis between local tradi-

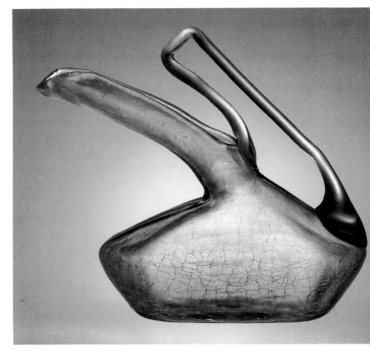

Marie Kirschnerová and Widow of Jan Lötz Glassworks, Klášterský Mlýn, cruet, 1901. Colourless glass, crackled, iridescent, h.: 17 cm. Prague, UPM.

tion and the ideal of the English family house and garden that was much in vogue at the time. Local tradition was predominant in the Trmal house (1902) in Prague-Strašnice (the Strašnice neighborhood of Prague), and the English style in the Sucharda villa (1904) in Prague-Bubeneč. Common to both was Kotěra's concern for opening up the houses onto the surrounding space, by means of loggias, balconies and bow windows.

The new notion of intimacy, in consonance with the melancholy poetic spirit of the time, also affected funerary design. The Elbogen tomb (1901) in the Jewish Cemetery at Prague-Strašnice is surprising for the plain unadorned simplicity that enhances the nobility of the stone. Its characteristic three-part arrangement, consisting of a central element flanked by two truncated towers, symbolized the idea of the gate of death, a very popular theme among Czech Secession architects. The Robitschek tomb beside it is more ornate, and its details display the sensitivity of Kotěra's sculptural talent.

Kotěra participated enthusiastically in the activities of the Mánes Union of Artists. He designed the Mánes Union's exhibition pavilion, which was built with great speed at the foot of Prague's Kinský Garden in the spring of 1902. The Manés Union was preparing an exhibition by Auguste Rodin at the time, and had taken advantage of the sculptor's renown to obtain a site and permission to build a temporary pavilion. In fact, this building was to house a good many other exhibitions organized by the Mánes Union, and helped to raise the status of modern art in Bohemia. Kotěra drew up his project for the pavilion in the space of three days, and the result was the poetic high point of his initial creative period. The motif of a central doorway flanked by two towers appeared here again, but the door in this case represented the gate of life, decorated with wreaths of flowers and a lunette painted by Karel Špillar. The plan of the pavilion was also interesting. It was designed around the constraints imposed by the exhibition, which required a small room for Rodin's drawings and a large space for the sculptures; from this starting point Kotěra created a lively structure that represented a significant expression of dynamic Art Nouveau style. He was later to use the same structure again for monumental projects.

Jan Kotěra, credenza, 1900. Wood, metal, glass and marble, 175 x 160 cm. Prague, UPM.

Jan Kotěra, divan, 1899. Wood and textiles, h.: 48 cm. Prague, UPM.

Even though he was only twenty-seven when he took up his appointment, the young Kotěra enjoyed great respect at the School of Applied Arts. In 1902 he wrote a book, *Meine und meiner Schüler Arbeiten* (My work and my students' work), published by the Viennese firm Schroll, which consisted of reproductions of work produced in his studio. It appears that the book came in for some criticism from Otto Wagner on the grounds of its "poeticism". The examples selected were mainly of interior architecture and showed a stylistic evolution away from his original naturalism. Furniture design focused on matching sets rather than single pieces, which sometimes led to the creation of rather heavy "walls" of furniture.

Kotěra's first opportunity to create a prestigious modern interior came from the Ministry of Religion and Education, which commissioned him to work on

Peterka building, facade and detail, 1899–1900. Prague New Town
(Wenceslas Square 12). Arch.: Jan Kotěra.

the space allotted to the School of Applied Arts at the 1904 World's Fair in St. Louis. He designed it as the hall of a villa, using oak "weathered" with ammonia; the saddle-shaped ceiling, supported by wooden beams, was covered with embroidered vellum, and the panelling was designed to display exhibition pieces. The entrance-axis was dominated by a red marble fireplace decorated with a large relief representing Prague and the Vltava River, by Stanislav Sucharda. The relief's predominant grey and yellow harmonized with the colours of the natural materials used. The usual Art Nouveau curves were already completely absent from the interior design, which, on the contrary, relied mainly on straight lines emphasizing the bulk of the space and the flatness of the panelling. One of Kotěra's pupils, Emanuel Pelant, designed the ornamental elements, which even then were geometrical in style, invoking the frequent repetition of a spiral motif at the end of long, barely inflected lines.

The glass bowl Kotěra exhibited in St. Louis is a perfect example of the early expression of the modern decorative style. Here there is a clearer statement of a geometrization that had been concealed by Art Nouveau's symmetrical effects. Although the recipient was basically round, Kotěra flattened out the curves. The resulting form seems to recede even further due to the transparency of the glass, while at the same time its plastic conception was set off to greater advantage. From a purely stylistic standpoint, Kotěra used this transparency of form in his treatment of glass in the same way that Vojtěch Preissig used his gouaches for wallpaper designs. Both artists had to address the problem of creating an ornamental treatment of the floral motif that would improve on the traditional use of a pattern set off against a neutral background. The single motif was retained, but instead of merely being repeated, a much more complex formal relationship was created. The repeating patterns in Preissig's wallpaper designs differ because the motifs were placed either diagonally or were superimposed on each other. This was not merely to create an illusionistic effect, but was a purely plastic development of pictorial structure, in which even the background had an active function. Preissig's design went beyond the traditional dualism between object and space. Furthermore, without abandoning the contrast between the natural and the ideal that so appealed to proponents of Art Nouveau, he

Trmal villa, 1902–1903. Strašnice (Vilová 11). Arch.: Jan Kotěra.

put these two qualities into a state of permanent interchange, creating a sense of ambiguity.

Each of these works featured its own solution to the question of the higher unity of the Art Nouveau style and significantly influenced other decorative artists. In the vases shown at the St. Louis World's Fair by Klouček's pupils Rudolf Hameršmid, Eman Stehlík and Václav Mach, the ornamental plant designs were stylized by means of a kind of flat collar turned up at the edges to form a wavy, slightly concave border. The concept of bas-relief also appeared in the decorative designs invented by the Klouček school. The same ornamentation, this time in the form of a ribbon, appeared again in jewelry made by Novák and his pupils, who flattened the relief as much as possible. At first sight such stylistic changes seemed esoteric but, like the earlier, more naturalistic style, they became widespread and, once adopted by the architectural profession, these decorative bas-reliefs became part of Prague's physical environment.

The development of the Art Nouveau style in Prague coincided with the project for revitalizing the

Sucharda's villa, 1906–1907. Bubeneč (Slavíčkova 6). Arch,: Jan Kotěra.

city centre. In 1887 Alfred Hurtig, Jan Heide and Matěj Štrunc won the open competition for the modernization and renovation of the Old Town and the Josefov neighbourhood. Their project was officially approved in 1893, and demolition work began shortly afterward, especially in the old Jewish quarter. The insalubrity of the old buildings provided the moral argument for this vast operation, but this was quickly superseded by the greed of contractors who had no compunction about destroying Prague's historical heritage. Cultural circles issued vigorous protest, which peaked in an emotional poleimcal text published by the naturalist writer Vilém Mrštík under the explicit title *Bestia triumfans*. The city council tried to cope with a flood of petitions in favour of "safeguarding Prague's historic character" as well as other energetic reactions, not least of which was the foundation of a "Save Ancient Prague Club". The council was forced to modify the renovation plans in 1902, and gave the architect Josef Sakař responsibility for the work. Sakař adhered to the theories of the urban planner Camillo Sitte, who, contrary to the roughshod methods practised by Baron Haussmann in Paris, urged the greatest respect for the environment and the everyday surroundings of the inhabitants, with the creation of small squares, attractive views, and so on.

The initial modernization project had envisaged opening up a great boulevard in the old part of Prague, beginning at Wenceslas Square, crossing Old Town Square, then continuing over a new bridge and on to the Letná plain, thus offering the possibility of expanding the city toward Bubeneč. Only part of the project was carried out: what is today Pařížská Avenue, and the bridge designed by Jan Koula. However, other areas were gradually demolished north of Old Town Square, then in the Petrská and Vojtesská neighbourhoods and on the New Town embankment. The character of the new buildings, which were to be constructed not only on newly cleared land but also beside extant housing blocks, deeply concerned both the public and the press, particularly at the beginning of the century, when the builders were very active. The situation therefore seemed highly favourable to the new Art Nouveau decorative style, which offered a solution to modernization and the preservation of the city's historic beauty. Architects proposed everything from Neo-Baroque to pure Art Nouveau, administrators then worked out a compromise, which was facilitated by the wide variety of skills of contractors and craftsmen. It was because of this building frenzy that Prague remains even today a city of Gothic, Baroque and Art Nouveau architecture.

In this context, the most successful architects were those who, instead of aiming like Kotěra for stylistic purity, were ready to experiment. Ohmann had already applied this kind of syncretism in his work, and it had been accepted precisely because it fitted in well with the existing architectural style of the city. His project for renovating Holy Trinity Church, published in *Volné směry* in 1898, was a characteristic mixture of Art Nouveau curves and Neo-Baroque.

Ohmann's Prague pupils (including, among others, Alois Dryák, Bedřich Bendelmayer and Jiří Justich) showed a greater preference for attractive plastic elements than did Kotěra. Bendelmayer and Dryák finished Ohmann's project for the Central Hotel on Hybernská Street, where, especially in the main room (later destroyed), they succeeded in expressing Art Nouveau's organic sense in structural terms, through the shape and rhythm of the lateral colonnades. There was a strong Neo-Baroque element in the decoration of the dais, which included an allegorical painting by Karel Špillar and sculptures by Ladislav Šaloun. Imaginative floral decoration extended as far as the elevator, where this paradoxical joining of nature and machinery seemed almost surrealist. Between 1903 and 1905 the two architects constructed the asymmetrical building on Wenceslas Square comprising the Hotel Archduke Štěpán and the Hotel Garni (today the Evropa Hotel), which clearly exemplified the curious presence of naturalism in the original conception of Art Nouveau style. The larger of the two, Bendelmayer's Hotel Archduke Štěpán, nevertheless incorporated details and interior design characteristic of a Viennese-influenced tendency, toward more geometrical shapes. At much the same time, Bendelmayer designed an apartment block, built by Q. Belsky, with a simplicity and elegance quite contrary to the hotel's rich decoration of coloured stucco, gilt and metal ornamentation. This

Vojtěch Preissig, wallpaper design, c. 1900. Gouache, 48.8 x 31.3 cm. Prague, National Gallery.

Vojtěch Preissig, wallpaper design, c. 1900. Gouache, 48.9 x 30.9 cm. Prague, National Gallery.

Following double page, left to right: Rudolf Hameršmid, vase, 1904. Colour-glazed earthenware, h.: 19 cm. Prague, UPM.

Václav Švec, vase, 1908. Colour-glazed ceramic, h.: 36.5 cm. Prague, UPM.

Anna Boudová-Suchardová, vase, c. 1900. Painted ceramic, h.: 38 cm. Prague, UPM.

Apartment building (1906–1907), bow-window detail. Josefov (Pařížská 17). Arch.: Richard Klenka and František Weyr.

FACING PAGE: Apartment building (1904–1905). Prague New Town (Gottwald Embankment 26), Arch.: Kamil Hilbert.

Art Nouveau apartment building was Bendelmayer's most modern work so far, and provoked an acrimonious article from the conservative critic of the journal *Architektonický obzor*: "Its smooth walls, flat frames and greenhouse look" make it "an arrogant and repugnant neighbour" for the medieval Prasná brána (Powder Tower).[10]

Besides the architects associated with the School of Applied Arts, the Art Nouveau movement included

those of the Technical Institute as well as architects from the older generation who had been trained in the historicist styles. An interest in Late Gothic linked Kamil Hilbert, the designer of the annex to Saint Guy's Cathedral at Hradčany, to Art Nouveau naturalism. Using both stucco with plant motifs and the coloured light of stained-glass windows, he created an interesting variant of the Art Nouveau building on the New Town embankment (1904–1905). An interest in modernity was already apparent in Josef Fanta's interior design for the Chamber of Commerce and Crafts at the Universal Exposition in 1900. He pursued this trend in some of his apartment buildings (including the Hlahol Association building on the New Town embankment between 1903 and 1906), and especially in his most important work, the Franz-Josef Station (now Main Station), which he built between 1901 and 1909.

The structure of the station clearly reflected the spirit of the times, if only in the way the working and public areas were linked together. The platforms were covered by a glass roof with two naves, a typical example of engineering architecture. At the front was a widespread complex of station buildings with interlinking wings. The central pavilion was designed as a great hall under a spherical vault, and the wall at the front of the hall was broken by a huge semi-circular window. The door was flanked by a pair of quadrangular towers surmounted by glass, globe-like cupolas, a motif that was repeated on the facade. The large, ornate marquise was the stylistic emblem of the whole and created a kind of artistic pole within the station that was counterposed to the railway lines. The richly decorative sculpture by Stanislav Sucharda, Ladislav Šaloun and Čeněk Vosmík among others, was particularly representative of Prague Art Nouveau. Its almost Neo-Baroque exuberance was held in check by the architecture, producing an integrated, overall decorative effect. That this huge prestigious building, which became an architectural showpiece of Prague, was designed in a modern decorative style – despite the inclusion of certain traditional elements – underscores Art Nouveau's success, especially in the eyes of the Prague bourgeoisie.

During the first decade of the twentieth century, Art Nouveau came to be a representative expression of Czech society, just as the Neo-Renaissance style had been before it. Yet unlike Neo-Renaissance architecture, whose main function was merely representative,

Apartment building, c. 1900. Josefov (Dlouhá 9). Architect unknown.

ABOVE LEFT: Gable decoration.

FACING PAGE: Stucco ornamentation.

ABOVE: View of residential buildings, c. 1900.
Prague Old Town (Pařížská).

RIGHT: Svatopluk Čech bridge, 1906–1908.
Prague Old Town. Arch.: Jan Koula and Jiří Soukup.

FACING PAGE: Hotel Central, 1899–1901.
Prague Old Town (Hybernská 10). Arch.: Friedrich Ohmann.

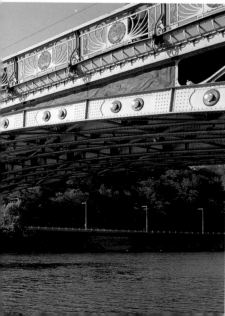

FACING PAGE AND RIGHT: Hotel Evropa, 1903–1905.
Prague New Town (Wenceslas Square 25–27).
Arch.: Bedřich Bendelmayer and Alois Dryák.

TOP LEFT: Hotel Evropa, stair railing.

BOTTOM LEFT: Second-floor café.

FACING PAGE: The entrance hall.

RIGHT: Apartment building, entrance-corridor stained-glass window, 1904–1905. Prague New Town (Masaryk Embankment 26). Arch.: Kamil Hilbert.

BELOW: Hotel Evropa, fireplace in the French Restaurant.

Art Nouveau architecture dominated the city's functioning in a complex way, and came to embody a change in the national mentality.

In this sense, proponents of the Art Nouveau style managed to create an urban environment with its own characteristics. The potential for doing this was inherent in the very nature of this art, in which reality and fantasy, the concrete and the ideal, and the commonplace and the ceremonial continually complemented and transformed each other.

In this context, the most enterprising and most adaptable architect of all was perhaps Osvald Polívka. In the 1890s he had succeeded in giving his buildings – the Zemská Bank, for example – an individual look, derived basically from late historicism. Since becoming the Commune of Prague's *de facto* official architect (though not explicitly appointed as such), Polívka had enjoyed privileged status, by virtue of which he received important commissions from banking institutions and insurance companies. He was not, however,

above working on numerous projects for construction firms, and between 1900 and 1903 he drew up the plans for a series of buildings in Vojtěška, Karlova and Haštalská Streets, located in areas that were being modernized. There, besides the still-popular Neo-Baroque idiom, he proposed a new Art Nouveau decor in a lyrical floral style, most of which was executed in stucco by Antonín Popp. Polívka attached considerable importance to working with artists, and liked his buildings to be heavily decorated.[11] This is particularly

The Hlahol building, general view and detail of the facade, 1903–1906. Prague New Town (Masaryk Embanknient 16). Arch.: Josef Fanta.

FACING PAGE: The entrance door.

FOLLOWING DOUBLE PAGE: Main Station, 1900–1909. Prague New Town (Vítězného února). Arch.: Josef Fanta.

TOP LEFT: Vault of the central hall.
BOTTOM LEFT: Side view of the building.
BOTTOM RIGHT: Side entrance door.

Main Station, mask decoration on facade.

FACING PAGE: Prague City Savings Bank, upper part of the facade, 1899–1901. Prague Old Town (Old Town Square 6). Arch.: Osvald Polívka.

apparent in those he designed for institutions. The facade of the Novák business premises on Vodičkova Street (1902–1904), for which his project was selected in preference to Kotěra's, returns to the Prague "painted building" tradition. For the large mosaic, he worked with Jan Preisler, who produced for the conventional barons of Commerce and Industry a delightfully refreshing spring celebration presided over by the beautiful allegory of Flora. The mosaics, stucco, stained glass and elaborate ornamental metal were completely Art Nouveau, while the architecture as a whole retained a traditional symmetrical layout.

Polívka's most successful facade was unquestionably the one he created for the Praha Insurance Company on Národní Avenue. Here the architecture was conceived as a vast surface broken by symmetrically placed projections of bow windows and balconies. The straightlined protruding cornice, the picturesque contours of Šaloun's sculptures on the attic storey, the flag-holders and the railings all break up the background surface with a liveliness that heightens the overall effect. In its extraordinarily colourful decoration, this facade bears a

marked affinity with the characteristic style of Art Nouveau posters. Polívka made even more extensive use of these devices in the project for the Municipal building, which in 1904 he was commissioned to do jointly with Antonín Balšánek, the architect of the new Franz-Josef bridge (1899–1901).

Construction work on the Municipal building, probably the best-known Art Nouveau edifice in Prague, lasted until 1912, which drew some vigorous criticism from modernists with purist convictions. The building's syncretism nonetheless is indicative of the way the Art Nouveau decorative style penetrated Prague architecture. The irregular shape of the site was handled ingeniously: the building was planned along an axis with the one-storey lateral wings linked at an obtuse angle to the central entrance area, which was itself designed as a slightly concave space surmounted by a high cupola. The great Smetana concert hall cut through the two floors in the centre of the building, with a number of public exhibition, catering and shopping areas in the surrounding wings. It is difficult to distinguish the respective contributions of the two architects, but it

Czech Insurance Bank, 1907–1909.
Prague New Town (Spálená 14).
Arch.: Osvald Polívka.

LEFT: The fountain.
RIGHT: Details of the stair rail
and staircase.

FOLLOWING DOUBLE PAGE, LEFT:
The former Novák department store,
detail of the facade with mosaics by
Jan Preisler, 1902. Prague New Town
(Vodičkova 30). Arch.: Osvald Polívka.

TOP RIGHT: Stained-glass entrance door.
BOTTOM RIGHT: Door of the Praha
Insurance Company building,
1903–1905. Prague Old Town
(Národní 7). Arch.: Osvald Polívka.

Osvald Polívka, project for the Praha Insurance Company building, 1903.
Watercolour, 42 x 43 cm. Prague, Národní technické muzeum.

Facing page: Municipal building, facade,
1904–1912. Prague Old Town (Republic Square 5).
Arch.: Osvald Polívka and Antonín Balšánek.

Top right: Elevator shaft.
Bottom right: Mural decoration in the
restaurant.

would seem that Polívka was responsible for the layout of the building, as well as for the predominant forms and decorative style. The walls of the facade are articulated by tall windows on either side of the monumental corner rotunda, giving the building a touch of historicism. Artist-craftsmen added Art Nouveau decorative motifs. The atmosphere of the Smetana concert hall and the facade is affected not only by the rather restrained work of the painter Karel Špillar, but also by Ladislav Šaloun's far more baroque sculptures. Despite the criticism leveled at the building's excessively ornate decoration, and even at "the decadence of its plastic conception", there is a certain grandeur in its theatricality and in the feeling of space suggested by the decorative elements.[12] Although these are admittedly exaggerated, they are balanced by other factors, and in this sense the solemn-looking marquise and its light-stands, designed by Karel Novák are necessary complements to the ornate corner rotunda.

The recent experience of post-modern architecture has made it possible to judge the Municipal building more favourably than did the modernists, who flatly condemned it. This was not the last building in which Polívka used an interplay of various styles, but he sometimes adopted a simpler decorative approach that tended toward mannerist classicism. Next to the Praha Insurance Company on Národní Avenue, he designed a building for the Topič publishing house, with no pictorial effects disturbing its symmetrical facade. It should be noted that these two buildings were erected at the same time, side by side, in a kind of stylistic counterpoint.

The Beaufort Editions building (1908–1909) on Jungmannova Street, and the Staroměstská Radnice – the Old Town's new Town Hall (1908–1911) – also date from the same period. The Beaufort building displays a decorative facade with reliefs representing the telegraph and the telephone, which are most interesting from an iconographic point of view. Rather classical in composition, they blend the concrete details of modern technology with an allegorical figure. In the other building, the new Town Hall, there is an obvious confrontation of styles in the juxtaposition of the rectilinear cornices

Municipal building, ceiling of the Mayor's Room, decorated by Alfons Mucha (1910–1911).

FACING PAGE: Municipal building, the small reception room, with an allegory of Prague by Alfons Mucha.

ABOVE LEFT: Door handle. Blue stained-glass window.

ABOVE RIGHT: Detail of metalwork in the Mayor's Room.

RIGHT: Stucco scroll work.

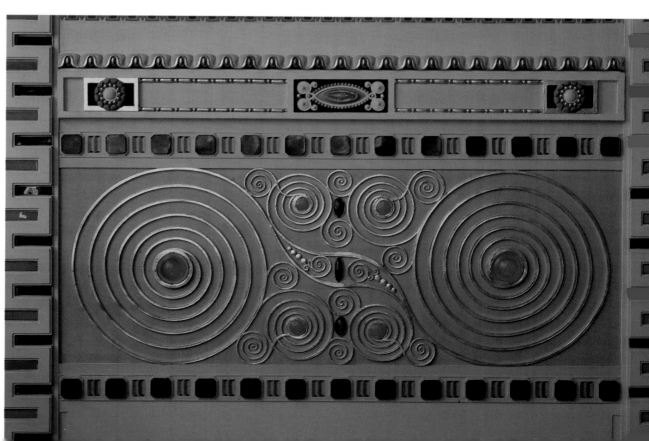

ABOVE LEFT: Topič building, 1903–1905.
Prague Old Town (Národní 9). Arch.: Osvald Polívka.

ABOVE RIGHT: Beaufort Editions building, 1908–1912.
Prague New Town (Jungmannova 15). Arch.: Osvald Polívka.

FACING PAGE: The new Town Hall, 1908–1911.
Prague Old Town (Mariánske náměstí 2). Arch.: Osvald Polívka.

PRECEDING DOUBLE PAGE: The Municipal building.
TOP LEFT: Ornamental fountain.
BOTTOM LEFT: The fountain in the cafeteria, sculptor: Josef Pekárek.
RIGHT: The Grégr Room decorated by František Ženíšek.

and the sculptures. Here Polívka was clearly aware of the heterogeneity of the work done by Sucharda and Mařatka – for which he was later harshly criticized – but respected their ideas and incorporated them into his architecture. The annex that he built to the Zemská Bank (1911–1912) was more homogeneous in plastic terms, and Polívka again called on Jan Preisler to create the mosaics on the facade. But here too, Polívka decided to make the new building fit in with the older one – the main building of the Zemská Bank – which he had built around 1895. It would be unfair to consider Polívka's attitude vis-a-vis the Zemská Bank annex as a

mere inclination to adapt. It lay rather in a conviction that what was new and modern did not contradict the old, but could be added to earlier forms and could enrich them without denying their worth. This same spirit characterized the new decorative style, which was adopted by a great many Prague architects and featured in works that fully respected the genius loci of Prague.

This does not mean that there was any lack of radical artists in Prague; they sprang up among the younger generation and noisily made their presence felt during the first decade of the century. However, it was first necessary to sweep away the concept of style as a formal

language that the architect could use in much the same way as a painter used colour, modulating it according to the effect required and giving it an original touch by mixing in more or less historical material. This purely pragmatic definition was countered by another, whereby style was attributed not merely an artistic value, but a value that was also cultural and spiritual, embracing the whole of life.

Šalda emerged as the main spokesman for this latter, emotive concept of style, for which he had already been prepared by the experience of Synthetism in the 1890s. In 1903, in an article entitled, significantly, "The Ethics

LEFT: Statues by Stanislav Sucharda and Josef Mařatka on the facade of the new Town Hall, 1910–1911. Stone.

FACING PAGE: Ladislav Šaloun, Rabbi Löw, 1910. Stone. Prague Old Town (Mariánské naměestí).

of the Present Renascence of the Applied Arts", he wrote: "We are turning away from convoluted imagination and accumulated formal conventions, and going back to essential, *simple and functional forms*, away from falsehood and pretense and back to honesty and solidity, from cosmetic ornamentation to structure and skeleton and from the secondary to the essential and original. All the arts are gradually coming out of their isolation and breaking out of their material imprisonment.

Artists feel with growing intensity that art's vital roots are *ornamental and symbolic,* and that their purpose is to strive to embellish life, to work on and to serve the whole: style as the highest cultural value, the unity of art and life, becomes the object of our hope. [...] Only now do we understand the significance and meaning of the word *style*: we understand that it is simply *this relationship and this permanent consideration of the whole,* wherein nothing lives for itself to the detriment of the other elements and parts, but lives for them and in harmony with them. That style is not limitation and material isolation, but consciousness of spiritual being, consciousness of the rhythmic life of the infinite, obedience to it and union with it."[13]

This affirmation of the organic nature of style reverted back to Jan Kotěra's pioneering ideas, and was to leave a deep imprint on Czech culture at the start of the new century.

The emotive
style

The enigma of life

LIVRE PREMIER

LES ANÇÈTRES

František Kupka, frontispiece for the first book of Élisée Reclus'
Man and Earth, Paris, 1905. Engraving, 19.5 x 27 cm.

PRECEDING DOUBLE PAGE: Josef Váchal, *Elemental Plain* (detail),
1907. India ink and watercolour, 30.6 x 52.3 cm.
Prague, Památník národního písemnictví.

FOLLOWING DOUBLE PAGE: Kupka cycle: *The Voices of Silence*.
Coloured aquatints.
LEFT TO RIGHT:
The Beginning of Life, 34.7 x 34.7 cm, 1900–1903.
The Silent Path, I, 34.6 x 34.4 cm, 1900.
Resistance, 34.7 x 34.7 cm, 1900–1903.
The Silent Path, II, 34.5 x 35 cm, 1903.

In 1902 František Kupka finished a painting in Paris
that, as his correspondence with the poet Machar
reveals, harboured great artistic ambition. He entitled it
Ballad. The Joys. His commentary was more explicit: "I
want to express, skilfully but simply, how I felt when I
was sitting alone and content on the seashore, and since
I have many sketches of things like that, I got to work.
There are two rather unattractive women who have
come riding up to the beach on horseback and are gazing out into the warm reflection of the setting sun. The
seashore and the clouds imbue the scene with a tone
suggestive of pleasures as yet unknown, and the clouds
look as though there were a thousand gnomes gaily
dancing and capering about in them. [...] All of us
have the desire to experience joy, an intangible sense
of happiness, and I should like everyone who sees this
to have the same feeling."[1]

The picture is painted with a rarely used encaustic
that produces an unusual effect of light in the colour.
This device is important, because the coloured light
unifies the somewhat disparate idealistic and naturalistic elements of the work. The scene is set on a beach
near Trégastel, where Kupka spent holidays, but it has
been transposed onto a mythological plane to represent
a meeting between land and sea. The tide is low, and
seaweed, the foaming waves and variegated strips of
sand form a typically Art Nouveau series of curves
fading off into the distance. These sinuous, serpentine
curves symbolize the vital elementary force that perme-
ates the whole of nature. The twofold source of Kupka's
imagination is even more obvious in the human figures.
The two nude women, depicted in an uncompromis-
ingly naturalistic manner, were personal acquaintances
of Kupka's, but their mounts belong to a prehistoric
race. The picture has another title, *Epona-Ballad. The
Joys*, after Epona, the Celto-Roman goddess, protector
of horses. This linked it with Kupka's extensive archeological and mythological research, often reflected in some
way in his work, which culminated a few years later in
his illustrations for Élisée Reclus' *Man and Earth*.

Kupka studied at the School of Fine Arts in Prague
for three years. In the autumn of 1892, he went to live
in Vienna, where his Neo-Romantic painting *Wine's
Deathbed Dream* met with great success. While in
Vienna he became familiar with the fashionable religious and philosophical ideas, theosophy, occultism
and the oriental mystics, and became a vegetarian. At

the Künstlerbund in 1895, he exhibited a large painting (now lost) entitled *Quam ad causam sumus?,* in which he attempted to answer this question from the sceptics with a great allegorical gathering around the "sphinx of life". In the spring of 1896, he settled in Paris and produced a lifetime of work that earned him a significant place in the history of modern art.

Kupka's course toward abstract painting was not without its side roads. His interests were wide-ranging, from philosophy and esoterism to a passion for the natural sciences. He also embarked on a campaign of vigorous social criticism graphically expressed in a series of drawings, *Money, Religion* and *Peace,* for the anarchist journal *L'Assiette au Beurre* in which he attacked the evils of international capitalism, religious superstition and militaristic imperialism. These drawings were much admired in Prague at the Workers' Exhibition in 1902, and have been the most popular of Kupka's drawings among the Czech public ever since.

For some time, Kupka's work incorporated contradictory naturalistic and idealistic elements. In Paris in 1897 he painted a large picture entitled *Bibliomaniac,* in which he made fun of his own passion for books and, in an illusionistic vein, turned confidently toward nature and the senses. Three years later he did a series of aquatints called *The Voices of Silence,* in which metaphysical subjects were evoked in eerie, fantastic settings. In *Obstinacy* (and also in *Revolt* and *The Black Idol*), a man is seen as a tiny, almost invisible speck. He is standing on a long ridge of land, surrounded by dark, murky water that leads toward an immense statue of a tense, rigid demon rising up menacingly into the empty

František Kupka, *Epona-Ballad. The Joys*. Oil on wood, 83.5 x 126.5 cm. Prague, National Gallery.

sky. The *Silent Path* shows a pilgrim walking along an alley of Egyptian sphinxes by the magical light of stars shining mysteriously in the night sky. In *The Beginning of Life*, two luminous circles float up from a calm sheet of water covered with lotus flowers. An umbilical chord links the two circles, one of which contains the embryo of a child, the other a shining body.

As his works show, Kupka found himself faced with the problem of the synthesis of apparently incompatible worlds: the world of thought and that of visually perceptible reality, of idealism and naturalisim, and of the invisible and the visible. The modern artist was helped here by the decorative features of the new style. The linear movement in Kupka's work at that time was sinuous, but not ornamental, and became more of a formal symbol of the transition between the savage, demoniacal "struggle for life" and ideal, sometimes Utopian redemption. Through his interest in photography, which enabled him to study body movement, Kupka's further experiments with line led him to develop a new compositional structure in abstract painting, in which his new concept of colour played an important part.[2]

In 1902, the year he painted *Epona-Ballad. The Joys*, this tendency was more marked in some of the preparatory drawings than in the final work. It was particularly apparent in the many studies for one of the riders, the athletically built Gabrielle, which were done in blue chalk with yellow and white highlights. Colour is no longer the usual "local colour": instead, the coloured light falling on the figure is used to express the fundamental cosmic energy essential to life and its pleasures. This transcendence, resulting from a phenomenon that was itself of a natural order, opened up new possibilities.

Over the next ten years, Kupka found solutions to these problems that were far more radical than those of his Czech contemporaries. It is true that they were working in a different environment, but they were all nonetheless presented with the same question. Symbolism, which had been predominant at the end of the century, was taken as a challenge – successfully meeting this challenge could throw open the door to modern art.

It was not easy for Czech artists to find their bearings in contemporary art and to distinguish the promising personalities and trends. Miloš Jiránek attended the retrospective exhibition covering one hundred years of painting at the 1900 Universal Exposition, and his

doubts and hesitations were apparent in his subsequent essay in *Volné směry*.[3] An idea similar to Ruskin's theory of "the two paths" gained ground among the young artists who belonged to the Mánes Union, which was the group most representative of modern Czech painting. This idea, published in the Manés Union's magazine, held that modern art should draw its inspiration first and foremost from events in modern life.

The young artists searched for models embodying this concept, and were first attracted by Luděk Marold, who left Paris and settled in Prague in 1897. Marold's life had given him the profile of a true Secessionist. He was an orphan whose father had died as an officer during the war between Austria and Prussia, and who joined the School of Fine Arts after being rejected for admission by the Cadet School. Shortly thereafter, he fell out with the conservative authorities at the school and left for Munich. In his draft autobiography, Marold wrote with ironic self-deprecation that all he had studied in Munich was good beer. But when he returned to Prague, he dazzled the public with his *Egg Market* (1888), in which he captured the atmosphere of the Old Prague market with great sensitivity, demonstrating the subtleties of the new naturalism in painting. Marold, whose talent was by then beyond question, was designated for appointment to the teaching staff at the Prague School of Applied Arts and was sent to Paris for training in decorative painting with Professor Pierre Victor Galland. The study of decoration was a torment to him, however, and he preferred to capture moments of everyday life on the Parisian boulevards. He very quickly achieved considerable success as an illustrator who could add lightness and charm to illusionistic naturalism. His younger compatriots admired his realistic technique: the way he seized fleeting instants of day-to-day existence showed presence of mind and the sharp awareness of a photographer, as well as penetrating psychological insight. His contemporaries said that they could almost hear his figures speak, and understood perfectly what they were saying.

Readers of Paris magazines, Munich's *Fliegende Blätter*, and *Světozor* or *Zlatá Praha* in Prague were all familiar with Marold as a lover of feminine beauty, but there was also Marold the painter, especially of oil portraits, who admired Rembrandt and longed to devote himself entirely to painting instead of illustration.[4] Then there was a third Marold, probably the best of all, who executed rapid drawings and sketches, free improvisations often reminiscent of Toulouse-Lautrec. In 1898, he used this particular talent to create a colour lithographic poster entitled *Our Building under Renovation*, for the theatre at the Architecture and Engineering Exhibition. This was a brilliant model of foreshortening that proved Marold's talent for surface decoration. However, illusionism was more to his taste, as reflected in his second work for the Exhibition, a sweeping, circular panorama of the Battle of Lipany. This exploit took Marold a step away from painting in the direction of cinematic technique, and underscored the modernity of an artist who did not hesitate to transgress the traditional conventions and boundaries of artistic genres.

Marold's sudden death was considered a national cultural catastrophe, but artistic circles, where there was an awareness that illusionistic naturalism had reached its limits, recovered quickly. Nonetheless, Marold's new sensualism, which lay at the heart of his vision of modern reality, remained very much a part of Czech art and became an integral part of the modern approach to art.

What critics at the time called "the renascence of the life of the senses" was often believed to be the source of a new art and literature, especially poetry. In the theory of synesthesia, common in poetry at the end of the century, the predominant sense was sight, which the others were largely used to enhance. By the 1890s, Antonín Sova's lyrical poetry, whose main subject was nature, had already become the literary paradigm of this new keen perception of the environment, represented mainly by landscape. In these landscapes, the sensation of objects through smell and hearing, which changes with the flow of time, was invariably dominated by a coloured image.

In 1901, Šalda published an essay in *Volné směry* called "The Heroic View", in which he likened sight to a kind of knight errant, "the creative organ of the soul" and, for the artist, the most important of the senses. This "eternal liberator could rejuvenate the world", could sweep away the mountains of accumulated literature, commentary, criticism, conventions, clichés and all the intricate rules and theories – "the whole ceremonious ritual of the decrepit, old-style courts" – by freeing the artist to fulfil his mission and change the world. This heroic vision challenged the artist to be

fearless in upsetting the hierarchy of the senses and to show an "honest primitiveness in times marked by a perverse false sophistication that tries to look artistic".[5]

It was in this context that Impressionism once again became fashionable in Czech art. In the 1890s, Czech artists occasionally encountered works by the French impressionists. Václav Radimský, a young landscape painter, even lived in Giverny for a while, and took up a method directly inspired by the mature work of Claude Monet. His pictures were exhibited at Topič's in Prague in 1899, and were appreciated by the critic Mádl, who described him as a "painter of light". However, Mádl expressed his true opinion of Impressionism when the Mánes Union organized an exhibition on "French Modern Art" in the autumn of 1902. The French critic Gabriel Mourey, President of the Societé Nouvelle des Peintres et Sculpteurs, was invited to curate the exhibition.

Jan Preisler's exhibition poster employed muted colours and depicted a white peacock stylized in the Art Nouveau manner, symbolizing the rarity and the exceptional nature of the works being exhibited. Mourey, whose idea was to show the wide range of contemporary French art, presented Albert Besnard, Eugène Carrière, Charles Cottet, Henri Aman-Jean, Henri Le Sidaner, Gaston de Latouche and several other famous names of the time. These were preceded by a small number of impressionists (Claude Monet, Alfred Sisley, Camille Pissarro, Auguste Renoir, Edgar Degas and Mary Cassatt). Mádl, probably influenced by R. Muther's then-popular manual on the history of nineteenth century French painting, shared the view of Impressionism as a historical revolution freeing painting from academicism. But if the impressionists were forever to be presented "like saints in the calendar of art", their innovative role had come to an end. Mádl believed that their art was one-sided, and could not transform the whole of new artistic creation. Their interest in the perception of light had led them to destroy form and line – not merely academic line, but also "the line deduced from the essence of nature and transformed into individual language". Mádl was more interested in their successors, Le Sidaner, Aman-Jean and Henri Martin, intimists and colourists who expressed themselves "through quality of color and harmony of line".[6]

Mádl's criticism of Impressionism reflected the criteria of Art Nouveau synthetism. Although not funda-

Luděk Marold, poster for the play *Our building under Renovation*, 1898. Colour lithograph, 124 x 92 cm. Prague, UPM.

guard have regained their prestige: they stood out from the others for their unique approach to art."[7]

This opinion of Impressionisin was shared by Šalda, who since 1902 had edited *Volné směry* and had been involved with its plastic arts section. In his preface to the catalogue for the "French Modern Art" exhibition, he spoke of Impressionism as a heroic experience, and one of the most beautiful and purest moral ideals ever to come out of art. When Šalda used the word "experience" he was referring not to a tentative, fleeting event, but to the deep commitment of an individual who makes art "the very function of life".[8]

To Šalda and Jiránek, the kind of art a painter produced was directly related to his psychological make-up. Modern artists were to have dramatic, heroic di-

Jan Preisler, poster for the 5th exhibition of the Mánes Union of Artists, French Modern Art, 1902. Colour lithograph, 98 x 68 cm. Prague, UPM.

mentally incorrect, his criticism was nevertheless flawed in the sense that its theoretical credo was applied to individual artists who could not play a truly decisive role in the general evolution of modern art. Miloš Jiránek later wrote that "behind Bastien-Lepage, Besnard and Harrison were hidden Manet, Degas, Monet and Renoir. It took us a long time to pick out the individual personalities that lay behind the uniformity of the common effort. And now the true old

Luděk Marold, study for the *Portrait of Anna Červená*, c. 1895. Oil on canvas, 52.2 x 36.5 cm. Prague, National Gallery.

mensions and were to be imbued with the moral pathos characteristic of authentic Secession. Their model was not the decadent pessimism of the 1890s, but a vigorous struggle for a new approach to art and to life. This ideal of action was undoubtedly linked to the increasing influence of the Mánes Union and of the entire younger generation, who played a co-ordinating role in national culture. The Mánes Union was also very active abroad. In 1902 it showed its work in the exhibition hall of the Hagenbund, a new Viennese association with which it had established friendly ties. The same exhibition was later presented in Krakow.

The conceptualization of modern art, which was a fundamental part of the Mánes Union's cultural development, could be ascribed chiefly to Šalda. His lecture on "The New Beauty: Its Nature and Origins" was published in *Volné směry* in 1903, and became a manifesto of the view that modern art sprang from creative spontaneity and a rejection of established conventions. In Šalda's view, art was above all an original creation. Art Nouveau did not seek its means of expression in the past, but "organized the chaos of the present moment into a new law, a new expression, a new rhythm". It pursued its own style, a new and superior union between art and life, and grew out of "a strange, mystical feeling about reality, the mystical cult of life and the paths that lead to it". This new relationship to reality was not based solely on its appearance, but on "its existence and its laws". The new works of art were the result of the objectivation of a new attitude toward reality and life – a monistic attitude according to which all "the forces of life and the universe" were one. It rejected exaggerated fantasies rooted in dualism: "We have abandoned fantasy and turned to reality, observation, feeling, intuition, interpretation. We want to feel reality and think it through to the end: this is how this new thinking and new aesthetic feeling came about."[9]

Šalda's rejection of the fantastic was of major importance to the status of a new art that still contained elements of Neo-Romanticism. In the same text, he proclaimed his admiration for architectural engineering, and praised the pure beauty of a "naked" railway bridge as an example of strong architectonic impact. What was important to him was concentrating the attention of artists and the public on the essentials in art. When he wrote that the new beauty was above all the beauty of function, logic and inner structure – which was the

primary postulate of modern aesthetics – he was not celebrating functionalism. The emphasis was on the individual creator whose values were based on creative inspiration and pathos working in an organic harmony whose model was the natural union between man and the universe. The heart of this union, Šalda wrote, was a rhythm like that of the human heartbeat. In beauty, this rhythm was condensed into the distilled essence of things. Beauty matched its rhythm to the world's. Modern rhythm was independent of conventional patterns; it was flexible and free, like the rhythm of Walt Whitman's poetry, contemporary music or modern design. This rhythm of life expressed by modern art was the echo and continuation of the "heartbeat of the world", and the source of modern style. This style was "everything that reflects and intensifies the continuity of life, its flow and the law governing its evolution; everything that disturbs this unity, isolates the details, separates the links of the chain or breaks the measure of the rhythm is in contradiction to it."[10]

Šalda's very broad and cosmologically based conception of style shows how important the new art and style were in forming the concept of modernity. At the same time, it seems obvious that, from this standpoint, Impressionism must be considered its first paradigm. Šalda attempted to provide an explanation for the fundamental change in aesthetic taste by inviting the public to compare what the old generation and the new generation respectively found attractive in nature. In the old days, nature was always expressed in terms of enclosed spaces and still lifes, whereas Impressionism demanded of a picture that, "even if it relates only to a tiny bit of the earth, it should be represented as closed off and materially and plastically complete. It should he bathed in the immensity of the sky and atmosphere, permeated with the lyricism of cosmic light, vibrating in infinity and attuned to all the harmonics of the universe. A determined shape should be no more than a point of departure that harbours the infinite; not rough, dead material subjected to minute scrutiny, but a pretext for seizing life and the rich atmosphere that surrounds it, the source of the most subtle and elusive cosmic life. We love best that land where the cosmic wind blows most violently and where the echo of the universe's Cyclopcan heart resounds most loudly."

This emotive declaration also shows that Šalda adapted Impressionism to suit the temper of the time.

It was impossible for the theoreticians and painters discovering Impressionism in reverse perspective, via their intimist successors, to turn back the clock several decades. They had understood the main techniques and exploited the new simultaneous perception of object and nature – which meant that life could be captured on the instant, spontaneously and all at once, in the colour matrix of natural light. However, they supplemented the French impressionists' analytical objectivism with a strong emotional content by means of which they tried to take possession of visual reality. This explains the marked expressive characteristics of this "second" Impressionism and its occasional tendency toward stereotyped painting.

Otakar Lebeda was one of the pioneers of this "second" style of impressionist painting. The studies he made in 1898 at Karlovy Vary were pure Impressionism and were noticed by Mádl. His language evolved perceptibly the following year with, for example, *On the Way*, a canvas featuring a team of oxen, in which his use of colour – thick, heavy off-white shades – reached beyond Impressionism. At that time, his landscapes began to include a dramatic human figure whose "cosmic affinity", to use Šalda's expression, was tinged with tragedy. Lebeda's last big painting, *Killed by Lightning* (1900–1901), was inspired by a real incident in the Chodsko region. At first, the work was seen as spinning out of the painter's control – which was supposedly confirmed by Lebeda's subsequent suicide – but actually was a harbinger of the emotive style that emerged shortly afterward.

The work of the young painter Antonín Slavíček later imbued the genre with far-reaching artistic significance. His paintings, which drew attention at the early Mánes Union exhibitions, consisted of a contrapuntal sequence of autumn and springtime atmospheres. Slavíček's powerful emotional make-up lent a combative strength to his youthful sensitivity, that was reinforced by an eventful life full of hopes and disappointments. One set-back occurred when he had to abandon hope of succeeding at the School of Fine Arts. He fell into depression, and looked around for a new setting in which he could recover his spirits. He found the very place at Hostišov, where the writer Jan Herben invited him to stay, and there painted works that were later shown at the fourth Hagenbund exhibition in Vienna. His approach to the landscape followed the usual Art Nouveau pattern of organization in decorative horizontal bands, but – and this was an original trait – the detail was not stylized, so that the picture hovered between a natural appearance and a decorative composition.

In reaction to the new interest shown in Impressionism, Slavíček did not remain passive before the natural features of landscapes; the atmosphere of his pictures was enhanced by an active interpretation of the subject. In *The Garden Wall,* a remarkable work dating from about 1902, the artist also creates a new spatial quality and the entire surface is covered with splashes of luminous colour. He moves completely away from the traditional viewpoint "from the wings": the eyes are drawn not to the centre of the picture but over a very wide field of vision, which causes them to lose their habitual orientation. This is achieved by the slight curving of the garden wall into a diagonal, in conjunction with an unusual distribution of light, that is at its most intense at the edge of the painting, resulting in the effect of literally pulling the viewer. The impression is made even

Otakar Lebeda, *On the Way*, 1899. Oil on canvas, 111 x 116.5 cm. Prague, National Gallery.

TOP LEFT: Antonín Slavíček,
Saint Mary's Square, 1906.
Oil and tempera on canvas.
109 x 131 cm.
Prague, National Gallery.

BOTTOM LEFT: Antonín Slavíček,
The Garden Wall, 1900–1902.
Tempera on cardboard.
88.5 x 100 cm.
Prague, National Gallery.

Antonín Slavíček, *Prague Seen from Letná*, 1908. Tempera, 188 x 390 cm. Prague, National Gallery.

more acute by the energy with which the colour splashes are applied, and the movement they create (the emotional identification with reality) dynamically draws the viewer's eye into the living organism of the picture. Paintings of this kind were a direct illustration of the ideas expounded by Šalda in his essay on the new beauty and the new landscape art: real form should be no more than a pretext for grasping the life of the universe and transmitting the cosmos through the lyricism of light.

This thought was masterfully put into effect in the work Slavíček carried out during his summer visits to Kameničky, in the Czecho-Moravian highlands, between 1903 and 1906. The barrenness of this high plateau was conducive to concentration and economy

of pictorial means, and Slavíček painted vast horizons whose stark musicality voiced the boundless union of sky and earth. An accumulation of details was unsuitable for expressing the immense space he found here, and he achieved a painting's unity, for example, not by a patch of sunlight, but by a luminous equivalent he encountered in the colours of the place itself, leading to a new procedure in the impressionist breakdown of colour and light. In no way did it reduce the compositional possibilities, and more "earthy" landscapes facilitated the rendering of new subjects that were more emotional than visual.

In the letters he wrote from Kameničky, Slavíček often expressed his need to capture the true feeling of the landscape, to understand it not as a tourist, but as

Antonín Slavíček, *Stromovka Park,* 1907. Oil, 18.7 x 24 cm. Roudnice nad Labem Gallery.

someone who lived and laboured there. Of course, this approach went far beyond the aesthetic preoccupations of the early impressionists, and Slavíček came under the influence of the Worpswede painters, who exhibited as a group under the aegis of the Mánes Union in Prague in the autumn of 1903. He wanted to create a similar colony of artists in Kameničky, where Bohuslav Dvořák, a friend from his days in Mařák's studio, and the young Otakar Nejedlý were already painting. This reflected Slavíček's desire to leave city life and find "Paradise Lost" in nature, among simple people. Describing an instant of pure artistic ecstasy in the open air, he wrote: "A man looks and forgets everything. He sees neither shapes nor lines. He sees only eerie colours spiralling down toward him, closer and closer; at that moment, a tree has no branches or leaves, only flashes of flame, ornaments whose existence we had never suspected."[11]

Slavíček's comments demonstrate that despite appearances, the spirit of the times was still present. He conceived even the very basis of his new paintings as ornamental. Yet the decorative element was hitherto unknown, or at least not yet understood by the artist, however widespread it was in the great book of nature. This ornament was not part of a "style" one conformed to, but rather the means through which art gained access to the essence of higher things and grasped it in its own way. Thus the mystery of the world finds expression, and man is overwhelmed by its endless depths.

The dream of Kameničky eventually faded, however. Slavíček went back to his native Prague, and in 1906 began work on a large series of pictures representing contemporary features of the city. Slavíček often complained of the demolition caused by the modernization of Old Prague, which eliminated the most picturesque parts of the town and destroyed its "patina". Even so, his attitude to the city was not one of mere nostalgia for the past. All of his pictures throb with "the pulse of colour" that is proof of the indestructibility of life and the constant interaction between past and present. To pin down his personal impressions, Slavíček painted in the open air on small wooden boards. This resulted in a series of sketches that are among the best work in early twentieth-century Czech painting. Afterward he put this material together in larger pictures, in which he managed to retain all the spontaneity of his vision. The same applied to the large panoramic views he painted of Prague in 1908. *Prague Seen from Ládví* was commissioned by the city council; he was well aware that a blue Prague was unlikely to be accepted easily, but he held to his convictions. Later, he painted Prague from Letná as a city buzzing with life under its Gothic roofs, the symbol of "the artery of life and the Czech bloodstream".[12] After that, he wanted to paint a third panoramic view of Prague in the colours of autumn showers, apparently intending to create a cycle of landscapes corresponding to the four seasons. With these paintings,

the moment of impressionist elation would be raised to the level of permanent ecstasy, expressing the rotation of cosmic energy through life.

Slavíček also painted a large-scale work of the Old Town Square and another of the tower of Saint Guy's Cathedral in Hradčany. In both, he achieved the virtually impossible feat of combining the immediacy of the impressionist vision with the monumentality of the subject and its plastic form. These works are permanent symbols of the heroic attitude that informed both the life and the art of Slavíček and his generation. To Slavíček, the new debate on Impressionism was merely a pretext for him to fully express the values of his life and art. The symbolist and ornamentalist works of the young artists of yesteryear were open to accusations of plagiarism and escapism, but the new conception's insistence on permanent contact with reality opened up a fresh space for creating an original artistic symbol out of a continual flow of perceptions and impressions. This conception respected the artist and put him in harmony with, not opposition to, the real, which was viewed from a pantheistic standpoint. It considered the work of art, and culture as a whole, as an open system for the exchange of expressive content between modern man and his environment. It was an active response to the enigma of life, formerly seen in a pessimistic light, and, even more, it was a challenge to the future.

THE EMOTIVE STYLE

The sources of intuition

The demand for a relationship between art and life became the guiding precept for Czech artists and writers of the modern movement at the beginning of the century. This involved far more than just a different way of seeing things: it represented an entirely new experience of the universe that brought into play all of the artist's mental powers, as well as his senses and emotions. This viewpoint inextricably linked visual appetite with an inner restlessness. It was felt that through the desire to discover the cosmic echo in nature and to become part of the oneness of life, artistic creation would provide the solution to modern man's crisis and would culminate in a dramatic, unmediated encounter with the powers of life and death.

Inspired by this emotive conception of the artist's role, Czech artists felt the need for an example to follow; they found it in Auguste Rodin. Their attention was first drawn to him by the scandal provoked by his monumental sculpture of Honoré de Balzac at the 1898 Salon de Paris. After that, Rodin completely won over the young Czechs with his exhibition in the Place de l'Alma pavilion at the Universal Exposition in 1900. Miloš Jiránek and Arnošt Hofbauer saw the exhibition and immediately started work on a special issue of *Volné směry* devoted to the sculptor. Jiránek contacted him, and as there was some difficulty about procuring photographs, he suggested to Rodin that drawings of some of the sculptures could be published instead. Not only did Rodin agree, but he made verbal corrections to the sketches. This method enabled Jiránek to gain deeper insight into the meaning of Rodin's drawings, whose apparent roughness and primitiveness had shocked him at first. He discovered the sculptor's flair for capturing the essence of bodily movement in its infinite variations, as well as his unusual expression of the unity of body and soul in gesture and movement: Rodin's art became accessible to him.

Jiránek wrote about all of this in the double issue of *Volné směry* on Rodin, published the spring of 1901. The cover was simple, showing a wood engraving of Hofbauer's version of *Man with a Broken Nose,* and the issue contained texts by the Parisian critics Arsène Alexandre, Gustave Geffroy, Roger Milès and Camille Mauclair, anecdotes by Jiránek and Hofbauer concern-ing the publication's preparation, and a conclusion written by Stanislav Sucharda, the president of the Mánes Union. Sucharda once again noted Rodin's pursuit of "natural beauty", based on the study of movements that expressed human emotions and were therefore the image "of love and suffering, hope and despair, abnegation and contempt". It was important that Sucharda, as a great Czech sculptor, also showed how Rodin succeeded in handling great monumental subjects such as *The Burghers of Calais* and *Balzac,* and how, independently of public taste for descriptive detail, he adhered in these works to "the idea of unity expressed on a monumental scale".[1]

Interest in Rodin by no means ended with this publication. There followed an exhibition of the master's work in Prague, an event made possible by the sculptor Josef Mařatka, who in 1900 had gone to Paris on a grant and was greatly impressed by the works he discovered in the pavilion on the Place de l'Alma. Through the recommendation of the painter Pierre Limet, he became Rodin's pupil and later his assistant. Mařatka himself, in his *Memories and Notes*, gave a particularly vivid description of his arrival at the famous workshop on the rue de l'Université and the work he did, which earned him the master's friendly approval.[2]

On Rodin's instructions, Mařatka began by studying feet and hands, learning how to exaggerate shapes freely to enhance their expressivity. A slight correction from the master along with words of encouragement – "Let it sing!" – would be enough for him to loosen up and get closer to the fundamentals of Rodin's conception of form. The French influence that Mařatka's first teacher, Myslbek, had introduced into Bohemia was now bearing fruit.

Mařatka was quick to understand that to Rodin the modelling of feet and hands was not merely a subject for study: he saw each individual part of the body as an autonomous sculptural entity. The fragment of the hand, for example, was identified with the theme of destiny in Rodin's psychophysical symbolism. Mařatka also executed diametrically opposed variants on a basic theme: alongside vigorous studies of convulsive, cropped limbs, he would also create hands drained of energy, limp, drooping and half closed, expressing the passive side of emotional tragedy

Mařatka later applied this experience to his preliminary sketches of female nudes created in 1902 and 1903,

Emil Filla, The *Reader of Dostoyevsky,* 1907. Oil on canvas, 98.5 x 80 cm. Prague, National Gallery.

Josef Mařatka, *Ariadne Abandoned*, 1903. Bronze, 30.5 cm.
Prague, National Gallery.

which represented a unique innovation in Czech sculpture. He succeeded in ridding himself of his preconceptions concerning composition, and transformed the subject of the nude into a free, unbridled expression of matter given life by the sculptor's sensitivity. He was aided in this by his drawings, in which, like Rodin, he captured impromptu and expressive attitudes of the moving or dancing model. In these sketches, Mařatka first of all made a relaxed rendering of hip movement to obtain a freer distribution of mass, and transformed the body into a flexible interplay of irregular rhythmic curves. The plastic achievement of his *Torsos* lay in the swirling, flamelike configuration imparted to the material, which lent the figure a vigorous upward thrust, but the upper part of the body was more often than not abruptly bent over in a dynamic, curvilinear motion.

This kind of movement became integral to the symbolization of the subject in the sculpture *Ariadne Abandoned* (c. 1903), in which the open space formed by the figure bending toward a rocky outcrop constitutes the sculptural focal point of the work and the most interesting feature of the composition. In Rodin's marble sculptures, light filters between the figures through a transparently thin sheet of stone, whereas Mařatka, in his bronzes, left an empty space. This radical plastic invention already encompassed modern sculpture's intuition of "inner" space, and fitted in with symbolist ideas of returning to nature through mythological poetic visions. In this case, however, it was no longer a matter of literature, but of a plastic symbol that seemed to appear quite naturally. The lack of a solid central point, a physical centre of gravity, put Mařatka's *Ariadne* among the works furthest removed from the traditional classical concept of sculpture.

Mařatka gave up the illustration of contemporaneous literary themes, and under Rodin's guidance moved in the direction of original, modern sculpture. This development is apparent in his nudes, in which his work took opposing forms of expression. At the other end of the scale from the classical serenity of *Ariadne*, for example, were his *Fat Woman* studies, where the predominant element is heavily expressive solid matter. One of these is a perfect piece of psychophysical analysis, another, sketchier work, of a seated woman leaning on her hands on the ground behind her, is more interesting from the sculptural standpoint. It brings to mind a passage from Mařatka's handwritten notes: "Rodin wanted me to give greater attention to the profiles, to study them from all angles. That is to say that, in the modelling, one should not work face on, but study the profiles and therefore the contours. This is the only way to obtain a firm shape (the solid core of form) that has to be first and foremost architectonic, or in other words, constructed."[3]

This principle is clearly apparent in the study: the core constructed from the solid matter is brought out on the surface by a slight asymmetry in the basic volumes, which are delineated by their outlines as seen from different angles. However, the contours are not closed off, and tend to spread out triumphantly into the surrounding space. The deformed shapes seen occasionally in his nudes heralded an important step in Mařatka's career: his association with the French sculpture emerging from a heretical development in Rodin's own studio in the work of the unruly Antoine Bourdelle, one of the Czech sculptor's contemporaries.

In 1902, however, Rodin still guaranteed a royal path to modern art in the eyes of Czech artists. His exhibition was held during May in the Mánes Union's pavilion, which had just been built according to Kotěra's design. It was not restricted to art alone. The undertaking was sponsored by the Prague city council and other important Czech institutions, and during the preparation of the exhibition, an official delegation headed by the mayor of Prague visited Rodin's studio and requested that he lend the model for his Victor Hugo monument to the exhibition. The artists them-

selves, in tune with the Czech politicians' unequivocally pro-French attitude, did their best to draw attention to their association's activities, its European orientation and its demanding criteria. The excitement reached a peak when Rodin visited Prague at the end of May. From the moment he reached the Bohemian frontier he was besieged by hordes of journalists and artists, and in Prague a great crowd fêted the representative of French culture. In addition to official receptions, the heavy schedule organized for him included meetings with Czech artists, a visit to Slavíček's studio, and a brief meeting with the professors Myslbek and Hynais at the School of Fine Arts. This hugely, successful trip culminated in a three-day visit to Moravia, which Alfons

Jan Kotěra, Mánes Union of Artists' pavilion in Prague, 1902. Now destroyed.

Mucha had organized around the theme of popular folklore.

Rodin's exhibition was the most widely visited of all the events organized by the Mánes Union before the First World War, although its success was due more to the press campaign surrounding it than to genuine interest on the public's part. The truth is that the public in Prague – as indeed in Paris and elsewhere – found Rodin's art particularly difficult to understand. The considerable gap between the taste of the public and that of the modern artists became evident on a number of occasions. There was, for instance, the accusation that the Rodin exhibition was part of a plot by the Mánes Union against the "national" sculptor, Myslbek. Also, the city authorities had bought (though not without hesitation) a bronze casting of *The Age of Bronze* at the exhibition, but a proposal to put it in the Žofín Gardens was rejected on the grounds that it might "offend public modesty".

The Rodin exhibition was nevertheless a major turning point in Czech art. The sculptor's enormous prestige, which was in part attributable to political considerations, provided a protective aura for the work of the modern artists; it validated their right to deform subject matter and to elaborate freely on themes. Even though some influential critics such as Mádl and Karel Čapek-Chod failed to grasp the meaning of Rodin's fragmented anatomical parts, and definitely preferred *The Kiss* to *Balzac*, nobody dared cast doubt on the greatness of his sculpture. With this endorsement, modernity was formally established in Czech art.

"The Mother Tongue of Genius", an analysis of Rodin's art written by Šalda in the exhibition catalogue, contributed significantly to developing a Rodin cult that glorified him as the perfect modern artist. This hero-worship grew to greater proportions in Bohemia during the first decade of the century, and has not disappeared entirely even today. The text presented the French sculptor not only as the great "renovator and restorer" of sculpture – which seemed to be no more than a "frozen, dead language from bygone days" – but also as the archetype of the creative artist capable of "making the natural language of the day and age sing out, with its warmth and unconventionality, the artery for the surges of the soul today". Rodin's talent for speaking the artistic language of his time and giving voice to its deepest tendencies was not due solely to his

Maxmilián Švabinský, *The Inspiration of Rodin*, 1901. Charcoal, 132 x 96 cm. Prague, National Gallery.

sense of the unusual. Šalda stressed Rodin's creative introspection and the psychological roots of his work: "There has never been a sculptor, and in the last century there have been only a few artists, who were capable of accompanying you to the depths of the dark sources of creative chaos, who by taking the sacred waters from it in such an original and unhesitating manner, gave it to you to drink straight from their hands outstretched toward your feverish lips, and who enabled you to gaze so closely upon the mystery of creation. [...] Rodin's art is completely immediate." Šalda saw Rodin essentially as an original, creative individual whose intense concentration gave him the ability to grasp universal values.[4]

Although Šalda was of course expressing his own views here, he was nonetheless also speaking on behalf of modernity as a whole. His influence, which had grown since he became editor-in-chief of *Volné směry*, derived from his flair for expressing the ideas artists needed and for giving their effort meaning. His portrait of Rodin as the ideal artist condensed a number of fundamental theses circulating among artists about the purpose and essence of art. These echoed the ideals of the time, especially those of the literary world, or else arose from the dynamics of the artists' own work. Their concept of the world included many elements reminiscent of the mythological model. Indeed, the mere effort of creating a new stylistic alternative to the decadence of eclecticism drew them to the myth of "Paradise Lost" that formed the essential framework of the Art Nouveau vision. The attempt to create a new style was in fact an attempt to create a new artistic world. This meant going back to the pure, original sources of creation, which explains why the artists spoke in terms of the unity of art and life. Initially they sought these sources in nature and in the naturalist outlook, but the centrality of the creative individual to the artistic process soon shifted interest toward the mind.

This displacement was reflected clearly in Šalda's article on Rodin. He particularly emphasized the artist's psychical "mother tongue", his ability to draw forth artistic symbols from the mysterious depths of his soul, and his tragic view of life. Here the artist was capable of creating a new world of artistic forms out of primordial chaos. The fundamentally cosmogonic nature of this viewpoint was also expressed theoretically with the qualification of Rodin as "an element of nature" and even "a cosmic force".[5] The origin of Rodin's exceptional standing and of the worship accorded him by the Czech modernists lay in the role attributed to him as a demiurge whose work was considered the archetype of creation. His sculptures and drawings became symbolic visions of the unity of biological, spiritual and mental elements transformed into the fundamental components of art by a conception of material, line, light and space. What nourished the artist's genius was no longer solely a phenomenon of nature, but also the psychophysical processes of a cosmic order that existed within the creative artist. This explains why, on the Rodin exhibition poster created by Županský depicting the monument to Balzac, and in Švabinský's ink drawing *The Inspiration of Rodin*, the artist himself is associated with the vision of the depths of the universe.

Quido Kocian, *The Artist's Fate*, 1900. Bronze, h.: 64 cm. Prague, National Gallery.

Bohumil Kafka, *The Mummies,* plaquette, 1905. Bronze, 31 x 44.5 cm. Prague, National Gallery.

Such a model was certainly an inducement to imitation, but it was above all an incitement to creation. Šalda ended his analysis of Rodin by saying, "The renovators can only be understood by those whom they have caused to be reborn, those who are born again through them. An artist whose mother tongue is his genius can only be addressed in his own language: You alone, in yourselves, in the depths of your own being, can discover his language, expressed in metal." It was an ambitious aim.

The influence of Rodin was most marked, of course, on Czech sculpture, which, with his assistance, attained extremely high standards. The sculptors Stanislav Sucharda, Ladislav Šaloun, and Josef Mařatka exhibited together at the sixteenth Mánes Union exhibition at the end of 1904, where they showed a number of small pieces that the dismayed conservative critics censured as a growing "cult of sketches".

Contact with Rodin's expressive tendencies recurred often among Czech sculptors, most of whom had been pupils of Myslbek. This took place all the more easily given that since the 1890s Czech sculpture had been animated by a radical Baroque tradition, which in sculpture had been considered a purely local phenomenon. Already in 1901, Quido Kocian – whose *Šárka,* sculpted in 1897, had brought him into conflict with Myslbek – was working on the model for *The Artist's Fate,* a sculp-

ture intended to express his feelings as an outcast. It could also be interpreted as a bitter satire on Myslbek's *Music.* The lyricism of *Music* is countered by the emaciated, nude figure of the artist wearing an augur's cap and twisted into a Neo-Baroque position. He is fiercely clutching his instrument – here, a palette – but instead of giving it the kiss of consecration, as in Myslbek's work, he is tearing into it with his teeth in torment, his eyes closed as though drinking an intoxicating, deadly brew. In this painful vision, form reaches a dramatic point of ecstasy at which it frays away, tears apart and leaps upward like a flame. Kocian's other sculptures, including the *Abel Dead* group that won him a grant to travel to Rome, were all based on the theme of irreparable loss. He managed to transfer what was initially still a Neo-Baroque naturalist form of expression onto a deeper symbolic level, to create a new genre in symbolist plasticism that was both profound and emotional. Kocian's *Sick Soul* (1903) used the absurd position of a young male nude figure, with the body's diagonal resting on an unpolished base, to express the tragic spirit of the age.

Bohumil Kafka was another artist who shared an affinity with Baroque sensibilities. He went to live in Paris in 1904 to acquire a knowledge of French art. During the ensuing years he created a series of works that, though directly inspired by Rodin, showed a marked individuality. His *Visionary, The Mummies, Head of John the Baptist, Bacchanalia* and *Madmen* evoked symbolist themes, but their forms were far more convulsive and erotically agitated than the fluid lines of Rodin. The decorative surface was particularly expressive, and in *Madmen* Kafka even achieved the destruction of form in space.

Kafka's style became more serene in 1906. On a preliminary sketch for *The Sleepwalker* he wrote: "The model must not pose in a standing position, so that the muscles do not harden, and everything remains fluid." The aim was to express weightlessness, to surmount the basic limitations facing the sculptor by means of a vague and psychic freedom of movement, which would release plastic principles from their traditional constraints. The treatment of light and the means of expressing it remained the essential element of *The Sleepwalker,* a flowing figure set on a base, covered with a finely worked naturalistic decoration. Kafka's fusion of impression and expression was reminiscent of Antonín

Slavíček's sketches of landscapes, but there was greater relief in his plastic rendering of the elements. In the sensory effect produced by light on solid matter, which infused the symbolist visions with their strength, line was used to interpret the psychological and conceptual elements. However, this was not a rational, straight line: as in Henry Van de Velde's well known definition, this was a force that derived its energy from the hand that drew it. Witness the arching curve of the nude in *The Sleepwalker,* whose physical mass creates a volume in space that appears open or closed according to the angle from which it is viewed. The treatment of light, which is handled in such a way as to obtain both strong highlights and deep shadow, further intensifies this duality. A complex effect is produced on the contours of the figure, where the action of light on the mass creates a union of the visual and the tangible that transmutes line into an expressive surface. The same idea appeared in an article on Rodin by Camille Mauclair, Kafka's patron in Paris, published in *Volné směry*: "Sculpture destroys the erroneous idea of line drawing and replaces it with drawing that consists of surfaces and volumes. Rodin himself insists that the limitation of a surface in the air is illusory, and in his own work he multiplies surfaces endlessly to give his sculptures silhouettes, maximizing the contact between the sculptures and the atmosphere in such a way that they seem to melt into one another."[6]

This expressive interpenetration of matter and space was deeply significant. It represented not only emergence from depression but also the quest for freedom and universality. In the spirit of the times, this search led to man's return to nature and to the earth-matrix at the origin of the work of art. This notion of universality was directly linked to that of renewal, of a fundamental emotional rebirth. In this sense the emotive tendency, far from opposing the idea of synthesis, gave it greater depth.

Kafka conveyed this idea in his *Embrace of Love and Death,* a funeral monument made between 1906 and 1907. The work depicts a symbolic angel of death, its outspread wings creating great hollows that devour the light. These hollows create space within the sculpture

Bohumil Kafka, *The Sleepwalker*, 1906. Bronze, h.: 78 cm. Prague, National Gallery.

Bohumil Kafka, *The Embrace of Love and Death*, 1906–1907. Bronze, h.: 176 cm. Prague, National Gallery.

Josef Mařatka, *Portrait of Antonín Dvořák,* 1906. Bronze, h.: 33 cm. Prague, National Gallery.

and emotionally express a fusion with that dark cave of origin, the womb. The feeling of negative space also seen in Mařatka's *Ariadne Abandoned* and elsewhere in Czech sculpture is monumentalized in this case. Indeed, Kafka worked it into a structure with his characteristic style: highlighted surface areas contrast with profound shadows, while the starkness of this effect is attenuated by the figure's lyricism.

Rodin, who was influenced by the emergence of psychology in France, was attentive to the phenomena of suggestion, hypnosis and the unconscious.[7] His sensibility made a positive impact on Czech sculptors in this early, Neo-Baroque period; it heightened their inner awareness and inspired them to a purer style. Josef Mařatka, in his bust of the composer Antonín Dvořák (1904–1908), introduced Rodin's followers to the closed, inward-looking eyes typical of French Symbolism, a theme that František Bílek had already managed to imbue with mystical significance. Mařatka, who had met Dvořák as a young man when they both lived on Žitná Street in Prague, wanted to represent the composer as a Slav musical genius, and so captured his likeness at the moment of utmost creative concentration, with the eyes shut and the face twisted with emotion. What Mařatka was representing, therefore, was the birth of a unique and brilliant musical idea. As a melody, it corresponded to the concept of the "new

Stanislav Sucharda, *Funerary Sculpture*, c. 1909. Bronze. Vysehrad National Cemetery.

line", a term used by Mauclair in reference to Rodin. This work was stripped of all the current conventions of portraiture, and Šalda's presence, with his "mother tongue of genius", can be felt in Mařatka's interpretation of the composer. Mařatka managed to have this bust placed in the main foyer of the National Theatre, thanks partly to Rodin's prestige and partly to Czech culture's acceptance of the Mánes Union's view of the artist-creator as hero, which implied respect for the artist's right to trial and error.

The theme of inner contemplation also appeared, with a distinctive elegiac accent, in Sucharda's *Funerary Sculpture,* in which a female head with closed eyes and a tragic expression looms above an imaginary funeral procession in bas-relief. But Mařatka's treatment of this same theme was more direct and sensual, and yielded a new conception of portrait sculpture.

This is shown in his remarkable series of studies for the portrait of Tereza Koseová (1906–1909). A crown of hair frames the woman's face, which is marked by conflicting emotions. The highly charged emotional content virtually eliminates any actual physical resemblance, as though Mařatka had set off on the same path that took his contemporary, Constantin Brancusi, to the *Sleeping Muse.* Mařatka, however, continued to be limited by his insistence on sensuality and emotivity.

Such psychologically induced emotivity became a principle for Ladislav Šaloun, who discovered in Friedrich Nietzsche the concept of Dionysian art – that true artistic creation is impossible without drunkenness. Šaloun's notes, some of which were later published, show that he considered art a manifestation of the basic force of the cosmos, with the artist its medium.[8] The artist needed an inner understanding of the work,

Stanislav Sucharda, plaquette from *The Beautiful Virgin Liliana*, 1903–1909. Copper, 9.9 x 10.3 cm. Prague, National Gallery.

by freely treated male heads such as *Flight from Life*, in which a face bearing an expression of resignation appears among rough waves, as well as the two extremely expressive faces in *Meditation and Concentration*: the former has its eyes shut and the latter's are open wide and staring. These works reflect Šaloun's interpretation of the symbolist theory of empathy, according to which man-the-creator must close himself off to the outside world so as to enable intuitive knowledge to burst forth from his inner being.

These heads formed part of the project for the great monument to Jan Hus that Šaloun was working on at the time, and which was to be installed in Prague's Old Town Square. The series of heads ended with an interesting grotesque mask that decorated the entrance to Šaloun's studio in Prague-Vinohrady. This was conceived around 1910 in the Secession spirit of the "total work of art", and represented a heroic mask of the horned god Pan, on whose swirling, stylized locks sat the erotic female nude of his Muse.[9] The mask recalls Bourdelle's *Beethoven* yet bears an even more distinct resemblance to the face of Schopenhauer; hence it is intensely expressive of the ideas and forms inherited by Czech art from French Symbolism. Philosophical pessimism and a conception of music more akin to Wagner than Beethoven as the direct incarnation of the world's volition were embodied in the form of the mask, and its placement on the door of Šaloun's studio celebrated the artist's workplace as a modern-day house of worship.

The mask's composition can also be linked to *In the Mind of Man* (1897), an engraving by Edvard Munch that was displayed at the major exhibition of the Norwegian painter's work organized by the Mánes Union in the spring of 1905.[10] Its strange syncretism thus reflected the second major influence – after Rodin – on the formation of Czech art.

The Munch exhibition is generally considered the turning point that marked the birth of a true avant-garde in Bohemia, influencing an entire generation of young painters who were later to revolutionize art under the banners of Expressionism and Cubism. A close look at the exhibition's history shows that it was the work of a more radical group within the Mánes Union, who hoped it would help them advance their own work. Munch, however, was not unknown in Bohemia. In 1896 *Moderní revue* had published his *Madonna*, in-

which he was to achieve through the senses rather than through an intellectual process. By increasing the range and depth of his feelings, he was reinforcing life. His task consisted of "firmly grasping the heart of the matter", and his work could not exist in the absence of his desire.

Šaloun received a great many commissions for decorative sculptures, and his remarkable capacity for work was put to full use. The facades and interiors of many Art Nouveart buildings in Prague featured works executed by Šaloun, whose dramatic movement was invariably held in check by the decorative curves of his contours. The essence of Šaloun's concept was particularly evident in the series of heads he created between 1905 and 1910, which showed interesting variations on the theme of the inward gaze borrowed by Czech sculptors from the symbolist repertoire. The series began with oneiric, self-contained female half-portraits, and seems to have been inspired by the spiritualism that Šaloun regularly practised with his friends. This was followed

Ladislav Šaloun, *Concentration*, c. 1905. Bronze, h.: 30 cm.
Prague, National Gallery.

cluding its legendary frame on which spermatozoa
were depicted, and later, *Self-Portrait* and *The Scream*.
These were published together with a monographic
study by Stanislaw Przybyszewski in which Munch was
described as the only artist besides Gustav Vigeland to
represent "each feeling as a shape and a line".[11]

At the time, *Moderní revue* and the Mánes Union
were in conflict over modern naturalism. The latter
was accused of not being modern in its insistence on
a profound study of nature and on protecting it from
"violation". After the sharp rise in appreciation of
Rodin, whose work was a major source of inspiration
to Munch, all of these problems were transposed into
a different context. Compunction about distorting
form became irrelevant, whereas the question of colour
remained a live issue. Indeed, it was Munch's "bleeding
colour" that created the scandal responsible for a great
split among art critics in 1905. The reason for this was
simple: Munch lacked Rodin's political weight and,
unlike the sculptor, was only received in Prague as a

representative of modern individualism. The critics
argued heatedly, and Mádl, in great indignation, violently condemned the exhibition, claiming that Munch
had no understanding of painting or form.[12] In Madl's
view, what the artist was trying to express had nothing to do with "the world of sensuality", and his "wild
ghosts" and "neuropathological convulsions" were
merely an infantile bid to "return to the nakedness
of prehistoric man by artificial means, with fumbling
uncertainty of hand and eye". By mounting this exhibition, the Mánes Union threatened "to undermine all
our values" and thereby replace a strong, healthy art
with one that was morbid and diseased.

The spokesmen for the Mánes Union could not let
such an attack go unanswered. Jiránek[13] and Šalda[14]
each replied in his own way, but only the young poet
Miloš Marten defended Munch unconditionally, even
though he did not approve of all of his paintings. It was
not entirely by chance that Marten's view prevailed in
Moderní revue. Unlike Jiránek and Šalda, he was not
burdened by the constraints of Impressionism, and the
issue of light in colour was of no interest to him. This
gave him all the more freedom to concentrate on refut-
ing the second argument against *Moderní revue*'s preferred artists: that their work was essentially literary.
Marten retorted that the "literary interest" of a true
creator reflected his attention to the inner life. Painters
chose these subjects because they saw in them "the
heart of life, a more powerful set of symbols of nature
and the soul". The only real issue was how a painter
managed to exploit them in terms of "the lines and
colours [that] are his natural language, just as words are
to the poet". Marten's defence of Munch, which was
based on Przybyszewski's analysis of his work in the
1890s, concluded by drawing parallels between the
artistic credos of these two "Decadents". "A relationship that was personal and artistic rather than historical, a kind of inner kinship between Munch and Stanislaw Przybyszewski, casts a clear light on the former's
work. [...] Their respective psychologies overlap in the
essentials: they are seeking man, his being and his purpose, through the eruptions of the wild, untamable
forces of a physical being whose activity begins where
the roots of consciousness and volition disappear. To
them, man is not merely a self-contained social unit, a
more or less clearly defined individual, but a conglom-
eration of an infinite variety of nerve centres, each of

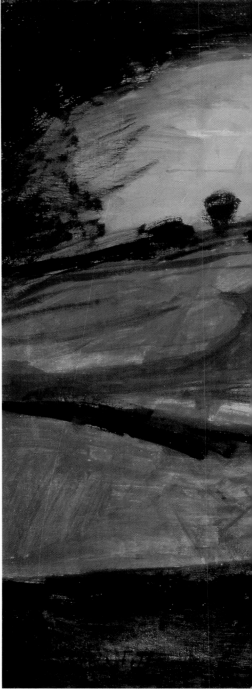

Emil Filla, *Love-Night*, 1907. Oil on canvas, 73 x 110 cm.
Prague, National Gallery.

Top left: Bohumil Kubišta, *The Card Players*, 1909. Oil on canvas,
65.5 x 82 cm. Prague, National Gallery.

Bottom left: Antonín Procházka, *The Circus*, 1907. Oil on
cardboard, 47.4 x 65 cm. Prague, National Gallery.

which has its own function and is capable of deranging the frail, artificially constituted human entity. In what is commonly thought of as aberration and mental disorder, they see the effervescence of the clean raw materials from which life is created. Hence, matter to them becomes the vehicle of the mystical fatality that in times past was situated in some otherworldly realm. The medieval satanic sphere is now within man himself, and from here [Munch and Przybyszewski] procure dark, red ecstasies as did the poets of the early Christian ages. [...] They love passion in a state of paroxysm, for it is like volcanic eruptions, throwing up the deep-buried, inchoate layers of the soul. They love fear and despair as the primal forms of consciousness, they love pain, for it inflames the mind with vertiginous thoughts and probes sin, crime and madness for the answer to the mystery of life and death. That is why to them art is an outward-leaping flame, the work of fever and ecstasy, a drama and a hallucination. Munch's painting resounds with the echo of Van Gogh's fatal words: 'The sicker I am, the more of an artist I become.' But the artist's illness is the explosion of his soul's energy, too violent for the body to bear, it is the inner life intensified, it is the self-sacrifice with which he redeems the frenzy of his thoughts. Sickness, with her burning embrace, is a cruel friend, and it is beauty itself in its entity that is pathological."[15]

Marten was aware of the lyricism of Munch's painting; he remarked on his ability to see things as "large, dissolving masses and [to] feel their rhythm", and noted that "in this anarchist's technique lie hidden shoots of new decorative stylization and form". Nevertheless, Marten based his whole assessment on an empathetic interpretation of Munch, a view that found an echo among the younger generation. Furthermore, his conceptualization of the psyche's "inner depths" as a conflict rather than a "mood" or an "impression", was in fact the first statement of Czech Expressionism.

Marten's comments seem to have been a preamble to Emil Filla's painting *The Reader of Dostoyevsky* (1907), a veritable manifesto of the younger generation of painters. Filla sems to have taken Marten's ideas on the "literary" value of a work quite literally, since the subject of his painting is a man reading Feodor Mikhailovich Dostoyevsky. In the eyes of the young artist, the Russian writer's pitiless scrutiny of the depths of the soul made him a literary authority of the highest order

(Dostoyevsky's subject matter greatly affected Filla's contemporaries). Here, Filla creates an atmosphere of crisis by the use of stark, Munch-like hues. The relief of the subject's head is modelled with a blue-green colour; the man is reading, collapsed into an armchair, and the dissonance between the reds and the blue-greens suggests a wrenching conflict between his body and his mind. The body, wracked by this inner contradiction, stretches diagonally and seems to be linked to a crucifix on the wall – which appears to offer no consolation – and also to the works of Dostoyevsky, lying on a table beside a glass of water. The universe of the modern writer, where the questions of life and death are confronted head-on, is thus presented as an alternative to the more humble past. The formless marks on the floor represent mental disorder and are a direct reference to Munch's *Melancholy.*

That same year, this use of colour as a pointed psychological indicator led Filla to create *The Night of Love*, then considered the most "barbaric" work in Czech painting. The subject is quite different from *Dostoyevsky*, and daylight is here replaced by mysterious night, with a moon worthy of Hlaváček, which evokes animal-like shapes. These are rendered by spontaneous strokes made with a wide brush, which distributes colours of poster-style harshness over the canvas. The use of the brush stroke to create form is significant. It functions here as an expressive colour surface, not as a line. Filla takes up Munch's symbolic concept of shadow: in the foreground, which is enlivened by a white cat, it induces the viewer to accept the strange harmony between the red colours and the blue-green moon. Filla, who had already moved a long way beyond the older generation's impressionist programme, demonstrated that experimental painting had toppled the last defences, and that other upheavals were on the way.

Filla was a leading light of The Eight, a group of young painters that had formed in reaction against the illusionism prevalent in the studio of their Art School professor, Vlaho Bukovac. In 1907 these young painters mounted their first exhibition, which went unnoticed. The following year, The Eight, which included Germans as well as Czechs (this was the period when the law on citizens' rights was voted in, and the times were conducive to democratic illusions), organized another show that took place this time in the prestigious Topič rooms. It met with a rather unfavourable reception, however, and the works shown were generally considered to be more exhibitionism. Even so, the younger generation took a deep interest in the most renowned of the new painting's "unclassifiable phenomena", such as Van Gogh, to whom *Volné směry* devoted an issue that year. Although the older generation may well have appreciated the enormity of Van Gogh's sacrifice, only the young drew a lesson from his paintings.

Bohumil Kubišta was another outstanding member of The Eight. In 1907 he painted a *Triple Portrait* of himself with his painter friends Bedřich Feigl and Emil Artur Pittermann, which seemed to challenge the viewer to a duel. In his paintings after 1908, the expressive line and hammered surface texture were clearly influenced by Van Gogh. Unlike the more introverted Filla, Kubišta at that time was interested in scenes of daily urban life, portraits and still lifes. Indeed, he was inspired by the traditional Mánes Union aesthetic, according to which the impact of an artistic vision should be brought to bear on "natural" objects. He soon began to show a strong leaning toward the theoretical analysis of artistic devices, together with a solid, critical mind. These qualities made him a spokesman for the young painters and helped to strengthen their interest in the conceptual aspect of their work. During The Eight period, Kubišta developed his style on the basis of everyday scenes, and continued to work in a range of yellows, greens and purples. His style was also affected by the evolution of his brushwork and his treatment of colour, but its decorative aspect was increasingly subordinated to elemental forms and the magical diffusion of colour emanating from objects, all of which he treated with a rather uncompromising seriousness.

The Eight also included another important painter, Antonín Procházka. Procházka was still painting in the impressionist manner in 1907, but he too caught the spirit of the evocative power of crowded city streets and the melancholy torment of Munch's portraits. He certainly did not disavow Impressionism – quite the contrary. In his paintings, light does not fall onto objects, but tends rather to be reflected off the white canvas in a way that imparts colour to it. His 1907 *Circus* is particularly remarkable for its vibrant transparency of colour, which shows a tendency toward Orphism and away from the highly charged emotionalism of his pictures inspired by Munch. An extremely receptive painter, Procházka was also affected by the renewed influence

of Honoré Daumier; this can be seen in a number of his allegories such as the biblical parable *Christ Casting the Merchants out of the Temple*, which he painted in 1909 as a commentary on the situation in art.

The exchanges among The Eight painters were reflected in a set of common themes that the artists treated, such as *The Card Players*, a subject dealt with by Filla, Procházka and Kubišta in 1908 and 1909. Filla's *Ace of Hearts* represented the confrontation between the "searching man", in the Dostoyevskian mould, and his treacherous destiny. Kubišta portrayed a scene of nervous players gathered at an inn, while Procházka treated his *Players* in a monumental style. Their common feature is a deliberate "primitivism" in both the choice of subject and, above all, the artistic means employed. Influenced by Munch, these young painters had adopted a psychological conception of colour that clashed with the previous generation's idea of a picture as an ensemble of sensations and emotions, which was adopted after the revival of Impressionism. In the young painters' work, colour was used more as a vehicle to express the permanent conflict between daily existence and the psychic inner life, and hence seemed to flow continually from the real toward the unreal. This state of psychological unrest – which can already be qualified as expressionist – shattered the illusionistic qualities and rhythmical patterns of the ornamental style.

These young painters must have had the impression of being card players themselves: they concentrated their entire attention on questions of art, and fought heated personal battles over it. The most innovative members of the Mánes Union of Artists, such as Preisler and Jiránek, urged the energetic young painters to join their association, which was how Filla came to join *Volné směry*. His first article in the magazine appeared in 1911 together with reproductions of works by Pablo Picasso; it was entitled "On the Virtue of Neo-Primitivism", and contended that all forms of naturalism, including Impressionism, were dead ends because they failed to address the basic principles underlying the construction of an artistic work.[16] The storm this provoked in the ranks of the older generation abated only with the memorable scission of the young members of the Mánes Union, who were accused of engaging in arid intellectualizing instead of creating paintings that were rich, original and full of life.[17] Yet, like Munch, in

Josef Váchal, *Elemental Plain*, 1907, India ink and watercolour,
30.6 x 52.3 cm. Prague, Památník národního písemnictví.

FACING PAGE: Josef Váchal, *Astral Plain*, 1906. India ink and
watercolour, 35.7 x 52 cm. Prague, Památník národního písemnictví.

their younger days they had been criticized for quite the
opposite – undisciplined anarchism.

As a doctrine and a political movement, anarchism
was attractive to many Czech intellectuals, especially
writers. The poet Stanislav Kostka Neumann had
already been publishing his anarchist trade union periodical *Nový kult* since 1897, and the anarchist ideal of a
social Utopia fathered Neumann's Decadent Satanism
of the 1890s. His doctrine appealed especially to a dis-
oriented intelligentsia unable to find its place in society.

František Gellner's first two collections of poems, *Live for the Moment* (1901) and *The Joys of Life* (1903), epitomized the movement, whose bohemian attitudes were a provocative challenge to the ordered lives of bourgeois society.

Josef Váchal was younger than Neumann and Gellner, and one of their greatest admirers. His multifaceted activities showed how far anarchist sentiment could be carried – in the case of The Eight painters, its limits were confined to plastic art. Váchal suffered from

the fact that he was an illegitimate child and reacted to this by honing his feelings of exclusion. His father had been an adept of crude spiritualism, and Váchal followed its growing popularization to become a member of the Prague Theosophical Society in 1903. He was employed in a printing shop when the following year he began to suffer distressing hallucinations. Subsequently, he decided to become an artist and after a brief spell of training with the landscape painter Alois Kalvoda, Váchal found that his artistic work enabled him to

Josef Váchal, *Black Mass*. Wood engraving, 23 x 32.5 cm. Prague, National Gallery.

handle his psychotic states. Later he even regained his self-control and mental equilibrium.

Characteristic of Váchal's art at this period are two large coloured drawings, *Astral Plain* (*A Séance of Spiritualism*) and *Elemental Plain* (*The Plain of Passions and Instincts*), on which the artist commented: "A séance of spiritualism. The fruit of thought. The inhabitants of the astral plain. [...] Passions and instincts. Eternal movement within the astral plain. Here walk the slaves of the senses, loosely defined bodies and thoughts that have shape and colour, furtively crossing each others' paths. All of this fused together in an immense chaos, but nonetheless having a certain goal. In the centre, music and sound, beauty and light, the shapes of passion and crime, tenderness and fornication, strength and resignation."[18]

Váchal took part in séances of spiritualism held in Šaloun's studio. In his drawings it is difficult to distinguish clearly between his own personal visions and those he came upon in his diligent investigations into occultism. Whatever the case may be, his work remains an excellent example of the strong influence exercised on some areas of Czech art by the novel conceptions of French "new psychology" during the 1890s. Jean Charcot's study of hypnosis, his emphasis on the irresistible force of perceptual images and "sensory hallucinations" in mental functioning, and especially his description of people's ghastly hypnotic visions largely account for Váchal's eerie fantasies. His demons' pictorial forms were still bound up with the pathological roots of this imagination, but Váchal's general emphasis on these ideas went beyond spiritualism's dualistic division of the world toward the "ideodynamism" expounded by Hippolyte Bernheim, who considered the kind of suggestion a hypnotist makes to a person's unconscious a normal part of spiritual life. Šalda's own "mystical sense of reality", and his concept of the cosmic dimension of the individual brought him closer to Henri Bergson's re-evaluation of human consciousness.

In any case, the function of the hypnotist, whose experimentation released the emotions by means of suggestion, was gradually taken over by the artist. The latter possessed a more sustained ability to probe the depths of intuition, to help surmount the barriers of egoism, and to lay the solid foundations of a new understanding of the universe.

Josef Váchal, cover for J. Šimánek's
Journey of a Little Elf, 1911.
Wood engraving, 31.5 x 24.5 cm.
Prague, UPM.

The national myth

In Paris during the 1890s, Alfons Mucha became familiar with the "new psychology" and its conception of the unconscious. He was also fascinated by spiritualism and sought to link this new area of awareness with ancient mystical and esoteric traditions, as well as with more recent theosophical teachings. In the company of Albert de Rochas, the famous astronomer Camille Flammarion, and the artist's model Line de Ferkel, who was also a medium, Mucha carried out a number of experiments in hypnosis and "extra-sensory perception".[1] During these sessions, Mme. de Ferkel responded to verbal or musical instructions with gestures and mime movements that Mucha considered of great value for their authenticity. Thus the way was paved for a far-reaching renewal of decorative art, which was often criticized as being artificial.

For Mucha, this renewal did not simply represent a new technique of working from a model, through the use of photography, for instance, but was the genesis of a new artistic framework and of a universally valid symbolism. Mucha's ambition reached its peak in the late 1890s with several major projects. For the 1900 Universal Exposition, he proposed a design for a gigantic pavilion dedicated to Mankind. One version called for the project to be built atop the first level of the Eiffel Tower, and consisted of an enormous globe with ramps leading up to entrances framed by great, crescent-shaped portals decorated with allegorical paintings. The building's conception was also to have been reflected in groups of monumental sculptures by James Vibert, representing the evolution of man from his earliest appearance on earth to his spiritual ascension, symbolized by the statue of a winged, heavenly Spirit of the Earth set on the highest point of the central globe. The proposed Mankind pavilion was so gigantic, however, that it was impossible to build for the 1900 Universal Exposition.

In Paris Mucha published a magnificent illustrated edition of the *Pater Noster* (1899) that was created in a similar vein. A recent study shows a clear link between the artist's symbolism and theosophy, as well as the striking resemblance his illustration of the seven petitions of the *Pater Noster* bears to the seven stages of the

Municipal building, the Mayor's Room, decorated by Alfons Mucha (1910–1911). Prague Old Town (Republic Square 5). Arch.: Osvald Polívka and Antonín Balsánek.

Alfons Mucha, project for the Mankind pavilion, 1897. Graphite and watercolour, 50.1 x 64.9 cm. Prague, National Gallery.

initiatory journey described in the esoteric work *Die chymische Hochzeit des Christian Rosenkreutz*, to Rosicrucian liturgy, and to a number of other sources.[2]

All this indicates the extent to which Mucha was inspired by the spiritualism of his day, and how closely his work was bound up with theosophical speculation – derived from Gnostic and Neoplatonic theories – concerning the spiritual evolution of mankind from formless basic matter toward self-knowledge and on, finally, to peace in the light of the cosmic divinity.

Mucha himself wrote that the idea for *Pater Noster* came to him when he found himself sighing "My God" at the overwhelming amount of purely commercial poster work he was doing, with little satisfaction. He may also have been piqued by criticism of his decorative work that was beginning to appear in certain Czech periodicals, including *Moderní revue,* accusing him of banality.[3] Jiránek acidly commented on his "machine-made dolls".[4]

Although Mucha's Mankind pavilion was never built, he did carry out the interior decoration of the Bosnia-Herzegovina pavilion at the 1900 Universal Exposition. In accepting this commission he was probably very conscious of a kinship with the Czech painter Jaroslav Čermák, whose pictures romanticizing the Southern Slavs had attracted attention in Paris. Mucha too turned his decorative friezes into a defence of the Slav peoples. On two strips ornamented with a lovely floral border, he gave a fluid rendering of the legendary Turkish oppression, and allegories from Life and History flanked a central painting, *Bosnia Presenting Her Wealth,* that linked the strips together. By adding sculptures, Mucha created a "total work of art" which, although it may not have had the universalist intent of the Mankind pavilion, nevertheless opened up new possibilities for decorative art.

It was a long time, however, before Mucha fully exploited the potential of this style. Immediately after he had finished his work for the Universal Exposition, he went into a period of crisis, which can be discerned in a series of freely treated drawings and pastels based on themes drawn from oneirical and mythological visions, as well as from life. These were dark visions reflecting the hidden, primitive, furtive sides of life, and were marked by the scars of depression, inner doubt and despair. These paintings, which never left Mucha's private collection, mirrored the conflict that beset him in the wake of his success.

Mucha spent the following years teaching design in the United States. He occasionally returned to his home country and seemed to feel an increasing nostalgia for it. Indeed, he never lost contact with Czech culture, and his continuing friendship with Mikoláš Aleš is testimony to the respect he felt for Czech "classics".

In 1903 Mucha created the stage scenery for Bedřich Smetana's prestigious "national" opera, *Libuše.* While in the United States, he had been deeply impressed by *Against All,* a novel by Alois Jirásek describing the heroic struggle of the Hussites. It appears that it was after hearing Smetana's moving symphonic poem *My Motherland* in 1908 that Mucha decided to devote his art to the defense of the Slav community and the promotion of Pan-Slavism.

The American art patron Charles R. Crane agreed to finance Mucha's project for a series of large works on the theme of *The Saga of the Slavs,* and by doing so enabled Mucha to return home for good in 1910. The famous decorative artist once again entered the Czech cultural arena, where he brought renewed strength to a field that had been somewhat undermined by a decade of concentration on a universal modern art.

While most Czech artists were influenced by nationalism, they found the most chauvinistic of Mucha's efforts disturbing. Yet there was one aspect of "national art" to which they could not remain indifferent: the tradition founded by the Romantic Josef Mánes, which exalted simple country folk as the guardians of the nation's autonomy and the life-blood of its culture. During the 1890s, it became obvious that this tradition

Alfons Mucha, *Pater Noster*, end page, 1899, Watercolour and India ink, 49 x 36.5 cm. Prague, Private Collection.

THE EMOTIVE STYLE

was a two-edged sword, and that idealism could be carried too far.

The great Czecho-Slav Ethnographic Exhibition was held in Prague in 1895. Preparations had begun several years earlier, and the event was the culmination of a far wider campaign that bore all the hallmarks of a Czech political event. Hynais' exhibition poster did not follow the conventional illusionistic style, and was immediately parodied by Otakar Lebeda in the Mánes Union's satirical review, *Špachtle* (Spatula). The Ethnographic Exhibition had a naturalist orientation; its planner's objective was to show the lives of country people throughout Bohemia and Moravia as accurately as possible by reproducing the decorative aspects of their surroundings. Folk architecture was an important element in these *tableaux vivants,* and the centre of the exhibition featured a circular-shaped village where different styles of peasant buildings, from the west of Domažlice to the eastern Slovak region of Oravia, were presented side by side.

The exhibition gave rise to an incredible proliferation of ethnographic eclecticism. In later years, Jiránek, looking back on his youth, wrote: "We saw 'national celebrations' that even today send shivers down my spine: there were processions and 'national costumes' that came straight from the Prague dressmakers, and 'folk art' from patrician households, with painted embroidery in varnished frames. There was so much talk about national art and keeping up old traditions that in the end the younger generation's sense of independence rebelled against this kind of moral pressure. [...] We felt that this folk art held up to us as an example was a dead end, something over and done with, a thing of the past. [...] We were much more interested in grasping everything that was going on abroad, and getting into step with the rest of Europe."[5]

Of course, this exhibition, a museum of ethnographic curiosities, did inspire some people, especially architects, who had been interested in folk architecture ever since Antonín Wiehl built his "Czech chalet" for the jubilee Exhibition. Subsequently, Jan Koula's specialist publications and some of his architectural works drew some attention to this phenomenon. Inspired by

Vojtěch Hynais, poster for the Czecho-Slav Ethnographic Exhibition, Prague, 1895. Colour lithograph, 104 x 134 cm. Prague, UPM.

folk architecture, Koula built a villa in Prague-Bubeneč in 1896 which focused not on decorative detail but on the essential relationship between the construction's mass and its roof structure. Already the impression of modernity was suggested by the counterpoint of the pebble-dashed surface of the wall and the supporting timbers under the roof line. Koula was also familiar with English garden houses, which were a further source of inspiration in his buildings. He used this dual influence to present the city-dweller with a healthier and more aesthetic habitat. He also created interiors, and in collaboration with the ceramics co-operative in Bechyně, developed a very modern use of tiling.

A similar folk-oriented spirit informed the work of Dušan Jurkovič, an architect of Slovak origin who had been brought up in close contact with the actual practice of folk architecture. At the Ethnographic Exhibition, he supervised the construction of the "Valašsku Village", as well as a large house that was the model for a people's collective residence. Since 1897 he had been building a pseudo-folk-style tourist complex entirely in

Alfons Mucha, *The Moravian Schoolteachers' Choir,* 1911.
Color lithograph, 111 x 80 cm. (43.3 x 31.2 in.). Prague, UPM.

wood on Radhošt, a mountain in Valašsku. This work simultaneously showed a poetic sense of wooden architecture, a fine conception of construction and a great sensitivity in the decorative work. Current ethnographic theories held that wooden constructions were characteristic of the ancient Slav tradition. Thus, the decor was tied to this basic element, employing appropriate motifs, and accomplished this in a way that transposed folk inspiration into modern terms. The saddle-shaped bracing of roof beams was integrated into the decoration, and became typical of the new villas being built in Prague by architects such as Kotěra and Mašek. Although wooden buildings had generally been considered provisional, they nevertheless provided scope for interesting formal innovation. A surviving example of this is Saint Adalbert's Church, which was built by Matěj Blecha's company in Prague-Libeň between 1904 and 1905. In this case, of course, the building also harks back to the structural qualities of Gothic art.

Before such local folk tradition could take hold in painting, however, it was necessary to transform the lingering echo of the peasant genre that had developed in art schools during the nineteenth century and that was greatly appreciated by the public at the major exhibitions. Even in the work of an official historical painter like Václav Brožík there was no lack of scenes portraying little shepherdesses, or the laborer's return home after a day's work in the fields. Salon painting of this kind, which was fairly common, was brought up to date with naturalism. In Munich, at the school of Professor Otto Seitz, young Czech artists found the inspiration to accomplish this transformation. One of the first young artists to be noticed was Joža Úprka, a native of Slovácko, a rural region on the frontier between Moravia and Slovakia, where local traditions were still very much alive. Úprka's training in Munich led him to produce large genre compositions with an anecdotal, descriptive bent. On his return to Prague in 1890 he met Hanuš Schwaiger, whom he took back with him to his native Slovácko; there the two painters discovered a new source of inspiration in the picturesque peasant faces and customs. Besides his Neo-Romantic and grotesque compositions, Schwaiger also executed medium-sized paintings on wood, depicting the peasant types characteristic of the foothills in Valašsku. The exotic finery of the national costume did not disguise the reality of rural life, where people bore the harsh

St. Adalbert's Church, 1904–1905. Libeň, Rudé armády. Arch.: Matěj Blecha.

traces of their exhausting, laborious struggle for existence. But social comment was not Schwaiger's purpose. Rather, his work was the product of a direct visual interest inspired by old Dutch painting, and was situated at the opposite pole from the heroic conception developed by Josef Mánes in his ethnographical studies.

Úprka went to live in Paris in 1893. The move resulted in a lighter palette, the abandoning of local naturalistic colour, and a nuanced rendering of atmosphere, while at the same time the artist introduced stronger tints in the colour surfaces that formed his work's decorative element. In 1897 Úprka first exhibited works in this style, on the theme of pilgrimages in the traditional dress of the Slovácko region, and these met with a favourable reception from the Prague public. The Mánes

Union even devoted a special issue of *Volné směry* to the show. Hlaváček, in *Moderní revue,* was the only one who criticized Úprka, claiming that the artist painted empty pictures in which viewers forced themselves to see things that were not there.[6] At about the same time, Hlaváček made a similar attack on an exhibition of Mašek's works, qualifying the painting's figures from the Slovácko region as "marionettes dressed up for the village fête" and "pure fabrication". "If Arcadia still exists today", he added, "it has to be in Slovácko."[7]

Hlaváček could not accept the idea that the ethnographic genre should be exploited for commercial purposes, particularly after the Ethnographic Exhibition. It is true that at the time almost all buildings, especially financial institutions, were decorated with mural paintings or sculptures depicting the daily life of the peasants -- who were also clients. The Savings Bank, and the Zemská Bank, decorated with Mašek's paintings, were the best examples of this genre. However, this was not just a matter of good business. The deeper reason behind Úprka's success was that he had revived the romantic myth of love of the fatherland. Certain writers like Vilem Mrštík, in his study of Joša Úprka, used Moravia's Slovácko region to illustrate Rousseau's myth of man as an inherently good being. The idea that somewhere in the world there existed a forgotten region where people had been preserved from the evils of civilization and lived full lives in the natural harmony of human grandeur drew a large number of fervent adepts of modern art to Slovácko. Antonín Hudeček did his "apprenticeship" there before becoming a great landscape painter; Zdenka Braunerová, Vojtěch Preissig, Alois Kalvoda, and especially Miloš Jiránek all spent memorable times in the region. The cult of Slovácko was at its height when Rodin ended his journey to Bohemia and Moravia with a visit to Úprka there. Rodin, incidentally, readily compared the women of Slovácko to those of ancient Greece.[8]

To Czech artists, Moravian Slovácko therefore became the first outstanding element in a primitivism that can be considered integral to modern art. It was no accident that Šalda evoked Gauguin in 1904 when he spoke with some nostalgia about Slovácko as a region where "the deepest wellsprings of instinct still flow freely".[9] Nonetheless, by that time a more critical view emerged of the "Arcadia" of which Hlaváček had been so contemptuous, and appreciation of Úprka's painting

accordingly became more circumspect. The exhibition of Úprka's work organized by the Mánes Union in early 1904 was, on the one hand, received enthusiastically by the critic Mádl, who saw a synthesis of the logical evolution of twentieth-century art in Úprka's "Impressionism in burning colors" and his emphasis on the union of art and life.[10] On the other hand, in *Moderní revue,* Miloš Marten criticized the uniformity and artificiality of Úprka's pictures.[11] It is true that on closer acquaintance Slovácko's admirers also realized that socially the region had a darker side; this strengthened the conviction that an ethnographic subject was not enough in itself to create a work of art. This was underscored by Jiránek's attitude and his resolute rejection of the ethnographic fad of the 1890s. Jiránek in fact nourished a very strong personal relationship with Slovácko, which comes through in his impressionist paintings and especially in his literary work, and he never censured Úprka, even when the latter fell out of favour. Jiránek was a convinced European, but he began to feel, as he wrote in 1909, that it was important for an artist to "clarify his membership to a race, which is his most intimate relationship. It is a return to one's source, not in reaction or in lassitude, but out of greater sincerity, so as to come closer to the roots of one's being." As an example of the correlation between folk and modern art Jiránek mentioned the typical Slovácko jug that Jan Preisler – "the most modern of our painters" – placed at the feet of his figures: its combination of lemon yellow and cobalt blue integrated perfectly with the colour harmony of the painting as a whole. Even though it was impossible for the artist to return to the instinctive primitiveness of simple folk life, he could nevertheless consider the creations of his naive forebears, those traditonal artists with "pure artistic instincts", as exemplary guides to his own efforts.

The Mánes Union painters also tried to modernize ethnographically inspired art. Jan Preisler's mosaic for the Novak department store, designed by Polívka, was still restrained by the client's specifications, but a better opportunity was afforded in 1901 by the illustration of a *Volné směry* issue commemorating the painter Jan Neruda. The publication contained an analysis of the work of this classic national figure written by Šalda, who pointed out the internalized heroism and nobility of the poetic language underlying the apparent everyday banality of Neruda's paintings. Šalda's praise of

THE EMOTIVE STYLE

Neruda was no doubt also influenced by French naturalism, and once again expressed his defence of the ardent union between art and life. Preisler's illustration accompanying the article was a new variation on his favourite theme of the inspired poet in a landscape setting. Here the Neo-Romantic knight is replaced by a healthy-looking peasant boy wearing an open-necked shirt. The boy's eyes are full of emotion, and he is standing under a pear tree – a symbol of life – with his native, rolling countryside in the background. These images also inspired Preisler's *Picture from a Larger Cycle* (1900), which is not unrelated to his *Spring* triptych. In the setting of a springtime landscape, *Picture from a Larger Cycle* depicts a simple country lad who encounters a female figure, a symbol of the homeland, who is dressed in a slightly opalescent gown that lends poetry to the stark surroundings. The colour is far removed from local hues. This was also one of the reasons that *Picture from a Larger Cycle* was considered the first truly modern Czech painting. The ethnographic inspiration was re-evaluated here in purely artistic terms, and with none of the succession of strident colours found in Úprka's folk costumes.

It was in this context that Alfons Mucha appeared at the end of the decade with his project for *The Saga of the Slavs*. Mucha aimed to give new life to historical painting by means of the same mythological concept that had earlier attracted attention to the folklore of Slovácko. In 1909 he began working on the preliminary sketches for the first picture of the series, and at the end of 1912 he delivered three gigantic canvases – *The Slavs in Their Prehistoric Setting*, *Introduction of the Slav Liturgy* and *Ceremony in Honour of Svantovit on Rügen Island* – to the Prague authorities.

This work did not prevent Mucha from simultaneously carrying out a prestigious official commission to decorate the mayor's reception room in the Prague Municipal building (1910–1911). This turned out to be the last major interior decoration executed in the deco-

rative Art Nouveau style of the 1890s, although it was monumentalized in spirit by an architectural historicism which confined the paintings to the circular dome and its lunettes and vaults. Mucha was also responsible for the stained glass in the great triple window, the richly embroidered door curtains, the side-entrance doors and the furnishings. The harmony of the predominant shades of orange, blue and black related symbolically to the subjects of the paintings in the lunettes. Courage is personified in the central painting by three young athletes in training. The other paintings, *Sacrifice* and *By His Own Strength*, followed one of Mucha's favourite principles of composition: the confrontation, in opposite extremes of scale, between ordinary human beings whose lives are filled with struggle and suffering, and ideal, super-human beings, heroes and divine symbols. The paintings on the vault were also conceived in terms of confrontation between the real and the ideal, and represented historical Czech figures personifying moral and civic virtues. In both substance and form, the ensemble culminates in the impressive painting on the ceiling, *Slav Solidarity*, which represents a mythological eagle with outspread wings flying away from fruit trees in the centre of a group of workers.

These paintings for the Municipal building sparked off controversy even before they were completed. As early as 1909, the spokesmen for the Mánes Union complained that a commission of such importance had not been subject to open competition. Shortly afterward Jiránek expressed reservations about Mucha's proposed "syrupy decoration from abroad" and scoffed at the "new Slavs as seen from Paris and New York". In the heat of the controversy Šalda even went so far as to publicly cast doubt on the originality of Mucha's art,[12] while Mucha himself felt that these attacks emanated from old-fashioned and jealous minds. The truth of the matter was quite different: since the end of the previous century when Mucha delighted the local public with his posters, art in Prague had undergone a rapid evolution and different values had emerged. Whereas Mucha continued to juxtapose naturalistically treated human figures and general symbols – the circle, for example – within the same work, the avant-garde artists of the Mánes Union nurtured a different conception of artistic synthesis which, although also founded on aesthetic criteria, was far more monistic than Mucha's.

The Saga of the Slavs widened the split between these two conceptions. The first three paintings, depicting the different origins of the Slavs, are generally considered the most successful of the series. They still retain the decorative style, combining symbolism and freezing of action, and their imbrication of reality and imagination is strikingly attractive. Later works in the series, however, drift away from mythological symbolism and tend toward the illusionistic unification of the pictorial field. This could be logically explained by the dynamics of the cycle itself, which proceeds from mythology to actual history, but it was mainly due to the gradual evolution of the paintings into a mere illustration of the artist's own historical conception. When Mucha exhibited twenty works from the *The Saga of the Slavs* at the Palace of Industry in 1928, criticism from the cultural avant-garde was uniformly negative.

Today, in light of the unusual correlation between Mucha's imaginary world and the cinema, and given the current assessment of both illusionism and Symbolism, *The Saga of the Slavs* can no longer be considered either an archaic curiosity or merely an interesting example of the nationalism then in vogue. It should be borne in mind that when these works were painted, this artistic vision of national history and pre-history was enormously popular with the public, and was respected as a contribution to social debate. Nor was this impassioned approach unique to Mucha; it was also shared by other great Czech artists of the time, and was instrumental in provoking reflection on individualism and modern psychology.

In Prague the new decorative style was invested with a special mission, especially in architecture: to reconcile technical demands and the requirements of urban planning imposed by modern civilization with the keenly felt need to retain the city's ancient historical character. Political implications were involved here, inasmuch as the Czech state's concept of history was an essential component of nationalist politics. Within this framework there was still considerable admiration for nineteenth-century historicism and its main representatives, František Palacký, the historian, Alois Jirásek, the author of historical novels, Bedřich Smetana, the composer of national operas, and Mikoláš Aleš, the painter. This historicism, however, needed a modern form of expression. Veering completely away from the idea of war, the Czechoslovak programme moved in the direction of an uplifting ideal, of freedom through education and art. This spirit of Slav moderation produced lyrical songs and melodious language, poetry and art. At the same time, however, the tragedies of Czech national history and centuries of "oppression" also demanded that artists work in more dramatic, emotional tones.

New psychology and the modern decorative style offered a rich repertoire of forms in response to this social demand. Sculptural and painted ornamentation were widely used, particularly on the facades of Prague's buildings, although their interiors were neglected. The facades were covered with decorative motifs, but symbolic themes could also be found. Groups of sculptures on the frequently recurring theme of national decadence and renascence featured side by side with the pantheon of mythological and historical national heroes.

This predilection for expressing "national identity" in decoration was even more apparent in major commissions for monumental works, which the City of Prague wanted to dominate the public squares in glorification of Czech sovereignty. Indeed, the turn of the century was the golden age of Czech monuments.

This fervour for monuments, and the generous donations and public subscriptions that accompanied it, stimulated sculptors to seek original solutions. Myslbek, the doyen of Czech sculpture, used a traditional style for his Monument to Saint Wenceslas, the founder of the Czech state: a symmetrical composition showed the central figure on horseback flanked by four "national" saints. But the monuments executed by the younger sculptors were far more daring.

It was not always possible for them to carry out their most venturesome ideas, however. A case in point was František Bílek's *Monument to the Nation*. This work embodied a conflict of ideas between Bílek and Stanislav Sucharda, who had designed a large monument on Prague's White Mountain, which had been the site of a terrible national catastrophe in 1620. Sucharda's large architectural construction was to be in brick, with an atrium to house the imaginary corpse of defeated Bohemia, personified by a figure lying on a tomb. Bílek criticized the project's funereal, pessimistic character, and in 1908 he created a model of his *Monument to the Nation* on a scale of one to ten. His work was an invocation of Czech history; it represented a huge sacrificial

altar with an undulating procession of the principal national figures crossing its outline. The cortège began with the first Czechs to arrive in the country, then rose upward with the kings and heroes of the Middle Ages to reach a peak with the Hussite movement, after which there was a downward sweep of figures symbolizing the fateful White Mountain. A large temple was to be erected within the mass of the monument.

Bílek's project was a new version of the wave theme, one of the key images of Secession Symbolism. Until then, waves generally took the form of a couple being swept off by destiny into the cosmos or into a whirlpool of water, as in the works of Rodin, Mucha and Kupka. Bílek, instead, envisioned a large group of people who were to summarize the nation's history.

This dynamic conception was characteristic of a number of monuments built in Prague at the beginning of the century, including those in honour of František Palacký and Jan Hus. Their sculptors, Stanislav Sucharda and Ladislav Šaloun respectively, produced the models for them between 1905 and 1910. The assistance of Josef Mařatka indicates that the sculptors also sought inspiration in Rodin's work, although the final result bore their own original imprint.

Sucharda's Palacký Monument had to form a coherent ensemble with the Palacký bridge, whose four pillars already bore large works of sculptures by Myslbek illustrating ancient Czech mythology. In collaboration with the architect Dryák, Sucharda designed an initial version of the project in which he attempted to enclose the complex within an exedra-like structure, using sculpture as a purely decorative element. Later, after seeing the Rodin exhibition, he decided to handle the sculpture for the monument in terms of dramatic effect.[13] He retained the original lateral composition based on three focal points in space: two groups of figures on opposite sides – *Oppression* and *The Awakening of the Nation* respectively – with a large, seated figure of Palacký in the centre, representing the catalyst for historical forces. This was the man who awakened the nation and gave birth to a vast spiritual movement. Behind Palacký stood a group of figures gradually spiralling up to a height of thirty feet, starting from a couple symbolizing the awakening of the Nation, then Victory, a beautiful woman with proudly upraised arm, Fame, represented as an old woman with clenched hands, and a group of Awakeners. The monument also

Jan Preisler, *Picture from a Greater Cycle*,
1902. Oil on canvas, 102.5 x 157 cm.
Prague, National Gallery.

Stanislav Sucharda, *Monument to Palacký*, 1912. Bronze.
Prague New Town (Palacký Square).

comprises other figures, including a beautifully sculpted
nude representing the White Mountain.

Despite the work's dramatic content and form, the
base of the composition nevertheless remained serenely
symmetrical, creating a harmonious balance between
expression and form that confirmed Sucharda's position
as a representative of the style of his day. He had also
become an increasingly prominent personality. The
official photograph of the monument's inauguration
in 1912 displays the conspicuous presence of two rows
of people wearing national costumes. These were the
members of *Sokol,* a bourgeois association to which
Sucharda belonged, and which was a ubiquitous force
in Czech political and social life.

Prague's second great monument dating from that
time, created in memory of the martyr Jan Hus, was
less lyrical in conception. The drawing with which
Šaloun won the competition for the commission in
1900 showed a marked naturalism and was riveting in
its evocation of cruel historical injustices. Subsequently,
Šaloun learned a great deal from his contacts with
Rodin, and he had large photographs of two of the
sculptor's works, *The Burghers of Calais* and *Balzac,*
hanging in his studio. In the early stages of his design
for the monument, Šaloun confronted problems of the
siting of the monument in the Old Town Square, am
cornerstone of the city's historical heritage. The square
was dominated by two towers, between which stood
the Baroque Mariale column erected to celebrate the
Treaties of Westphalia. The Czechs viewed this column
as a symbol of Hapsburg domination, a continual
reminder of the cruel execution of Czech leaders after
the rebellion of the estates was crushed on White Mountain, marking the start of three centuries of oppression.

The column was ceremonially destroyed after the pro-
clamation of independence in 1918, but as far as Šaloun
was concerned in the pre-war years, it posed not only a
problem in siting the *Monument to Jan Hus,* but also an
unavoidable ideological challenge.

After trial sitings using a full-scale model of the work,
in 1907 Šaloun decided to erect a horizontal monument
to contrast with the Mariale column's vertical thrust
and to use the effects of volume and mass to heighten
its impact. The monument represents Jan Hus standing
in a kind of wheel of Czech history, composed of groups
of figures; at the wheel's highest point stand the *Fighters
for God,* while the *Exiles,* facing the site of the 1621 exe-
cutions, are at the lowest part. At the back is a more
discreet group consisting of a mother and child symbolizing the source of national renewal.

Šaloun conceived of the Old Town Square as a sensitive area charged with ever-present historical forces.
In his notes he wrote that to the Czech nation Hus
symbolized not only the struggle against the outside
world, but also an inner struggle, the mobilization of
energies and a near-fatal defeat. But Šaloun felt that all
this could not be appropriately illustrated by a neutral
form determined solely by decorative aesthetic criteria.
"Hus! What seething spiritual activity!"[14] And so he
translated this into the dynamic curvilinear base of the
monument, and above all into an intensely emotional
modelling that infused the entire mass of rock with an
overwhelming sense of pathos. The monument's artistic
value was later called into question, and it was inaugur-
ated very discreetly during the war, in 1915.

Thus, the new art quickly swept into the monumental domain, which until then had remained the preserve
of the official traditionalists. Its influence was felt by
the less youthful artists as well. Even the uncompromising Myslbek conceived a series of models for his *Monument to Saint Wenceslas* that reflected Rodin's influence,
while Josef Mauder's monument to Julius Zeyer was
inspired by a Symbolism with more than a hint of Neo-
Romanticism.

However, these new artistic works won public
approval at a cost, for their content had to be amenable
to that section of the Czech bourgeois political class
that considered itself the mouthpiece of the nation's
aspirations. And so this gave rise to a form of "national
art", especially sculpture, that was also modern insofar
as it took into account the new psychology and Rodin's

values. Ideas of suggestion and "ideodynamism" transformed the view of the past so that historical figures became the incarnation of national and racial virtues, manifestations of that collective will which, in tune with history, insisted on the nation's right to a higher spiritual existence. With this, the notion of historicism blossomed. Mucha, pursuing the idea of Neo-Slavism even further, concluded that if only by virtue of the cruel sufferings they had endured, the Slavs were a people virtually predestined to conceive a transcendent vision of a new human ideal. This lofty idealism was expressed through ornamental stylization.

This endeavour to harness artistic expression to the ideological and political situation for the explicit purpose of arousing the emotions of the viewer was the direct target of opposition from the Mánes Union's spokesmen, for whom artistic synthesis had very different aims.

Ladislav Šaloun, *Monument to Jan Hus*, 1915. Bronze. Prague (Old Town Square).

Modernism

The synthetist programme

František Kysela, poster for the 23rd exhibition of the Mánes Union of Artists, The French Impressionists, 1907. Colour lithograph, 107 x 77 cm. Prague, UPM.

The synthetist program for literary criticism that had been formulated by Šalda in the 1890s had an effect on the entire spectrum of Czech culture. Indeed, Šalda's optimistic vision of style presupposed that all artistic disciplines would be collectively involved in linking art and life and elevating the national spirit to a higher plane through the creative vitality of culture. Because of his influence on the artists in the Mánes Union, which expanded after he joined *Volné směry,* Šalda occupied the central place in the association, whose authority increasingly marked Czech cultural life.

In 1902, the Mánes Union organized the French Modern Art exhibition; this provided a splendid occasion to put the synthetist program into effect. During the exhibition, its curator, Gabriel Mourey, gave a lecture on Puvis de Chavannes, whose paintings had interested the Prague public ever since *Volné směry* had reproduced some of his work two years earlier, including *The Poor Fisherman,* with a commentary by Georges Rodenbach. Rodenbach had stressed that Puvis had "revived the decorative painting of our day", for which he had invented a new style combining the two main currents in modern painting: Realism, which held that painters should "only imitate Nature", and Symbolism, which held that there was "no such thing as Nature".[1] Preisler's *Picture from a Larger Cycle* (1902), whose synthetic concept of colour made it the first truly modern Czech painting, was to a large extent a manifestation of the artist's interest in the work of the first French synthetist. Preisler demonstrated that the decorative values of mural painting could be transposed into pictorial work, thereby setting himself in opposition to the illusionism and naturalism that were still prevalent at the time.

This initial synthetic approach was later partly eclipsed by the emotive concept of style, as well as by Vitalism, with its heavy influence of Rodin and Munch. Synthetism was nonetheless later revived and updated for a number of reasons, including the desire to prove that modern art was not the arbitrary outcome of chance but instead the essential and inevitable expression of the development of modern life and of art itself. In his introduction to the French Modern Art exhibition catalogue, Šalda emphasized that what he admired in this art was both its spontaneous nature and the logical underpinnings of its individualism, which derived from its ability to capture life's vital essence in an unbroken artistic flow of beautiful, powerful and authentic forms. Continuity of this kind was the sign of a great culture: "French art is a continuous line. Beside it, other arts are no more than series of disconnected dots."[2]

Arguments in defence of modern art strove to prove its independence from external contingencies. In *Volné směry*, the young artists published James McNeill Whistler's famous "Ten O'Clock Lecture", in which the English-based American painter presented a very humorous defence of the artist's professionalism and his independence from the dictates of both society and nature. Preisler introduced the "Ten O'Clock Lecture" with an illustration of a young man leaning in a meditative pose against a white horse, above a creek and a dark sea.

Preisler drew this theme out of a sublimated memory of the sea in Italy, where he had travelled with Antonín Hudeček in 1902. His wanderings in Italy had given rise to a series of large oil paintings of black lakes, in which his synthetic conception grew more pronounced. He later wrote that "a picture must be a precise set of elements that are organically constructed, like a piece of architecture or a musical composition. [...] Everything in the picture has to be justified. Either by instinct or by logic. [...] And it was exactly the things that made people's hair stand on end that brought me closer to that artistic logic, for instance, when the colour black played an important part in the picture. [...] Or, for example, the painting in which you can see a young man with a white horse in front of a black lake, and which could be called *Melancholy* or something of the kind. The black shades with which the artist can brilliantly portray this subject are already found in the subject itself. Then the whole picture was permeated with the colour, from the darkest shades through broken and greenish grey tones into the vibrant light grey and bright white of the horse against which the young man is leaning. So, far from being a black or grey picture, it's full of colours. [...] In this work I was also instinctively very precise about the linear composition. By 'precision' I don't mean exact, or what might be called 'correct' drawing, but that each object and each shape used in the picture function as real elements of an organism. Because nothing must be put into a picture merely by chance."[3]

Although this attitude appears to focus solely on form, in fact it perfectly articulates the painting's sym-

bolic devices and its artistic qualities, the large predominant colour surfaces and the concrete objects in the picture: the tree of life springs out of the rocks, the black lake gives life to the white horse, and the black drapery encircles the "inspired" nude of the young poet. The profound interconnection between these symbols is structured by the alternation of black and white, that is, the negative and positive poles in the symbolic evolution of the colour hierarchy, where each symbolic object casts light on the entire range of its meanings. The black, fathomless lake is associated in legend with the land of the dead, but its surface is a mirror reflecting one's own image. The horse, associated with water in Greek mythology, is the demoniacal symbol of instinct and desire, but the white horse is a sacred beast linked to the divine powers of intuitive knowledge. Finally, man in all his physical beauty is beckoned toward the spiritual universe, and thus becomes the true centre of the macrocosm of natural forces.

At that time, Preisler also drew a pastel in which a young man was standing beside or even entering the dark water. Other symbolic figures appeared: a pair of lovers, a nude woman unbraiding her hair, and a woman sitting stone-still by the deadly water. Rather than illustrations, these pastels were free variants of Preisler's poetic visions, although the motif of the young man beside the water does recall the narcissism already visible in the artist's work at the end of the 1890s. His illustration of the first page of *Poisons and Remedies* (1901), a collection of Decadent poetry by Jan Opolsky, clearly represented a Narcissus amid swirling currents of air that imparted a cosmological dimension to his self-contemplation. Preisler's paintings, and especially his drawings on the black lake theme, increasingly emphasized the hero's physique, which he studied assiduously. The still immature body was twisted in the *contrapposto* typical of Classical sculpture, traditionally used to represent "the gods and heroes, as though they were standing in those sacred places where peace reigns."[4]

This return to idealism was born out of the desire to attribute a more substantial purpose to art. At the beginning of its ninth year (1904–1905), *Volné směry* – under the direction of Preisler, Hofbauer, Županský and Šalda – published an article by the new member of the Mánes Union, Camille Mauclair, who brought the idea of a fresh strategy into the debate on modern art.

Jan Preisler, *The Black Lake,* 1904. Oil on canvas, 73 x 113 cm. Prague, Pražského hradu Gallery.

The article, entitled "Classicism and Academicism", proposed replacing these two customarily paired concepts with the notion of a unitary "national classicism" to which the inflexible rules of the academic school would no longer apply. Within this proposed framework, even the impressionists and the younger Intimists emerged as the heirs to the Greeks, who were also "radiant, blooming, authentic, sensual lovers of the spontaneous act and of life in the open air".[5] Modern art became impervious to charges of decadence and elitism

and would to be recognized as the main current of contemporary creativity, where "beauty of character and expression dethroned beauty of proportion". Mauclair's rehabilitation of Classicism incorporated the notion that there was an internal logic to the evolution of French art, which in turn determined the evolution of modern art. In *Living Ideas,* Mauclair reformulated the notion of Synthetism in the new art. He treated the Wagnerian *Gesamtkunstwerk* (total work of art) as a materialist error; he rejected the amalgamation of artistic genres and sought the deep-seated identity of art in an "ultimate synthesis", which he conceived as "the final vibration of the rhythm" provoked by music in the modern arts.

The French insistence on art as a "glorious life of the senses" shaped the thinking of Julius Meier-Graefe, an art critic who was far more fervent than Mauclair and who influenced Czech Synthetism. Meier-Graefe's theory of unities and his books, *History and Evolution of Modern Art* and, more especially, *The Böcklin Case,*

Jan Preisler, *Yellow Landscape,* 1908. Oil on canvas, 94 x 95 cm. Prague, National Gallery.

proceeded from a sweeping evaluation of modern art in terms of "living" tradition and attacked all obstacles to its development. The author's engaging idea was that modern painting was heir to the great non-official tradition of "pure painting" (Meier-Graefe traced its evolution through Rubens, Delacroix, and Manet). Its aesthetic criterion was a specific visual form that was subordinate to the formal imagination and determined the organic untiy of all the plastic elements in a picture, a unity that varied with the personal vision of the artist.

Šalda made a detailed analysis of Meier-Graefe's book on Arnold Böcklin, which he considered extremely valuable. Meier-Graefe's dramatic description of Böcklin's artistic failure and his "pursuit of popularity" recalls Nietzsche's critique of Richard Wagner. In Šalda's opinion, Böcklin's case was more than just a strictly German affair. Indeed, many Czech artists were his devoted followers, and such a cult was anathema to Šalda, for it "seduces and tempts the mind with passionate artistic dreams, with the desire to soar in flight and cast off the shackles of time. Those who trust in this as a guide on the path to artistic freedom are led astray into uncouth licentiousness and brutal violence. It blocks the way to the future. If there is a desire to create wholesome, vigorous painting and to attain an art of the pure senses, a sparkling enchantment of the soul, an art that would truly embody the cosmos, an entire universe balanced in inner harmony, then such an influence must be destroyed."[6]

The real issue was not so much the external pressures brought to bear on art as the artist's own self-confidence. Czech artists had great difficulty in throwing off the melancholic syndrome that had submerged them in the 1890s – an atmosphere of melancholy was still predominant, as evident in Preisler's series of black lakes. The lyrical feeling of the world's decay also attracted the younger artists, especially the more talented ones. The sculptor Jan Štursa became a member of the Mánes Union in 1904, the year in which he first visited Paris and saw the wax sculptures by Medardo Rosso at the Salon d'Automne. These works immediately elicited a study, *The Drowned Cat* – perhaps the most informal work in Czech sculpture – as well as *Life Escaping,* the face of a young girl with tuberculosis, which was conceived in more lyrical terms and sculpted in alabaster from a wax model. Štursa had an intuitive understanding of the meaning of the union in Rosso's

work between naturalism and the breaking up of the object by means of light, and was also aware of the decadent character of this union. However, he could hardly have imagined that this opened up the possibility for a re-evaluation of the aesthetic category of the sublime, which was only to be achieved by Brancusi.[7] Štursa himself attempted his own solution to the problem through the use of naive art and transcendental themes, but these never replaced the appeal of Decadence. In this spirit, Štursa entered the *Moderní revue* circle. He made a portrait of the late Karel Hlaváček in 1906 that was etched on the surface of the limestone rather than actually modelled.

An article by Miloš Marten, who was the only critic to unconditionally defend Edvard Munch's 1905 exhibition in Prague, proved to be a veritable discovery for Štursa. The article, "On Lyrical Impressionism", published in *Moderní revue,* was a remarkable analysis of this phenomenon, that exerted a powerful influence on Czech artists and critics alike. Marten argued that there was a paradox in late lyrical Impressionism, which combined "an erotic, passionate relationship with the earth" and an amazing capacity for enriching the artist's sensitivity through refinement of the senses, with an interior-

Jan Štursa, *Portrait of the Poet K. Dewetter,* 1906. Limestone, h.: 22.5 cm. Prague, National Gallery.

ization of vital instincts without which modern art was inconceivable. Thus the paradox lay in the "dissociation of mind and heart". As the artist's sensibility became increasingly productive and he abandoned himself with almost fateful passivity to its suggestion, he neglected the development of creative imagination, and fell victim to the double negative of "the absence of spiritual concentration and the lack of faith in the essence and meaning of beauty". The magic intrinsic to impressionist lyricism lay in the atmosphere it conveyed, the "synthesis of all the components of emotional life". This was most magnificent in the spellbinding sensuality of perceptions united in a musical harmony, when it extracted a kind of transcendental force out of the chaos of ecstasy and sensual intoxication. However, this new pathos formed "a relationship with fatality as dark as, if not darker, than in the times of Antiquity". Free verse was an invention of lyrical Impressionism that made it possible to transcribe mental experience and emotionally communicate artistic feeling to the reader. However, it was in the symbolist prose poem that impressionist intuition fully blossomed; this form gave scope to the crystallization of ideas in a more genuine synthetic expression, with a more definitive style. Poetry had to be an "absolute vision of the human soul", which in art was translated into increased stylization.[8]

Marten's re-evaluation of lyrical Impressionism is essential to a full understanding of Štursa's limestone sculpture, *Melancholic Girl,* from 1906. The first sketch for this work, which was drawn above other small sketches for tombstones, survives today. In this work, art grows out of the sorrowful emotions stirred up by the harsh events of life and death. The feeling of infinity is expressed in the youthful, arched body of the seated adolescent, her face resembles a mask. The sculptor used the curving twist of the hands cradling the face and the perfect inflections of the body as a spatially dynamic ornamental element fully expressive of the Absolute in the Art Nouveau manner. At the time, this was probably the Czech sculpture with the most distinct style; the work was infused with a light similar to Rodin's, and its modelling was somewhat removed from the usual lyrical Impressionism. *Melancholic Girl* was truly symbolic of the times; it turned the poetic concept of youth into a major theme in Czech art, and incontestably put Štursa on an equal footing with Preisler.

Jan Štursa, *Melancholic Girl*, 1906. Limestone, 43 cm. Prague, National Gallery.

Together with Miloš Marten, Paul Gauguin was the model for Štursa's new concept of style. In February 1906, *Volné směry* published the translation of Maurice Denis's article, "The Influence of Paul Gauguin", which was illustrated with reproductions of Gauguin's paintings (*Te arii vahine, Three Tahitians, The Yellow Christ* and *The Horsemen*), sculptures in wood (*War and Peace*) and earthenware (Oviri), and other works. Gauguin's Symbolism was to have an impact on Czech art in various ways in the years that followed.

Jan Preisler, who saw Gauguin's paintings in Paris in 1906, also contributed to the development of a cult of this French painter, whose work affected most of the artists, of whatever age, who claimed kinship with modern art. Jan Zrzavý, a very young pupil at the School of Applied Arts, signed his early pictures with the name of Gauguin. In 1909 Otakar Nejedlý was still searching in Ceylon for a virgin land to paint in the style of Gauguin, while Josef Váchal sculpted grotesque figurines inspired by the French painter. Gauguin's simple decorative style also influenced major works such as Bohumil Kafka's reliefs of reclining nudes in the Municipal building (1909), and especially Štursa's *Eva* (1908).

The extent of Gauguin's influence can be explained partly by Czech artists' search for an authentic, modern model to aid in the transition from the naturalist heritage, and partly by the vigorous backing given the painter by determinedly contemporary art critics. The occasion for the critics' support was provided by the great exhibition of nineteenth-century French art mounted in the autumn of 1907 by the Mánes Union, entitled The French Impressionists. This exhibition, which was heavily influenced by Meier-Graefe and his *History and Evolution of Modern Art*, was designed to show the evolution from the ancestral figures of Honoré Daumier and Adolphe Monticelli, through Johan Barthold Jongkind and Eugène Boudin, up to the Impressionists, Neo-Impressionists and above all, the Gauguin-Van Gogh duo (along the lines of the subjective and objective deformations developed by Maurice Denis) and the Nabis. *Volné směry* primed the public beforehand by publishing special issues on Manet, Cézanne, Renoir, Degas and Monet. Even though the curators never really managed to carry out their original plan to assemble completely representative works, the show had a far-reaching impact.

Once again it was Šalda who best summed up the exhibition. His view was that Impressionism had taught modern man the immediate perception of totality, which had until then been blocked by artists' love of detail in the objects they painted. It had created a new awareness of the intensity of the moment, and perfected

Jan Preisler, *Diana*, 1908. Pastel, 21 x 23 cm. Prague. Litoměřice Gallery.

Jan Štursa, *Eva*, 1908. Limestone, h.: 55 cm.
Prague, National Gallery.

surfaces, and to conceive of the painting as a serene harmony. This gave painting a new objective that went beyond naturalism to create a decorative art based on broad, harmonious, flat colour surfaces. For Šalda, the more scientifically minded Neo-Impressionist painting followed along these lines, further developing the style and decorative elements found in Impressionism. It removed the object from the picture and retained a geometric, abstract formal composition; it reduced the importance of matter and gravity and, on the contrary, gave an enhanced role to the beauty of the law of rhythm. F. X. Šalda concluded that Impressionism resolved the problem of creating art on a higher plane. "This marvelous, ambitious goal – the creation of a new decorative art that is grandiose and of great beauty and purity – is becoming ever more visible on the horizon of art today; all paths lead to it."[9]

Today it may seem that announcing the ideal of "decorative art" in 1907 was not extraordinarily progressive, but it should be remembered that Šalda made a very clear distinction between mere decorative style produced according to a borrowed formula (for which he criticized not only the Russian artist Nikolaï Konstantinovich Roerich when he exhibited in Prague, but also Albert Besnard, who was defended by Mauclair), and authentic, creative decoration rooted in the "eurythmy of the soul", as illustrated by both Puvis de Chavannes and Gauguin.[10] Šalda's view and conceptions lay behind pictures such as Preisler's *Green Landscape* and *Yellow Landscape* (1908), depicting female figures in ideal landscapes, which the extremely self-critical painter found satisfying for their pictorial unity. Šalda's ideal of the association of wholesome instinct and law was embodied here in a manner not far removed from French Fauvism. Here too was a solution to the basic theme of a figure set in a landscape – a subject that had been much in favour in Czech art ten years earlier. All this gave the concept of a new synthesis its full significance.

The term "Synthetism" can be understood as a tendency to maintain a fundamental balance between subjective experience and objective order. However, balance should not be taken here to mean measured quantities, but rather a living process that makes it seem as though the intensity of the painting also heightens the intensity of the life it expresses. The apparent quiescence and decorative serenity of Preisler's paintings belie

the visual culture in which the eye was the focal point for the artist's soul. For Šalda, impressionist painters were capable of the unbiased observation found only in dreams, and they had turned seeing into a spiritual function. This explains why, instead of creating mirror-images of reality, the Impressionists expressed it in a purely pictorial style that heightened its sensual impact. In this way, Impressionism engendered the next stage of its own evolution, whose most outstanding figure was Cézanne. Šalda believed that Cézanne had understood the possibilities opened up by the Impressionists' liberation of colour, and converted this into a principle of pictorial composition, much as the Venetians had done centuries earlier, but now using more dynamic colour values. Cézanne taught Gauguin how to create a painting from few elements, with large, uncomplicated colour an ever-present undercurrent of expressive tension, while the psychological conflict of his earlier days is progressively resolved as the pictures acquire greater artistic unity.

A moderation akin to the synthetic balance, and with a somewhat decorative quality, characterizes Vojtěch Preissig's colour engravings. Their rather difficult technique of superimposed colours fostered an artistic attitude very different from the cult of sketchy impressions and more immediate experience. Preissig founded his own engraving workshop in Prague, and in 1906 he printed an album of his twenty best engravings, with a preface by Jiránek. By printing a succession of colour plates in such a way that the radiance of colour emanated from the entire surface of the picture, he achieved effects unobtainable by the impressionist painter. The results of this work were exhibited at the Topič Gallery in 1907. Preissig's poster announcing the show was faithful to Art Nouveau in its use of greens and purples, while the use of a floral motif underlined the need for simplicity and economy of form. Although the exhibition was very well received, unfortunately it did not ameliorate the artist's financial situation, and he was obliged to leave for the United States, where he worked until the beginning of the 1930s.

The sober elegance of Preissig's poster drew attention to the existence of a certain style of decorative Synthetism then apparent in Czech art, which was evident in the white-glazed ceramic vases created by Robert Hájek in collaboration with the ceramics workshop in Bechyně, and in Josef Ladislav Němec's jewellery, with their simple and yet meaningful shapes. The refined taste of this art was reflected in a greater simplicity and more effective exploitation of the plastic potential of the materials used. The stylization was still closely linked to natural motifs, but naturalism was discarded and inspiration was channelled into pure, poetic formulae. The new synthetic plasticism also appeared in architecture, as a decorative pattern of harmoniously arranged colour surfaces. The Náhlovský villa in Prague-Bubeneč (1907–1909) designed by Dušan Jurkovič is a good example of this, while a similar decorative interplay can also be detected in the series of landscapes Antonín Hudeček painted during his visit to Machov in 1910.

All these works, which come under the heading of "decorative Synthetism", appear to be individual expressions of the general spiritual and artistic concept of mature modern Czech culture. Its programme was outlined in *Struggle for the Future,* a collection of Šalda's essays first published in 1905. Šalda was both passionate and sarcastic, which inevitably aroused vigorous controversy and stirred up rivalries, but he was also one of the spokesmen for the widespread conviction that Czech culture was very much alive and that it was succeeding in creating a modern universe. The constant emergence of individuals who, as a group, had dropped the melancholy and depression of earlier days in favour of a more vigorous and triumphant concept of art was symptomatic of this vitality. The same was true in literature, whose new generation of poets included Fráňa Šrámek, Karel Toman and František Gellner, who had already passed through Anarchism and Vitalism. The same phenomenon was occurring in the theatre, and in music with composers like Josef Suk, who returned to the work of Antonín Dvořák, transposing into his own style the principal melodic theme of the latter's music for *Raduz a Mahulena,* a narrative play by Julius Zeyer that had opened at the National Theatre in 1898. The public was also impressed with the great emotional strength of *Praga* (1904), a symphonic poem in honour of the city, which was an original composition by Suk.

This cumulative effort took hold during the first decade of the twentieth century and from then on the new culture was an established fact. Creative artists in all fields, however, found themselves confronted with a dissatisfying contradiction between the ideal and the actual results. Even Jan Preisler, whose pictures evince a strong feeling of harmony, complained in a letter to Stanislav Sucharda, "It seems to me that we have achieved very little, and that we are not much closer to the goals we discussed with such excitement."

This feeling was fuelled by several incidents that occurred in 1909, including Šalda's withdrawal from the Mánes Union and *Volné směry.* His resignation, a harbinger of the imminent crisis, was provoked by the criticism made at the Union's general assembly that the periodical did not pay enough attention to local art and was too much a reflection of the editor-in-chief's personal taste. From then on, under the management of Max Švabinský, the magazine dealt with subjects relating to the history of art, and its committed, avant-garde character was gradually pushed into the background.

Conflict also arose over the exhibition of works by Émile Bernard, a veteran of the Pont-Aven School, which was curated by Miloš Marten. Preisler, president of the Mánes Union, had invited Bernard, thinking that he shared common inspiration with Gauguin. However, Bernard's views, which were passionately supported by Marten, proved controversial. Although they certainly fitted into the new strategy developed by *Volné směry* since its ninth year – developing artistic discipline, renewing ties with living tradition, and shedding an esoteric anarchism and individualism – these views were nonetheless limited to an imitation of earlier art, which had become the idol of the "Neo-Idealist Renaissance". The youngest artists who had exhibited in The Eight shows were most vehemently opposed to these eclectic processes. The most outspoken of them was the intransigent Bohumil Kubišta, who wrote an

LEFT: Vojtěch Preissig, *Evening*, 1903. Coloured aquatint, 36.8 x 27.7 cm. Prague, National Gallery.

BELOW: Vojtěch Preissig, *Deserted Island*, 1904. Coloured aquatint, 26.5 x 38.3 cm. Prague, National Gallery.

Municipal building, the Palacký Room, decorated by Jan Preisler (1910–1912).

article criticizing Bernard's exhibition that, after some hesitation, was published in *Volné směry*. Kubišta demonstrated the necessity of moving away from the moods, "Impressionism", and haphazardness prevalent in the work of Czech artists.[11]

Jiránek argued along similar lines in an important lecture, "Modern Czech Painting", given before the Mánes Union of Artists in April 1909. Here he discussed the logic of artistic evolution and expressed scepticism as to the cohesiveness of the nation's artistic tradition. In his view, there were sufficient numbers of gifted individuals in Czech art, but too few who were

capable of working according to a systematically conceived order. French art was once again held up as an example to Czech artists: there, composition of line and colour was conceived according to certain rules, and this could be taken as a lesson in how to create a picture as an autonomous, organic entity.

The reputation of French art was further consolidated in Prague in 1909, with the visit of the sculptor Antoine Bourdelle, who exhibited works on the Mánes Union's premises. During his visit, he saw the most influential workshops in Prague and gave a highly anticipated lecture. Bourdelle, of course, was not received

Education pavilion at the Chamber of Commerce and Crafts jubilee exhibition, Prague, 1907–1908. Arch.: Jan Kotěra. Now destroyed.

with the grandiose welcome accorded to Rodin seven years earlier, but Czech artists who were already familiar with his work and knew him personally felt that he would be a good judge of the current art scene. And since he was considered Rodin's successor, this hot-blooded Frenchman's judgments carried a good deal of weight. Bourdelle's lecture was structured around the question of how to determine whether a work of art was the product of an "ordered mind" or of the "soul of an adventurer". He criticized Rodin for lacking a decorative system and for having made virtually indiscriminate use of high and low relief in his *Gates of Hell*. Bourdelle had greater esteem for the figure in the *Whistler Monument* and for some other lesser-known sculptures, which in his opinion were capable of giving rise to a "new synthesis". In his view, sculptors should attach greater importance to matters of form, the beauty of surface, profile and proportion, and, above all, they should conceive a statue as if it were a work of architecture.[12]

The stricture that a work of art should be seen in "architectonic" terms very soon spread to all fields of artistic activity. The studies Bourdelle exhibited in Prague, including those for his *Beethoven* and *Heracles Archer,* demonstrated that this constraint did not obstruct sensitive expression. While the vigour and dynamism of his ideas encouraged young artists,

Bourdelle's plastic achievements, which shared some of Gauguin's characteristics, were also an example and a stimulus to modern creative art.

Štursa's later work often displays the breakdown of volume into planar surfaces that was the basis of Bourdelle's style, as well as archaistic subjects deriving from the Primitivist's research into new sources of art. The first of Štursa's really public works were the larger-than-life figures decorating the entrance door to the Commerce Pavilion built by Jan Kotěra for the Chamber of Commerce and Crafts jubilee exhibition in 1908.

Jan Kotěra's personal character, as well as his activities in the Mánes Union and at the School of Applied Arts, placed him at the forefront of the major Czech architects of his day. However, his most important works were located outside of Prague, in Hradec Krá-lové and Prostějov, because commissions within the city were granted mostly to architects who were amenable to compromise and who had better contacts among the civic authorities. This may also explain why Kotěra quickly went beyond Art Nouveau naturalism and headed in the direction of the more abstract decorative Synthetism. He was also influenced by some modern works by foreign artists.

In 1908 work was completed on the Bank of Vienna's building on Na Příkopě Street, built by the German-born Prague architect, Josef Zasche. Its elegant, pol-ished-granite facade, placed symmetrically around the two axes of the main door, featured simple but strikingly attractive geometrical ornamentation. The large, stylized figures by Franz Metzner illustrated the new possibilities of decorative sculpture, and the interior, designed by the Viennese architect Alexander Neumann, also reflected the new style in the treatment of surfaces, both in its use of precious, subtly coloured materials and in its figurative detail. Zasche attracted further attention with his large concert hall for the Chamber of Commerce and Crafts jubilee exhibition, which again underscored his leanings toward Classicism. Together with his major architectural work from 1908, Zasche's simple residential buildings (the "Three Horsemen" house in Prague's New Town, 1906–1907) and his villas (the Wilfert villa in Prague-Bubeneč, 1904–1905) constituted a special chapter in Prague architecture, and contributed to the development of decorative Synthetism.[13]

The principle of putting decorative elements on a geometrically handled surface can be traced back to Vienna, which was a magnet for an increasing number of Prague's architects. This attraction was reflected in the opening issues of *Styl*, a periodical first published in 1908 by the Architects' Association, a group within the Mánes Union that consisted essentially of young artists trained by Kotěra at the School of Applied Arts. *Styl* published an article by Pavel Janák analysing Otto Wagner's "new style", first of all from the plastic standpoint: "These are geometrical shapes, prisms and cubes, the bare bones of all shapes, where everything secondary has been stripped away. The new principles of composition deal with the assembly of these shapes, and the sole function of decoration is to accentuate them. The elements used to frame and underline them lose all autonomous form." Janák went on to explain: "This is a natural, virile form of expression, contrary to all the weaknesses of creation, an ideal of our times

The former Bank of Vienna, 1906–1908. Prague Old Town (Na Příkopě 1). Arch.: Josef Zasche and Alexander Neumann. Sculptures by Franz Metzner.

opposed to sentimentalism, colour, picturesqueness, intimist feelings and atmosphere, which have nothing to do with the strong, wholesome nature of modern man."[14] This intractable purism was to have consequences in the years to come.

Kotěra also introduced other important figures into the new Czech architectural scene, for example the Dutch architect Hendrik Petrus Berlage, whose Amsterdam Stock Exchange building was profiled in *Volné směry*. Kotěra also appears to have seen Frank Lloyd Wright's work during his visit to the United States in 1904. With the decline of Impressionism and the emphasis on principles of composition, he seems to have been won over by the advantages of exposed masonry. Plain brick offered not only the possibility of "true" straight surfaces but also new forms of ornamentation that moved beyond the naturalism of malleable stucco while meeting the requirements imposed by the rhythm of the construction materials. Kotěra first displayed this interest in his buildings for the water tower at Vršovice in Prague (1906–1907), in which the brick is consonant with the building's function. Kotěra gave plain masonry a monumental effect in the Departmental Museum in Hradec Králové (1906–1912), which was actually an updated version of his plan for the Mánes Union Pavilion, whose spatial organization created a brilliant equilibrium between the functional and public elements of this modern cultural institution.

Between 1908 and 1909, Kotěra built only private homes: a house for the publisher Laichter in Prague-Vinohrady and his own house, dominated by his prism-like studio. But among the traditional Art Nouveau and stuccoed architecture in Prague, even these buildings looked like something from another world. It cannot be said that they were not decorative. The facade of the Laichter residence showed a remarkably heterogeneous use of materials. Brick, stone and different kinds of pebble-dashed surfaces were interspersed with the large areas of glass in the windows and the lacquered parts of their frames, in an attempt to create a new decorative system. A similar effect was achieved with the ornamental brickwork over the doors and windows. In this house the architecture is functional and sound, but nevertheless gives old-fashioned poetic imagination universal value. Kotěra again applied this conception of the "new style" in Urbánek's house in Prague New Town (1912–1913). The large scale of this somewhat classical

composition was attenuated by the use of plain brick and harmonious proportion, and it became the medium for a warm and democratic architecture.

Kotěra's students and collaborators adopted and further developed this new direction, which ran parallel to the evolution of European architecture. Otakar Novotný, who designed Jan Štenc's house in Prague Old Town (1909) used brick in a more lyrical style than did Kotěra, who was more sensitive to its plastic qualities. Novotný also worked in a combination of red and white brickwork and copper sheeting. With this building, Novotný popularized the new purist aesthetic and established its place in the Czech architectonic repertoire.

After this, large office or residential buildings were handled in a very direct manner by young architects trained in Vienna under Otto Wagner. Antonín Engel (the architect of the Civil Servants' Co-operative building in Prague-Josefov in 1910) wrote an article in *Styl* expressing his disapproval of the "distasteful pseudo-splendours of tenement blocks that are mere tawdry finery to hide the dire poverty of the cities". He suggested that there should be instead "a concern for honesty in building facades as utilitarian objects with no pretensions to a higher vocation".[15] Yet like his former fellow pupil Bohumil Hypšman, who created the Jewish Funeral Fraternity building in Prague-Josefov in 1910, Engel himself demonstrated that these severe principles did not necessarily imply resignation on the aesthetic front. Even at such an early stage, however, it did limit decoration to simple lines, a checker-board design in the surface-coating on the walls, and non-integrated, rather classical-style sculpture.

The emergence and development of this kind of architecture took place rapidly, and in the public building sector even began to break the monopoly of traditionalist architects and official representatives of Art Nouveau. Kotěra, appointed professor of architecture at the School of Fine Arts in 1910, had been working on the prestigious project for the new Czech University

TOP LEFT: Jan Kotěra's house, 1908–1909. Vinohrady (Hradešínská 6). Arch.: Jan Kotěra.

BOTTOM LEFT: Drawing room in Jan Kotěra's house. Period photograph.

FACING PAGE: The Laichter house, hall and staircase, 1908–1909. Vinohrady (Chopínova 4). Arch.: Jan Kotěra.

The Laichter house, detail of the facade.

Gauguin and Van Gogh. *Volné směry* published an issue on Cézanne in March 1907 praising the purity of his painting, with a reproduction of one of the most controversial of his *Bathers* canvases. The following year, however, *Volné směry*'s attention shifted to Hans von Marées and Ludwig Hofmann. The term "evolutive logic" reverted to the young artists of The Eight group, including Bohumil Kubišta, who devoted a long theoretical article to Cézanne. He made a particular study of how Cézanne resolved the correlation of colours, and tried to discover the thread that structured his works. However, the young Czech's attempts to apply the lesson to his own work revealed the fundamental differences between the two personalities: Kubišta's expressionist feeling for colour took precedence over rationally conceived harmony of composition.[16]

Jan Preisler became aware of Kubišta's theoretical conclusions in 1909, at a time when he dreamed that logic could determine pictorial composition "to the last brushstroke". Preisler himself did not feel such a need to rationalize the act of painting. His was an intuitive "logic", which, true to symbolist tradition, unveiled not only how forms and colours represented impressions and feelings in spatial counterpoint, but also how a melodic system should be generated from particular formal relationships that would elucidate the rules governing an image's appearance.

Preisler developed this notion further in his inaugural class at the School of Fine Arts, where he received a professorial appointment in 1913. His analysis of Cézanne's synthesis was embodied in a grand series of paintings on the theme of bathers, and here too, his interest in spatial composition led to greater plasticity in the modelling of the figures.

Like other artists who adhered to Synthetism's programme, Preisler's later work showed a Classicism that was the corollary to this conception. The large panels in the Palacký Room at the Prague Municipal building, which Preisler worked on for three years, have come to represent the high point of Czech efforts to create great mural painting. In this utopian vision of the golden age of humanity, with its unsullied image of the "feminine" and the "masculine", lies the pictorial equivalent of Neo-Classical thinking. At the time, Šalda defended these panels as a synthetic expression of the "inner need for order as an organizing principle of abundance and richness of life" – an objective that could be attained

building since 1907. Such success showed that the "struggle for tomorrow" encouraged by Šalda and his *Volné směry* friends was not mere tilting at windmills, but of far-reaching cultural importance. The precepts of Synthetism, which found concrete expression in the artistic style, also represented an intellectual and ethical renewal. As such, they gave the artist a sense of responsibility for the wider impact of his work, which spurred a crusade against superficial decorative style and a search for a more interesting paradigm.

Liberation of form had to be accompanied by liberation of the mind, in a harmony of all creative forces. The painters who developed these ideas were fascinated by Paul Cézanne, although their passion for the "evolutive logic" of modern painting prevented them from deriving the greatest possible benefit from his work. Cezanne proposed a living synthesis of the polarity of subjective and objective deformation represented by without any contradiction between "revolutionary and traditional meaning" or between freedom and law, since what was involved was an "artistic principle", creative work based on cultural archetypes.[17]

In this way, the idea of Classicism as an apogee in art and culture was fully restored in the Czech context.

Even in 1911, Emil Filla, who belonged to a younger, more restive generation, still considered Neo-Primitivism as one more preparatory stage on the way to Classicism, the ultimate ideal of all art.[18] However, just as Classicism appeared to be coming onto the stage, ideas turned in another direction.

The Štenc house, 1909–1911. Prague Old Town (Salvatorska 8–10). Arch.: Otakar Novotný.

Apartment building, 1910–1911 Josefov (Široká 5–7). Arch.: Bohumil Hypšman.

The second wave of symbolism

Symbolism had taken far deeper root in Czech literature and arts than it might seem from a superficial look at their evolution. This was no doubt due to the work of the poet Otakar Březina, whose poetry and essays, frequently published by *Volné směry*, addressed the fundamental questions of artistic creation, the relationship between sensual and spiritual beauty, and the artist's place in the world. Even though Březina abandoned poetry after 1908, his spiritual vision of life continued to have a major influence on Czech artists.

Indeed, Březina also had considerable personal impact on the sculptor František Bílek, who in 1901 had illustrated his poetry anthology, *Hands*. The poem, "Music of the Blind", a song about souls blinded by "the mystical sin of their birth", suggested to Bílek the image of a wandering couple, the man's arm stretched out dreamily toward the unknown, and the woman clutching a lyre, the instrument of prophecy. Březina's imaginary world was also the source of inspiration for *Dazzlement*, a beechwood sculpture made by Bílek in 1907. This larger-than-life work, representing a mystic struck with the ecstatic vision of "the true essence of all things", showed an arched figure in initiate's garb contemplating the depths of the universe and being dazzled by its grandeur and beauty. The light falling on him is caught in the broad indentations of the surface-hatching in such a way that the optical effect lightens the mass to create an impression of upward movement. *Dazzlement* can also be construed as Bílek's reaction to Munch's famous *The Scream*, which the Norwegian painter exhibited in 1905; Březina's "cosmic" optimism in this sculpture was undoubtedly the deliberately polemical antithesis of Munch's pessimism. Contrary to what its subject matter might suggest, however, *Dazzlement* was not intended for an outdoor setting, but for the middle of a room accessible only to adepts of the cosmic religion, the antechamber to the ideal temple depicted by Bílek in a book of illustrations entitled *The Building of the Future Temple within Us* (1908). During the same period Bílek conceived a series of architectural projects, one of which included his villa-workshop in Prague-Hradčany, built between 1910 and 1911. His guiding concept was the idea of a wheat-

František Bílek, *Moses*, 1905. Bronze. Prague Old Town (Pařízská).

field, representing spiritual fertility and the harvest of creative work, expressed by large pillars freely styled after ancient Egyptian models. The brick construction was topped by the first flat roof in Prague, and the ensemble – which also included the soberly decorated furnishings designed by Bílek himself – was an original illustration of the Secession's major hallmark, "the total work of art".

Bílek's enthusiasm and his fertile imagination led him to create a number of ambitious projects that were impossible to implement on the scale he had originally intended; his *Monument to the Nation*, dating from this same period, is one of these. It was easier to find an outlet for his seething creativity in albums of illustrations, in which material constraints did not stifle his metaphysical visions. Books of this kind were indeed among the essential elements in the symbolist poetic scheme, where they were seen as parables on the mysterious spiritual order of the universe.

This was how in 1909 Bílek came to publish *The Way,* with a preface by Miloš Marten. It contains thirty-eight illustrations of what Marten called "the epic of

František Kupka, *Prometheus in Red and Blue*, 1908. Watercolour, 32.1 x 29.3 cm. Prague, National Gallery.

František Bílek, *Chamber of Horrors,* 1912. Wood engraving,
29.5 x 22.7 cm. Prague, National Gallery.

The Way recalls the popular stations of the cross,
which to Catholics evoke the Passion of Christ, and
which are still found today in places of pilgrimage in
Bohemia. This work demonstrates Bílek's effort to
make his images of spirituality easily understandable;
in the early drawings for the project he drew the path
as a shaky double line to represent both the "arterial
pulse" – the fundamental rhythm of all life – and an
earthly path. He also added a drawing showing the
path meandering round trees and stretches of water,
and disappearing into the distance. Bílek's view was
that the very reason for the existence of plastic art was
its ability to make spiritual truth accessible to people.

Bílek never succeeded in completing *The Way,* but
he worked constantly on one stage of the work or another in different scales. Only the sculpture for *Moses,*
made in 1905, was produced on the monumental scale
originally intended. This work, which combines stylization with Neo-Baroque naturalism, represents a kneeling, seemingly angry figure recalling the fatal Fall of
the first man, whose name he is inscribing on a roll of
parchment. The sculpture is conceived in such a way
that the position of the prophet's knees creates a concave area that catches a pool of light. This embodies
the concept of spiritual light, a fire generating moral
strength, conveying the traditional sense of Moses as a
key figure in the spiritual evolution of mankind. This
work is marked by the same baroque pathos often seen
in Bílek's sculptural deformations that affronted the
public, such as his gravestone monument, *Grief* (1909),
created for the historical novelist Beneš Třebízský, in
the Vyšehrad National Cemetery. The conservative
journal *Dílo* compared the monument to "a monster
in a theatrical pose of despair". Šalda, however, rose to
Bílek's defence, lauding his courageous and unconventional style, although Šalda's own classically inclined
conception of Synthetism also led him to recommend
"greater order of the plastic elements".[2]

By that time Bílek was no longer a member of the
Mánes Union, but he still fascinated younger artists
interested in reviving the poetic force of Symbolism.
Moderní revue was the first to encourage this revival,
and its editors, Arnošt Procházka and Jiří Karásek, res-
olutely continued to defend the Decadence and Symbolism of the 1890s. In 1907, Karásek published *Dream
of a Kingdom of Beauty,* an exotic tale illustrated with
vignettes by Zdenka Braunerová. The author, who

man's earthly journey".[1] Bílek envisioned it as a path
between rows of gigantic statues, leading from the aero-
lite – half man, half burning rock – lips parched with
thirst, to the statues of Adam and Eve falling, and
through the Deluge and Sodom toward the Divine
Child, humanity's new hope, playing in the shadow
of the ruins. Then come Rama, Krishna, Egypt and
Moses, representing all those initiated into the true way
of life. The path goes on through a number of perilous
events (the dance around the Golden Calf, the cruelty
of war) until it comes to an end amid the assembled
prophets of the Old Testament, where the first Apostles
answer the question "What seek ye?" with a question of
their own: "Lord, where art Thou?"

thought that no flesh-and-blood actor could possibly translate his message in all its subtlety, conceived it as a play for marionettes. The scene was set in ancient China and evoked an imaginary empire whose emperor could only be the most handsome person in the realm. When the new young emperor refused to put his pre-

František Bílek, *Grief,* 1909. Stone. Vyšehrad National Cemetery.

decessor to death, and replaced the cult of physical beauty with that of spiritual beauty, his empire vanished. The story was highly symbolic and reinforced the aristocratic rejection of the mundane that led *Moderní revue* toward unequivocal elitism.

In 1906, Arnošt Procházka published *The Way of Beauty,* a volume of essays on artists close to Symbolism and Decadence. Two years earlier, he had published an essay, or, more correctly, a prose poem, on Odilon Redon, in which he used metaphors to suggest the artist's fantastical universe. Redon was not unknown in Bohemia. Zdenka Braunerová had visited him several times in Paris during the early 1890s, and had already introduced him to many Czech artists, including Julius Zeyer. Even Jiránek, although a convinced Impressionist, knew Redon personally. Procházka's essay was a manifesto against the Mánes Union's effort to pinpoint an "evolutive logic" in modern art. Procházka used examples of Redon's work to underline its immense value, and emphasized how it steadfastly ignored problems of topical interest: "Faces whose eyes have never seen the light of this world peer out of Redon's little sketches. Faces veiled by dreams. And others, branded with the indestructible stamp of proud renunciation, resignation and silence. His art too is proud and silent; he speaks only to the few. With his noble simplicity, his thoughtful interiorization and hieratic gesture, he is not suited to the democratic, utilitarian common crowd. He needs souls enamoured of enigma, wrapped in dreams of mystery, awake to the mystical voices calling from infinite worlds and time immemorial, and able and willing to live the higher, richer reality of vision and dream, which give true value and individuality to human existence."[3] With this distinctive approach, Redon emerged as the major figure of the new Symbolism.

Moderní revue's reputation was considerably enhanced by the collaboration of Miloš Marten, who joined the editorial staff after his rupture with Šalda. Early in 1908, Marten met Émile Bernard in Paris. He had been interested for some time in Bernard's *Reflexions d'un témoin de la décadence du beau* (Reflections of a witness to the decadence of the beautiful) as well as in the ideas of the review *La Rénovation esthétique,* which Bernard had founded. The encounter with Bernard was to have a great influence on his art.[4] Marten was deeply fascinated by Bernard's basic contention that it was

František Kobliha, last sheet of the *Tristan* cycle, 1909. Wood
engraving, 29.3 x 23.3 cm. Prague, National Gallery.

beside the point to talk about ancient or modern art:
there was only one art, the manifestation of the eternal
ideal. This idea seemed to offer a clear alternative to the
anarchism and individualism introduced by the impressionist revolt. Its new idealism rejoined the Péladan
branch of French Symbolism in its Latin, Catholic
interpretation of the core of Western culture, but at the
same time its retrospective aspect contradicted Šalda's
synthetist conception of modern culture as a new creation born out of direct contact with contemporary life.
In 1909, Šalda published *Des conditions modernes de la
beauté* (On modern conditions for beauty), the book/
manifesto of French Synthetism written by Charles
Morice, who had already inspired Šalda during the

1890s, and whom Šalda had persuaded to contribute
regularly to *Volné směry*. Marten immediately reacted
with a critical broadside in *Moderní revue* that countered the conclusions in Morice's book, and which bore
the characteristic subtitle "Reflections on Artistic Ethics
and Sociology". Marten insisted on the artist's independence and the "solitary energy of his creative enter-
prise".[5] This rebuttal was further confirmation of *Moderní revue*'s artistocratic conception of art.

However, promoting individualism was not Marten's
intention, and when he left *Moderní revue* in 1912 it was
for personal as much as ideological reasons. Marten no
longer defended Munch, as he had earlier, and the failure of Bernard's Prague exhibition in 1909, which he saw
as the result of a conspiracy against himself, strengthened his conviction that Czech art was in need of a
thorough "renaissance". It also cut him off from Czech
artists. In Marten's opinion, it was František Bílek,
whose work he had been following since the latter's
arrival in Prague at the turn of the century, who was the
key to understanding the problematic issues of Czech
art. But here, too, Bernard made it clear to Marten that
a rich imagination was still not enough, that Bílek the
mystic was also a "deformer" and an "ideist", who put
idea before the Ideal, which can only express itself in
serene perfection.[6]

Marten's views on art were prey to constant conflict
between pessimism and optimism, individual revolt
and general harmony, Romanticism and Classicism.
The clash between the latter especially marked his last
important essay, "Above the City". In this work, a Czech,
Michal, and a foreigner, Allan – who resembles Bernard
less than he resembles Paul Claudel, a friend of Marten's
while he was consul in Prague – are together on "the
terrace of a seventeenth-century patrician house" overlooking Prague in the twilight. They discuss the two
spiritual forces that have always dominated the basic
principles and the vital nerve-centre of Czech culture:
the demon of Reform, purveyor of dissent and revolt,
and the chaos that challenges order and solicits the liberation of its "imprisoned soul".[7]

During the first decade of the century, *Moderní revue* attracted all artists who declined to follow the path
of Impressionism and who preferred the poetic elements
of Decadence and Symbolism. Alongside the poets were
also a number of plastic artists, especially those who
drew their inspiration from poetry. Procházka defended

these artists' originality and autonomy in his essay on Redon: "Theirs is the creation of beauty through line, hand in hand with the beauty of words created by the poet, each playing the same melody in his own individual style on his own instrument. In this way, a single inspiration, mirrored in two creative artistic minds, is reflected in a dual interpretation that produces an effect of greater unity." The strange form of narcissism represented in the idea of two artistic genres reflecting one another, which evokes the theme of the hermaphrodite so popular with the Symbolists, is also a statement of the distinctive aesthetic of the synthesis of the arts.

One of the most interesting artists accepted into the relatively closed *Moderní revue* circle was the engraver František Kobliha. At the turn of the century, Kobliha had started out as a decorative illustrator in the naturalistic Art Nouveau style, but had gradually moved toward engraving. During the first decade of the century, he did numerous sensitive charcoal drawings, which constituted the stock of images he was to draw on for the rest of his life. The style and melancholic content was reminiscent of Preisler in his black lake period, and like Preisler the richly modulated interplay of black and white provided Kobliha with a space that gave huge scope for his imagination, as well as for an impressive form of modernism. Kobliha was delighted by Odilon Redon's velvet black and would have liked to do lithographs, but he had to content himself with wood engravings. This gave a certain primitive cast to his first *Simple Motifs* (1908), based on a collection of Neruda's poems, which corresponded to the Pont-Aven School's contemporaneous interest in engraving. Kobliha's other series – *In the Early Hours* (1909) and *The Vindictive Cantilena* (1910), after the poems of Karel Hlaváček, then *Tristan* (1909–1910), followed by *May* (1911), illustrating the work of the greatest Czech romantic poet, Karel Hynek Mácha – represent the high point of his work and reveal his consummate mastery of technique.

Kobliha's symbolist programme was also apparent in his choice of night scenes, lit by dull moonlight, as opposed to impressionist daylight. In these eerily luminescent nocturnal landscapes, seen from above, the poet is haunted by oneiric visions of pale women dancing or wandering in the throes of desire, as well as various kinds of ghosts. In his essay on Odilon Redon, Kobliha

František Kobliha, *The Vampire*, 1909. Wood engraving, 20.8 x 15 cm. Prague, National Gallery.

later wrote that this somnambulistic atmosphere should evoke everything "that would otherwise remain concealed and unknown" in the silence of the night.[8] Kobliha turned from the poetically abstracted surface beneath his feet toward both the cosmic expanses and the depths of the earth. The first of these themes – the cosmic expanse – is seen in *The Sphinx*, which watches the night sky and all its starry convolutions, or in the Hlaváček-like nude sleepwalker staring at the moon, while the opening image from *May* shows the poet gazing in wonderment at the star-studded sky. The second theme goes back to a subject introduced by "mood-landscape" painting in the 1890s, in which there was often a figure gazing at a body of water. The last illustration in *Tristan,* for example, evokes lethal, deep-running water; on other occasions, Kobliha represented the fantastic vegetation of underwater forests. He used these symbols to illustrate the psychological process of sublimation, which instinctively seeks out archetypal images. A certain decadent stylization of his own self also appears at this time, for example in his wood engraving *The Vampire,* whose disturbing figure takes the place of the white swan favoured by poetic Symbolism.

One reason Kobliha's graphic style matured so rapidly was his exposure to Bílek's engravings. During the first decade of the century, Bílek applied his talent for drawing to wood engraving, in which he expressed his Neoplatonic concept of the symbolism of light. There is no doubt whatsoever as to the originality of his technique: short parallel hatchings and sometimes long, vertical furrows were used to dematerialize the object represented. Bílek's uses of light was as subtly nuanced as that of the Impressionists, but it appeared like a negative on the black surface. His handling of light captured the "inner scrutiny" of self-meditation.

Kobliha lacked such spiritual intensity, but he was more poetic. The *Moderní revue* environment influenced his evolution, even if its traditionalist leanings sometimes stifled his imagination. In 1911, he created the frontispiece for one of Marten's books, *Cortigiana,* using Neo-Renaissance elements. His poetic, fragile side vanished with his *Woman* series (1911), in which dreamlike scenes evoke heady, intoxicating atmospheres. Kobliha also resuscitated the traditional symbolist heroines, Herodias, Salome and Salammbo.

Prague (1913), Kobliha's album of engravings of the city's monuments and landscapes, belonged to the earliest trend of decadent art; Procházka commented that the work still retained "the inner feeling" of this beautiful city, which was "being destroyed by vulgarity and indifference". He was particularly impressed by the melancholy of the images, but also noted how closely their "grandiose and somber" quality was attuned to the atmosphere of tragic, historical Prague.[9]

Like Kobliha's engravings, Jakub Schikaneder's paintings were superb illustrations of picturesque old Prague, in which he captured the strange hue of its misty evenings. Paradoxically, the musical harmony of colour in these paintings is developed around sub-

Jakub Schikaneder, *Nightfall at Hradčany,* 1909–1913. Oil on canvas, 86.5 x 107.5 cm. Prague, National Gallery.

FACING PAGE:
TOP LEFT: Vladimír Županský, title page for G. Moore's *Modern Painters,* Prague, 1909. Prague, UPM.

TOP RIGHT: Josef Váchal, title page for J. Deml's *Castle of Death,* Prague, 1912. Prague, UPM.

BOTTOM: Jan Konůpek, title page for K. H. Mácha's *May,* 1910. Prague, UPM.

GEORGE·MOORE
MODERNI
MALIRI

···

Z·ANGLICKEHO·PRE
LOZIL·V·A·JUNG·PECI
VOLNYG·SMERU·A·NA
KLADEM·S·V·U·MANES
V·PRAZE·1900

JAKUB DEML
HRAD SMRTI

KARLA HYNKA
MÁCHY

MÁJ

jects from everyday life, and natural and artificial light are invariably mingled. All the authenticity of Schikaneder's paintings of Prague resides in this characteristic approach.

"Art books" occupied a special place in Kobliha's output, and even if he only produced a few of them, he was fully aware of the importance Symbolism attached to them as art objects. In the 1890s, Alfons Mucha's impressions of Paris had already demonstrated the potential scope of "art books", but for a long time local efforts produced far more modest works. Zdenka Braunerová's version of Mrštík's *May Tale* (1897) is generally considered the first "modern" Czech illustrated book. During the first decade of the century, Zdenka Braunerová's work – especially her illustrations for Marten's essay "Style and Stylization" (1906) and her album *The Cycle of Pleasure and Death* (1907) – showed illustration's evolution toward a new decorative conception respecting the plastic qualities of the paper's surface. Vojtěch Preissig, inspired by English models, was one of the main instigators of this evolution; the graphic elements in his books took on a decorative style (Jan Karafiát's *Fireflies,* in 1903, for example)

and a typographical architecture that was at once well conceived, elegant and sober (*Silesian Songs,* by Petr Bezruč, 1909).

Since 1905 *Typography,* the journal of an association of the same name, was instrumental in improving the quality of Czech books, even those of commercial publishers. In 1908 the Czech Bibliophiles' Association was founded, which published a model collection of books under the heading "Edition". An increasing number of publishers who specialized in modern literature, including Josef Florian in the Moravian town of Stará Ríse, and Kamila Neumannová in Prague, sought a presentation worthy of the content. This evolution in Czech book production had really been initiated, however, in 1895 by *Moderní revue,* with its publication of *Knižnice* (Library).

Kobliha's cover designs found scope for a richness of form akin to the floral naturalism of the Secession, but his fantastical handling of the ornamental motif as a metaphor for the contents of the book took him to the brink of Surrealism (Huysmans' *À rebours* [Against Nature] in 1913, *Aurelia,* by Gérard de Nerval in 1911, and *Works* by Jiří Karásek in 1912–1913). Kobliha possessed a very personal idiom; generally Czech book ornamentation was based on more stylized decorative elements similar to those of architecture, which were gradually transformed.

It was mainly the young engravers who took this direction, which allowed them to handle stylization in a new way. Vratislav Hugo Brunner's cover for *Small Flames* (a collection of poetry by Jiří Mahen published in 1907 by the Prague *Progressive Students' Review*), for example, used a spiral motif – rather like an archery target – entwined with vegetation, together with a female "bearer of light". Spirals of a similar kind also appeared in the ornamentation of Kotěra's interior decoration for the School of Applied Arts at the 1904 World's Fair in St. Louis, and they later became a typical motif of synthetic decorative art. They transformed what was initially an organic Art Nouveau curve into a design heavy with latent potential and with its own rich symbolic value.

Spirals were more than an ornamental motif: they were the emblem of modern Primitivism, which restored their prehistoric significance. For primitive communities, they had constituted a cosmological symbol associated with the labyrinth, which in ancient religions represented the kingdom of the dead and a ritual passageway for achieving adulthood.[10] In mythology, immortality was intimately linked with this ritual passage. These non-discursive ideas were expressed in dance or in graphic representations of sacral movements like the spiral, which evolves through free organic forms to the double and quadruple spiral and into the right-angled geometric Greek meander and other variations. It is interesting to note that a similar, though accelerated, evolution occurred in Czech decorative ornamentation, so that by 1908 the illustration for the twelfth-year cover of *Volné směry* was a geometric meander in the purest style, signed by the young graphic artist Jaroslav Benda.

It was not simply a matter of applying theorems learned in cultural anthropology classes, however; the inner logic of the plastic forms expressed a striking, ornamentally refined graphic form. Benda's geometric purism represented the most radical version of this phenomenon. Decorators from the previous generation introduced a liveliness of expression and a sensitivity that led to an unusual proliferation of decoration. The title page of George Moore's book *Modern Painters,* published in 1909 by the Mánes Union, was illustrated by Vladimír Županský with an ornamental frame partly formed of floral stems and stylized more geometric circular and spiral forms, giving it an almost baroque appearance. This mirrored exactly the type of ornamentation used in the decoration of Prague architecture around 1910. Another example illustrating the transformation which occurred in ornamental style is František Kysela's poster for the twenty-third exhibition organized by the Mánes Union, French Impressionists, in 1907. The peacock emblem recalls the poster designed by Preisler for the Mánes Union's exhibition of French art in 1902, but the use of new colours, the work's primitivist texture, its typography and ornamental details all clearly show the stylistic progression.

A number of significant events fuelled this evolution, including the 1909 exhibition of works by Bourdelle, whose powerful influence on decorative sculpture very quickly spread to all areas of art.

Although the increasing demand for a fundamental change at the beginning of the century produced another decorative style – a second wave usually known as Art Deco – it really arose from a number of different sources. Bourdelle's idea fitted better into the frame-

Jan Konůpek, project for the cover of the journal *Meditace*, 1909. India ink, 49.4 x 37.4 cm. Prague, National Gallery.

work of modernist Synthetism; his archaism still set the struggling hero in the central position. Modernist optimism of a similar kind is found in the works of František Kupka from the same date. In his 1908 *Prometheus in Red and Blue,* the Titan, full of the joys of life and the vigour of spring, is represented in unblended colours, standing amid luxuriant vegetation in osmosis with the earth, from which shimmering spirals of light seem to rise. In a later version, Prometheus holds a ball of scintillating light representing himself, as god of the

Sun, and his gift of fire to mankind. The cult of the classical ideal embodied in the work of Marten and Bernard belongs to this same artistic conception.

However, the new decorative style also had an additional, entirely different source, which was visible in the cover illustration of the spiritual journal *Meditace* (Meditation), started in 1909 by another young graphic artist, Jan Konůpek. Here, spirals form a symmetrical system that totally integrates an extremely stylized praying figure invoking an unknown divinity, or rather, cosmic forces symbolized by an ornamental design.

Konůpek's treatment of the figure was very different from Bourdelle's or Kupka's: although set in the centre of the composition, it is conceived simply as an intermediary, a medium for the larger symbolized whole. Konůpek subsequently employed this new ornamental concept for subjects on the fringes between earthly and otherworldly existence (*Hamlet* and *Charon of the Underworld,* in 1908). In his *Vanitas* (1908), magnificent oriental robes envelop a skeleton that is relentlessly squeezing the blood out of a human heart, while a cherub sits at its feet blowing phantasmagorical bubbles into a spiral motif.

Konůpek did not idealize the figure or make it into a model, but he did present it as an alternative to simply disappearing, as a form of integration into some higher order. *Vanitas* also shows the vulnerability of the sensitive human in this unequal relationship. Indeed, Konůpek found himself confronted with the psychological predicament of modern individualism, associated with Decadence from the 1890s on, and sought to express this in an image that went beyond the original ornamentalism. In *Black Flame-Salome,* a drawing from 1908, the praying-figure motif was handled in an illusionistic style, with the figure's hair sweeping upward in a whirlwind of flames. Other versions show Salome in profile, stylized in Egyptian fashion, to indicate that she has been consecrated. Her antithesis appears simultaneously in *Alteration,* an etching of a woman with a great mass of hair, who seems to be consumed by some morbid passion. An Egyptian-style flame runs triumphantly across the picture like a fountain of light and fizzles out in the hand of an anaemic-looking male nude with sunken eyes. In 1909 Konůpek made another etching, *Decapitation,* where Salome is depicted kneeling before the executioner instead of St. John the Baptist, as though it were she who was to be castigated and put to death. With *Ecstasy* (1912), a frontal version of Salome is transformed into a hideous ghost; although the "living" skull recalls *Vanitas,* the work is already far removed from the original ornamentalism.

Konůpek's variations on the Salome theme appear somewhat capricious, but the workings of his fantasy are by no means disordered. In fact, the imagery he

Jan Konůpek, *Ecstasy*, 1912. Etching, 10 x 7 cm. Prague, Private Collection.

Josef Váchal, *Invocation to the Devil*, 1909. Oil, 100 x 100 cm. Hradec Králové, Krajská Gallery.

used for this theme is far more modern and versatile than that which he had previously taken from the older Symbolists. Unlike Bílek, for example, Konůpek did not pursue the construction of antitheses, but worked on the inversion of a single theme. Salome, who was also a symbol of spiritual vitality, was treated as an archetypal vehicle for the representation of an inner struggle in which the opposing psychic forces were interchangeable. One of the last works in this series shows Salome dancing wildly over the decapitated head of St. John the Baptist (1912–1913), observed by a man on a throne who bears a closer resemblance to a modern philosopher than to Herod. The highlighting of both the naked dancer's sensuality and the prophet's head emphasizes that, for Konůpek, the conflict between the body and ascetic spirituality is to be resolved by strength of will.

It was Emil Pacovský, the dynamic editor-in-chief of the journal *Meditace,* who grouped the youngest of the Symbolists into an independent association: in 1910 Sursum was born. This association, of which Kobliha was president for a short while, rapidly organized its first exhibition the following October in Brno, and added Joself Váchal and Jan Zrzavý to its membership. Sursum set itself high ideals. It created a literary section that soon attracted many members, although these were fewer and less well known than the artists. The association's activity peaked in 1912 with an exhibition at the Prague Municipal building, which, besides Konůpek, included Váchal, Zrzavý, the painters Rudolf Adámek and Miroslav Sylla, and the sculptor Jaroslav Horejc, who was invited as a guest artist. The exhibition met with a cool reception from the public, and the group broke up shortly thereafter.[11]

Despite this setback, the fact remains that Sursum was founded by some remarkable individuals. Josef Váchal, for example, was already an established artist at the time. The dreadful hallucinations he had suffered in earlier years, in addition to his spiritualistic experiences, had convinced him that the artist was a medium for unknown forces. Váchal felt that the power of these unknown forces was potentially dangerous, so that they had to be fully understood and kept under control. This explains his interest in magic and his passion for ancient sources and authorities on the subject, through which he acquired the strange accumulation of knowledge that marks his books and paintings. This syncretic body of wisdom on ancient religions and practices of magic, together with his youthful anarchism, kindled an interest in the heretical movements in spiritual history. Váchal tried to find out about all religious sects, including those of the past as well as those that had marked the ferment of spiritual sensitivity at the turn of the century, but he did not investigate any of them in great depth. Váchal, however, did use his undisputable talent for grotesque satire to treat his subjects in a highly personalized way, and displayed a sense of humour and a rather folksy taste in the representation of metaphysical ideas.

Jan Konůpek, *Contemplation*, post-1909. Etching, 10 x 5 cm. Prague, Private Collection.

Magic, a pastel-coloured wood engraving made in 1909, summarizes Váchal's evolution between 1905 and 1910. It represents a magician invoking the hierarchical chain through which he takes possession of the individual's body and soul. The rough technique used for this wood engraving imparts a strong expressivity to the esoteric symbols. Váchal was certainly influenced by Gauguin, but his own personal exoticism lay in the psychic domain and in hermeticism. Váchal made unconventional use of every possible means of plastic expression to achieve his intentions. His 1909 picture *Invocation to the Devil* is a mysterious representation of a somber scene with a dazzling background, whose theme is carried over into the carving of the frame. Here, although Váchal has some points in common with Bílek, he was really his antithesis. In *Mother!*, Bílek used a cosmic subject to express the metaphysical aspirations of mysticism, whereas for Váchal Satan was the incarnation of forces lurking deep in the bowels of the earth. His cycle of birth and death did not occure in the transcendental light of Good and Evil, but on the earth itself, as was signified in *Invocation* by the skulls in the trees. Váchal's wood engravings, as well as his relief carvings, teem with demons leading man into temptation. Strangely, a terrifyingly powerful force is suggested by their slightly comic appearance.

Váchal's conception of art is further expressed in an engraving called *Fantasy* (1912), depicting a bird perched on the bars of his studio window. This represented the mysterious bird that, according to Váchal, several years earlier used to appear to him at midnight in "long, loud and beautiful" song – none of which was ever heard by his neighbours. An allegorical figure of Art – a woman meditating beside a palette – merges

Josef Váchal, illustration from the book *On the Ritual of the Heretics of Toledo,* 1911. Wood engraving, 12 x 10 cm.
Prague, Private Collection.

Josef Váchal, *Fantasy*, pre-1912. Wood engraving, 9 x 9.7 cm.
Hradec Králové, Krajská Gallery.

into her own astral wraith and stares intently at the bird, while a vague form, the materialization of the bird's spiritual song, presses against her heart. In a primitive manner, Váchal integrates his theme into the Neoplatonic conception of the imagination as the most advanced state of perception of the world in its entirety. A powerful but immaterial medium intervenes between the mysterious messenger of the universe and Art, who lends a fascinated ear. The inclusion of this medium as an instrument to express emotional union is characteristic not only of Váchal, but of the whole of the second wave of Czech Symbolism, which rejected the enthusiastic monism of the prevailing lyrical Impressionism. This was also why the remarkable books Váchal wrote, decorated, printed and bound himself were not produced like the usual "art books", but looked more like ancient books of incantations (*On the Ritual of the*

Heretics of Toledo, in 1911, *The New Psalter of Darkness*, in 1913, and *Vigil at the Hour of Terror*, between 1911 and 1914). In *The Perfect Magic of the Future* (1922), in which he analysed the whole of his previous evolution, Váchal wrote that in contrast to all forms of religion, which encourage passivity in the face of death, art alone unfailingly continues to resist its siren song.

Jan Zrzavý was the youngest, but also the greatest, of the second generation of Symbolists. He was sixteen years old when he arrived in Prague in the autumn of 1906; although he enrolled at the School of Applied Arts, he was expelled almost immediately. His themes, although very personal, were remarkably in tune with the symbolist tradition, and he claimed to have been initiated into art by Julius Zeyer. Zrzavý's work, which he sometimes signed "Gauguin", displayed a determination to fuse the poetic universe of Neo-Romanticism with the new decorative conception of painting. *The Persian Garden* (1907) is composed of symbols – trees, a path, a mysterious magus figure – created with ornamental lines and flat colour surfaces. Zrzavý was captivated by French art, which had been fashionable in Prague ever since the Mánes Union's Impressionist exhibition, and the artist made a brief excursion to Paris. This visit resulted in his *Vale of Sorrows* – a work that he held onto like a talisman all his life – depicting mountains inspired by the *Mona Lisa,* which he saw in the Louvre, and a pallid Art Nouveau-style female figure, beside a tree bearing exotic flowers. With Jan Preisler's encouragement, Zrzavý made a larger picture from the initial pastel drawing.

Although Zrzavý's painting was expressive, lyricism was his truly personal style. In *Nocturne* (1909), blurred colours similar to those in *Vale of Sorrows* imbue the picture with the magical charm of the night-time world of poetry. Zrzavý is very close to Kobliha in this work, but his conception remains purely pictorial; indeed, Zrzavý's work is fascinating mainly for the emotional

Top left: Bohumil Kubišta, *St. Sebastian*, 1912. Oil on canvas, 98 x 74.5 cm. Prague, National Gallery.

Bottom left: Jan Zrzavý, *Zeyer's Garden*, 1908. Pastel, 22.6 x 26 cm. Prague, National Gallery.

Facing page: Jan Zrzavý, *Meditation*, 1915. Oil on canvas, 50.2 x 37.5 cm. Prague, National Gallery.

Bohumil Kubišta, *Lazarus Raised from the Dead,* 1911. Oil on canvas, 163.5 x 126.5 cm. Plzeň, Západočeská Gallery.

Paris in 1909 and 1910, which had been made in difficult circumstances, he had discovered the Fauves, whose concept of colour he eventually rejected through the influence of Cubism. Kubišta became increasingly convinced that the value of a picture depended on its intellectual conception.

In "The Premises of Style", an essay he wrote in 1911, Kubišta made a fundamental distinction between internal and external form: external form was sensual, whereas internal form, which comprised the basic geometrical formulae organizing the structure of the picture, was "transcendental" and determined the relationship between the creator and infinity.[12] Kubišta became a fanatical analyst of the composition of both traditional and modern works, whether by Poussin, Munch or Cézanne. He used the golden section as a reference, and, later, the symbolic geometrical figures that were the basis of his own works from 1911 on (such as *Lazarus Raised from the Dead* and *The Epileptic Woman*) were structured around a magical pentagon. However, the dynamism imparted by this geometric infrastructure, which could well have originated with Seurat's doctrine on the expressive value of angles, is itself highly interesting. Although it is unclear why Kubišta adopted these structures, they fitted in with his desire to investigate the content of the new form in the greatest possible depth. In another article, "On the Spiritual Fundamentals of Modern Times" (1912), he focused on the "force of action" that is channelled through the creative will of the artist, and which transforms the cosmic forces sustaining life into real symbols, thereby exerting a magical effect on the viewer.

Kubišta emphasized the importance of seizing and using to the fullest the psychic energies contained in the magic of a picture's infrastructure. *St. Sebastian* was a key work painted between the end of 1911 and the beginning of 1912, in which the complex composition of triangular forms and tilted elliptical spirals is developed out of the basic motif of two triangles descending into a circle.[13] This dynamic projection was not intended to glorify the beauty of life, but to complement an imaginary self-portrait that was used to express the passion and torment of the artist's self-sacrifice. Such content was given greater intensity by the use of a colour harmony in tones of purple-brown and cold green.

Destitute, Kubišta joined the army in 1913, leaving Zrzavý with a greatly enhanced capacity to articulate

intensity of his colours – not in the usual sense of pictorial "atmosphere", but as symbolic evocations. The naive side of his art went hand in hand with an economy of means and a capacity for poetic expression achieved through elementary symbols, which he developed in a cyclical way by contrasting his paintings with each other. *The Merry Pilgrim-Women* (1908), for example, was juxtaposed with the sentimental melancholy of *Vale of Sorrows*.

After his meeting with Bohumil Kubišta in 1911, the orientalism and naive Symbolism of Zrzavý's early works acquired a new dimension. For personal and ideological reasons, Kubišta had by then already separated from his friends in The Eight. During his visits to the universe born of his poetic unconscious. The triangular structure apparent in *Sermon on the Mount* (1911–1912) indicates Kubišta's influence, but Zrzavý's total authenticity reappears intact in his *Sleeping Boy* (1912) – the sleeping boy was the characteristic symbol of the oneiric interiorization of the world – and again in *The Moon and the Lily of the Valley* in 1913. Here he brought new means into play to communicate the idea of the mysterious influence of the universe on mankind and on the earth itself.

Zrzavý's major contribution was a renewed interest in colour. Colour had been swamped by Kubišta's geometrism, but now came bounding back into the forefront, brimming with vigour. This was no longer the impressionist colour inherent in the local tone of the object, nor the sentimental hues impulsively adopted by young painters influenced by Munch and Van Gogh, nor even the decorative colour of Gauguin's Synthetism. Instead Primitivism was subjected to an inner discipline, its passion and vitality were subdued and given greater spirituality by the dream world.

In Zrzavý's mature works, an extraordinary luminescence emanates from the colours themselves, imparting a new plastic quality divorced from the traditional expression of volume. This can be seen in *Meditation* (1915), a mediumistic drawing transposed into plastic terms; here, Zrzavý seemed to be emerging from the

phase in which he was inspired directly by symbolist themes. A white figure with crossed hands and closed eyes is reaching out through prayer to a higher force, indicated by the white aura in the transcendent blue background and by the upward sweep of the leafy branches. It is not the figure itself but its form that is important, for its minimal outline divides the canvas in such a way that the figure seems to be simultaneously advancing out of the picture and sinking backward behind its flat surface. This illusion has a particular significance: to illustrate communication between the visible and the invisible.

In many respects, the artists grouped here under the heading of the "second wave of Symbolism" seem to remain traditionalists, and as such they were often seen as loners on the fringes of modern art. Yet the attention they drew to poetry and to the dream world that constituted the reverse side of everyday existence brought about a better understanding of the role of art in civilization as a whole. They countered the monistic tendencies of Impressionism and Synthetism by advancing the view that the world was not a clearly perceptible whole offered to the artist's sensitivity, but a process in which the mystery of the universe could be revealed only gradually. For these artists, art, though rooted in the protean dream-world, eventually came face to face with the problem of the conscious intent of the creative artist.

Decorative and geometric style

The Chamber of Commerce and Crafts jubilee exhibition was held in Prague's Exhibition Park in 1908. The buildings were designed by Jan Kotěra, his students and Josef Zasche and reflected the new decorative style of Synthetism. The exhibition also featured a small sales kiosk with a Japanese-inspired roof, designed by Otto Wagner's pupil Pavel Janák for the young decorative artists' co-operative known as Artěl. Beside it stood a pole bearing the Artěl flag, embroidered by Marie Teinitzerová, who was later to become famous for her rugs and tapestries. The flag depicted a small stylized horse after a drawing by Vratislav Hugo Brunner, the head of the co-operative. On sale inside the kiosk were gingerbread figures in amusing shapes conceived by Brunner, wooden boxes with painted lids, necklaces of coloured beads made by Helena Johnová, and figurative wooden toys in simple, machine-turned shapes, designed by Brunner and Jaroslav Benda. The highly artistic stylization and great simplicity of these first objects by Artěl immediately attracted attention. From 1909 on, the association also produced furniture (designed by Janák) as well as engravings (Jan Konůpek), interior sculpture, glassware (Jaroslav Horejc) and pottery. Artěl was the first Czech art co-operative that attempted to produce work in all fields of decorative art, and by doing so it fulfilled the Secession's primordial aim of influencing public taste through new art objects.

Like the new architecture defended by the periodical *Styl*, Artěl's artistic conception of production was to a large extent inspired by the decorative style that had developed in Vienna with the creation of the Wiener Werkstätte. This style had also been apparent in the Klimt group, of which Josef Hoffmann was the leading force, at their Kunstschau Wien exhibition. Hoffmann took note of what could be learnt from the Glasgow School and from Otto Wagner and succeeded in creating an elegant, refined style that was far more intimate than Wagner's monumentalism. His success carried over into several fields. Toward 1910, he began to design glass objects, including vases with simple geometric shapes, made of marbled white opaline and distinguished by a strongly graphic linear ornamentation.

These vases were produced by glassworks of such renown as the Widow of Jan Lötz Glassworks at Klášterský Mlýn, and were even more popular than the traditional Japanese-inspired coloured glass created earlier by Adolf Beckert. Hoffmann did not synthesize the object, but separated the basic form and the decoration into two distinct elements. This was an interesting conception, in that it left room for establishing a harmony between the two elements, but his production soon moved toward a symbiosis of pure transparent form and subtle decoration.

This differentiation between basic form and surface decoration did, however, generate purist tendencies. For an exhibition on English engraving organized by the Mánes Union in 1908, Jaroslav Benda created a poster consisting entirely of letters, in a design free of decorative ornamentation. The decorative element lay instead in the actual structure of the design. Benda took this concept to even further extremes with the monumental typography of his poster for the posthumous Hanuš Schweiger exhibition in 1912.

Ceramic objects, to which Artěl attached considerable importance, were a subtle indication of stylistic evolution. Vlastislav Hofman's tea and coffee service (1911), whose elements were designed as geometric volumes and decorated with simple checked patterns, reflected the interest shown in the "simple" elegance already advocated by Hofman's Viennese namesake. The large range of ceramics made by Pavel Janák the same year was an almost classic example of the way the younger generation of Czechs had pared down style. Particularly interesting is a set of boxes, in which one forms an octagonal cylinder with a decorative pattern of parallelograms created by undulating lines bent into a diamond-shaped meshwork. The richness of the design, which is further enhanced by the gilding and the organic, cyclical repetition of the pattern, brings to mind the spiral motif. Other works include pyramidal and hexagonal boxes comprising four sections set one on top of the other and decorated with a lozenge pattern. The superimposed pyramids create a broken surface pattern revealing an independent structure that runs through the object and ultimately seems to eclipse it.

The significance of this interplay between form and ornament was made clear in several articles by Janák. As early as 1910 he published an article in *Styl* with the

Marie Krikankova, pendant with chain, post-1910. Gold, emerald and mother-of-pearl, h.: 7 cm. Prague, UPM.

Pavel Jának, box, 1911. Faience with over-glaze, h.: 12 cm.
Prague, Private Collection.

created matter on either a vertical or a horizontal plane, and that all other, more complicated geometric forms were brought into being through the action of a "third force" that deformed matter and deflected it from its natural simplicity. This applied to the slanted plane, which showed the dynamics of "inert matter" becoming spiritual: as an architectural example he cited the pyramid, which is derived from a prism.[2] Jának saw the process of crystallization, on which the weight of matter has virtually no influence, as the most beautiful manifestation of this force: "The force of crystallization seems to be the gravitation of matter toward its own interior, so concentrated and powerful that it takes place in all circumstances, in a world circumscribed by itself." In a ceramic set designed by Jának (1911), the surface of a white, square-shaped box crystallizes into spherical triangles. A black design on the angles indicates "the ideal skeleton of the piece", while "the outer surfaces remain on the skin of the object and make it possible to follow the path of reality in all stages up to the picture".[3] In this way, Jának completely reversed Wagner's "rule of three" – function, construction, decoration. Poetic decoration took front stage, but at the same time was transformed from simple ornamentation into an active, spiritual conception of the object.

Jának's approach to ceramics was illustrative of the evolution followed by young Czech artists. The painters belonging to The Eight, who were gradually accepted in the Mánes Union, did everything possible to pursue their activities within its fold. The 1910 exhibition of French contemporary art, "The Independents", which had been partly prepared in Paris by Kubišta, was an event of major importance. In his introduction to the catalogue, the young theorist Antonín Matějček made much of Expressionism (he was one of the first in Europe to do so). He considered that, contrary to Impressionism, it offered a synthesis of the new expressions, of symbols that transcribed the feelings and concerns of the time in a more profound and relevant way.

The young artists' first choice among the works exhibited was André Derain's *Bathers,* which seemed to correspond best with their ideas on Primitivism. A public subscription organized in the town's cafés kept the painting in Prague, where it became the model for everyone to emulate. This canvas simply represented the accumulated essentials of a few high points of art: its subject matter and conception were inspired by

provocative title "From Modern Architecture to Architecture", in which he criticized the Wagner school's doctrine of the priority of function over construction and decoration.[1] In Jának's opinion, this produced work that was filled with "extraneous poetry", but lacked any inherent architectonic beauty.

This cult of functionality led to the flatness of modern architecture – parallel walls, naked surfaces, geometric configurations and straight lines. Jának felt that architecture should give up its flat, unidimensional look and become a creation in which "after functionality, thought and abstraction should be heard. This will evolve out of the effort to find a plastic form and to translate architectural ideas into plastic terms." Once that point was reached, architecture would have no further need to declare itself "modern" and would follow its own course, as the best architecture always had.

It is interesting to observe that Jának considered right-angled geometry, which was characteristic of the second phase of modern Synthetism, as being innate to nature and the laws of gravity. He believed that nature

Pavel Janák, pieces from a coffee-service in white faience, c. 1912. h.: 22.14 and 11.5 cm. Prague, UPM.

Cézanne's *Bathers,* while the stylization of the figures corresponded to the synthetic decorative style, and its limited colour range of grey, brown and green linked it to Analytic Cubism.

The imaginary competition with Derain opened by the young artists in 1910 quickly revealed that there were great differences among them. Filla, who had been the most active in the drive to keep the Derain painting in Prague, produced *Autumn,* whose expressive, hammered-looking figures are at the opposite pole from the Frenchman's elegant composition. Filla's colour was also more emotional, despite its reduction to predominantly blue and mauve tones. The decorative aspect was retained to a greater degree in Vincenc Beneš' *Idyll,* but its Cézanne-style handling had pseudo-Cubist overtones. Bohumil Kubišta showed no reaction to the Derain until 1911, when he produced *Spring, Bathing Women* and *Bathers.* In these works, Kubišta – whose compositions were thought out down to the last detail and who, unlike his companions, used the golden section and triangular grid-systems – seems to have

retained the lessons of Nicolas Poussin, the Japanese, Classical Antiquity and, especially, El Greco. The spiritual intensity of the recently rediscovered El Greco also exerted a powerful influence on Filla and affected the new Czech Expressionism as well.

Within a short time, a conflict arose out of which the avant-garde crystallized. It started between Filla, editor of *Volné směry*, and the board of the Mánes Union, and then its general assembly; an article by Filla on Neo-Primitivism, accompanied by reproductions of work by Picasso and Georges Braque, sparked it off. The controversy turned into a deep-rooted conflict of generations and provoked the departure of fifteen young painters, architects, decorators and theoreticians from the Mánes Union. These dissidents went on to establish their own Group of Plastic Artists, and produced the review *Umělecký měsíčník* (Art Monthly), which remained a source and focal point of radical thinking until the First World War. The group's efforts to establish a wider cultural base for contemporary ideas in philosophy, aesthetics and psychology suggest that it

Bor Professional Training School, vase, post-1915. Matt colourless glass enamelled in different colours and black, h.: 13.5 cm. Prague, UPM.

FACING PAGE:
TOP LEFT: Pavel Janák, box, c. 1912. Lid in ceramic clay with coloured glazing, h.: 7.9 cm. Prague, UPM.
BOTTOM LEFT: Jaroslav Horejc, vase, 1911. Ceramic clay with black and white glazing, h.: 22 cm. Prague, UPM.
FAR RIGHT: Kamenický Šenov Glassworks, vase, 1912. Black glass, with white and gold enamel-painting, h.: 19.3 cm. Prague, UPM.

Bor Professional Training School and Oertel Glassworks, vase, 1913. Colourless glass lid with overlaid white and black opaque engraved glass, h.: 33.8 cm. Prague, UPM.

Bor Professional Training School, vase, 1914. Colour-less glass overlaid with white, black and gold enamel, h.: 15.3 cm. Prague, UPM.

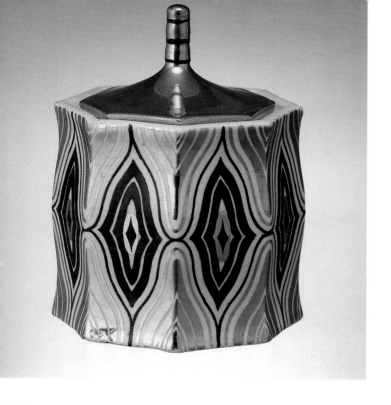

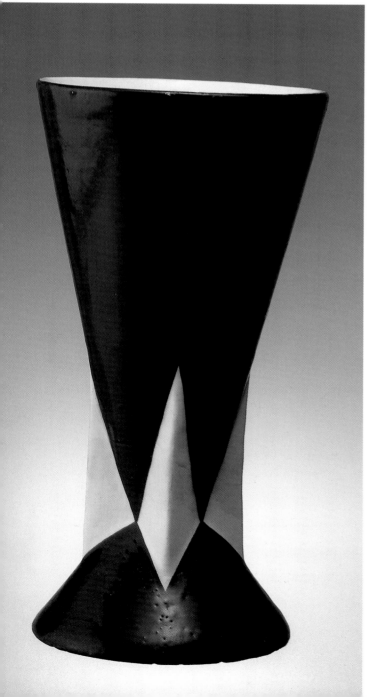

DECORATIVE AND GEOMETRIC STYLE   **235**

shared the synthetic inspiration of Šalda, and hence treated style as a link between art and life. For them, these efforts became part of acquiring a new spiritual dimension, using a style that grew gradually closer to Cubism.

Bohumil Kubišta discovered Picasso's and Braque's cubist work during his visit to Paris in the spring of 1910; their innuence can be seen in a self-portrait drawing and in a letter to Vincenc Beneš predicting the tremendous impact these painters would have.[4] The major lesson Kubišta drew from this encounter was the possibility not only of going beyond the separation of colour and composition but also of heightening the plastic expression of the objects represented. In his *Still Life with Funnel* and the monumental *The Quarry at Braník*, he succeeded in creating a dramatic tension in plastic form on the basis of two colours, using the principle of clearly separate light and dark surfaces. These two paintings were the first examples of Czech Cubo-Expressionism.

This movement developed further with the important contribution of the sculptor Otto Gutfreund, who joined Bourdelle's class at the Grande-Chaumière Academy in the autumn of 1909. At the time, Gutfreund noted that "Bourdelle … puts the figures into a single surface and sculpts them all in the same way … But he also obtains light effects by heavily and deeply emphasizing certain details, thereby creating waves and breaking up the surface into small, overlapping, wave-like facets, which gives an impression of movement …"[5] The sculptures produced by Gutfreund between 1911 and 1912, when he was still a member of the Mánes Union, seem to have come straight out of these notes. However, their titles – *Anguish, Hamlet, Don Quixote* – indicate that the sculptor's interest was not confined to form. Other members of the group also depicted "literary" subjects in cubo-expressionist terms: for example, Filla's *Salome* and Procházka's *Prometheus Unchained,* with its traces of El Greco. The group's review, *Umělecký měsíčník,* carried articles on Gothic, Renaissance and Baroque art. The lineage of Gutfreund's Cubo-Expressionism could clearly be traced back through Czech Baroque, while his new explanation of Donatello's concept of space (an open, fluid area, contrary to Aristide Maillol's concept of a containing space) linked him to Daumier – whose *Ratapoil* he admired – and Rodin.

While the Czech Cubo-Expressionists did not reject tradition out of hand, they felt that it needed radical renewal. Physiognomy became an element of inspiration in their symbolism, and they were convinced that every change of mood harboured a feeling that was directly translated into a physical movement. To them the human body and subjects of literary inspiration alike were merely channels of expression for this movement, which came from a purely spiritual source. In general, they turned from exteriority to interiority, and attributed a metaphysical dimension to the drama of human existence that had so fascinated them a few years earlier in Munch's work.

Kubišta, who never became a member of the young group, considered issues of style to be differences in the treatment of relationships between an art work's visible, empirical forms and its transcendental, infrastructural forms. But he too spoke of the need to surmount the current chaos by means of a new "concentration", and he called for the "radiant crystal of transcendental form", the very core of art, to manifest itself through its emotional content.[6] Certain works by the most radical members of the group, whose creative euphoria had led to the organization of two large exhibitions, seemed close to answering Kubišta's call in 1912. In Filla's *Bathers*, the luminous centre of the work is created by two analytically detached figures united by a crystal formation rotating around a fixed centre.[7]

The significance of adopting the crystal form as the new art's general symbol was interpreted in various ways. In his article "Prism and Pyramid" in 1911, Pavel Janák contrasted natural form on "two planes" with crystallization, which he considered the result of a "third force" bringing the slanted plane into play. In Janák's view, artistic creation was the analogical action of this distorting force, although it involved more complex mental states. A year later, in an analysis of cubist furniture in *Umělecký měsíčník,* he declared that its form derived from a "feeling projected into space". It was an expression of "spiritual activity" that drew the artist toward a perception of the material world as an "ensemble of matter" in which each separate entity loses its particularity. When such an ensemble was created in space, its surface was "in motion", and was characterized by "an extraordinarily concentrated, tense impression that is never created by solely functional objects".[8] Janák's conception of the superiority of art and mind

Otto Gutfreund, *Anguish*, 1911. Bronze, 148 cm. Prague, National Gallery.

over nature, and his conviction that technique consisted of "active", dynamic creativity, was typical of Cubo-Expressionism. Although completely opposed to naturalistic "lyrical Impressionism", it showed a similar globalization of the relationship between life and art, dictated here by creative intent.

Otto Gutfreund, who was also an enthusiastic constructor of theories at the time, developed a different analysis. He conceived sculpture as "the work of a creative will external to it; this creates sculpture according to its own laws, which are different from the laws of the organism." Sculpture was the materialization in space of an image that was itself a fragment of the unceasing ebb and flow of man's spiritual and intellectual activity. The artist's task was to make this "abstract" notion concrete in such a way that on seeing a work of art, the viewer could go back to the original starting point. To do this, it was essential to break the object down, because in reality it was impossible to imagine the statue as an entity. The final perception of a sculpture was the sum total of the different viewpoints that go into creating a single, but still divided, mental image. Such a perception was obstructed by naturalistic sculpture, in which the work was envisaged as the imitation of a living organism expressed in terms of volume. This obliged the viewer to go around the sculpture, which in turn served to heighten its naturalistic effect. The modern sculptor could restore art's spiritual vocation by exploiting the possibilities offered by treating the surface as planar projections; in this way, "it is possible to capture the whole richness of the work in a single point, and to enrich this point by the suggestion of other points". And this was feasible for Gutfreund because sculpture's vision was a vision of surface. Even the real space within which the sculptor's work took shape could be thought of as an ensemble of surfaces.

Thus, for Gutfreund, the flatness of the image suggested that it was only possible to construct form that was geometrical, and that the abstract geometric surface was the basis of the sculptor's vision. This was the *raison d'être* of the new relief sculpture, which remained close to the surface – the mother of the image. The final creation was the ensemble of the geometric body born of abstract vision and real form.[9]

As far as the members of the group were concerned, the result of this fusion of abstraction and geometry was a reduced expression of sensibility in favour of investigations into the structure of the image's projection. The more advanced Parisian Cubism was also beginning to gain influence, thanks in part to the art historian Vincenc Kramar. Since 1911, Kramar had established a remarkable collection of works, mainly by Picasso and Braque, purchased from the Kahnweiler

Josef Čapek, *The Accordionist,* 1913. Oil on canvas, 99 x 72 cm. Prague, National Gallery.

collage as a device, except to imitate it in paint. He gradually reinstated colour, and his new symbols became increasingly lyrical and intimist. Beneš later destroyed the many paintings he produced during this period. In Procházka's work, Parisian Cubism was reflected in more decorative paintings with a more spontaneous use of colour. Gutfreund remained closest to Filla. The lapidary forms of his sculptures from 1912 to 1914 became more structured and his work along this line reached its peak with wood sculptures – still intact today – that bordered on concrete art.

From the outset, the group's cubist leanings met with incomprehension from the older critics. By 1912, even Šalda, who took the young artists seriously and gave them his personal encouragement, was perplexed

Emil Filla, *Bathers,* 1912. Oil on canvas, 125 x 83.5 cm. Prague, National Gallery.

Gallery; some of these were included in the group's exhibitions, which greatly stimulated Czech artists. The third exhibition organized by the group in Prague in May 1913 showed nine works by Picasso, eleven by Braque, five by Derain and two by Gris.

Filla and Gutfreund were the first to be inspired by the great Cubists in Paris, followed, although less intensely, by Vincenc Beneš and Antonín Procházka. Initially, Filla combined various analytic, hermetic and synthetic aspects of Cubism in his work; he rarely used

Václav Špála, *The Three Washerwomen*, 1913. Oil on canvas, 72 x 81.5 cm. Prague, National Gallery.

by their new conceptualization: "These gentlemen are serving up formulae and diagrams, not works of art or individual expressions of their rich experiences. It could be that this kind of art is what will be fed to people in centuries to come, but such drastic abstraction has no charm for me other than that of cold, detached astonishment in the face of a bizarre hypothesis."[10] As for Arnošt Procházka, whose *Moderní revue* had become extremely isolated since Marten's departure, he adopted a totally negative attitude toward this art.

But there was also dissidence within the group itself, and by the end of 1912 the painters Josef Čapek, Václav Špála and Ladislav Šíma, the decorator Vratislav Hugo Brunner and the architects Vlastislav Hofman and Josef Chochol had left in protest against the "orthodox" cubist wing. The seceding group was headed by Josef Čapek, who, together with the French poet Alexandre Mercereau, organized the exhibition entitled Modern Art on the Mánes Union's premises. This event was the pretext for a tremendous confrontation, including a certain amount of personal vituperation, between the two different wings of the young avant-garde. Čapek's stance was vaguely labelled "futurist" and his overall attitude condemned as being detrimental to modern

Vratislav Nechleba, poster for the 31st exhibition of the Mánes Union of Artists, The Independents, 1910. Colour lithograph, 126 x 95 cm. Prague, UPM.

went to Paris in 1914. Even to painters who were not unconditional admirers of Picasso and Braque, Cubism represented the fundamental possibility of moving away from the traditional concept of art that respected life in its natural appearances. Basing their work on Cubism, Čapek and Špála created a new type of figurative painting, for which Čapek drew his inspiration from the city and Špála from the countryside. Their achievements were to become particularly important after the war, when they found themselves addressing a transformed society in the name of modern art.

As a form of expression, pre-war Cubism was also apparent in the work of artists who did not adhere to modernism, among them Jan Konůpek and even Jan Štursa, whose Neo-Classicism occasionally showed expressive features borrowed from Cubism (the reliefs on the Mánes bridge in 1913, for example). However, it was the competition organized in 1913 for the monument to the national hero Jan Žižka that really brought out the influence of Cubism. The monument was to be built on Vitkov Hill, on the site of Žižka's legendary victorious battle in 1420 against the anti-Hussites, which saved Prague. The site overlooks the city, and it is easy to understand the project's importance to national artistic prestige. Competitors even submitted projects for restructuring the entire summit of the hill, as well as for combining the monument with a commemorative building, and artists of every generation took part in the contest.

The event caught the attention of Czech journalists of all political persuasions, and this so complicated the jury's task of selection that they retained none of the projects submitted to them, although two were considered particularly interesting. One was František Bílek's, which proposed a ten-metre-high Žižka approached by an avenue formed of twenty great rocks whose obscure form suggested the personification of the entire Hussite epic. Although the "Czech" and "Slav" dimension of the project was easily acceptable, the jury found Bílek's conception of the main figure too emotive and religious, and too far from Žižka's warrior image. The other project of interest was submitted by Jan Štursa and Jan Kotěra, and emphasized Žižka's military image with an

art. The exhibition presented works by "small-time Cubists" such as Louis Marcoussis, Albert Gleizes, Jean Metzinger and André Lhote, but also works by Robert Delaunay, Raoul Dufy, Piet Mondrian, Alexander Archipenko, Constantin Brancusi and other Modernists who were shortly to become famous. At that point, however, conditions were still not ripe for their works to be understood or well received in Prague.

Be that as it may, this contact with Cubism was extremely fruitful for Czech art. Filla and Gutfreund were determined to get to the heart of Cubism and so

The Šupich building, 1913–1916.
Prague New Town (Wenceslas Square 38). Arch.: Matěj Blecha.

imposing statue of the hero on horse-back, accompanied by fighting men brandishing shields. Realism was less important here than the overall rhythm in the mass of the whole monument, which expressed offensive resistance. This time, the monumentality of the project could be appreciated from a distance, but not at close quarters. Furthermore, the jury found even less congenial the "irritating Germanic touch" suggested by the attempt to command impact through the strength of brute matter alone.

The unresolved outcome of the competition revealed the great difficulty presented by the confrontation between the conceptions of independent artists, on the one hand, and on the other, a public opinion shaped by "typical" ideas about national heroes that derived from the work of artists such as Josef Václav Myslbek and

The Adam Pharmacy, 1911–1913. Prague New Town (Wenceslas Square 8). Arch.: Matěj Blecha and Emil Králíček.

Mikoláš Aleš in the second half of the nineteenth century. It was significant, however, that the artists themselves – even the most avant-garde among them – were ready to accept such a confrontation. A fairly marked cubist influence was apparent in the projects submitted for the competition, particularly those for architectural works. Besides the architects Vlastislav Hofman and Josef Gočár, Ladislav Machoň, Čenek Vořech, Vladimír Fultner and the young Bedřich Feuerstein also made daring use of the cubist principle of crystallization. The most radical of the projects in this vein, however, was that presented by Otto Gutfreund and Pavel Janák, whose Žižka was totally integrated into a dynamic cubic structure. This was a fundamental departure from the static quality of the traditional monument.

Such massive participation by the avant-garde Cubists in a major official competition throws a clear light on the particularity of Czech Cubism. Whereas in Paris at that time Cubism was the concern of an elite, in Prague it was seen as the basis for a new style expressing a modern creativity, an artistic concept that started from the social *Zeitgeist* in examining its own epoch. This explains why Czech Cubism spread from painting and sculpture to architecture and the applied arts, and even into other cultural areas such as the theatre.

Architecture was key to this implantation of the new modern style. Naturalist Art Nouveau architecture survived in Prague almost until the 1920s, and still had a high profile when the Municipal building was erected in 1904–1912. The emergence of the synthetist decorative style, represented especially by Jan Kotěra and his students at the School of Applied Arts, had began around 1905. Nonetheless, older architects, with different training, also adopted the new trend toward planar geometry and the Viennese-inspired decorative concepts. There was also an influential wave of orientalism and exoticism, though it was related less to primitive Synthetism than to esoteric and hermetic Symbolism. This led to a proliferation of strange adornments on apartment buildings in Prague around 1910, with a decorative geometrism ranging from abstract ornamentation to figurative representation of every kind.

The most important of these works were executed by the building firm owned by Matěj Blecha. Young architects worked with Blecha, including Kotěra's pupil Bohumil Waigant and Emil Králíček, who had studied with Josef Maria Olbrich in Darmstadt. Their collaboration produced some interesting buildings on Wenceslas Square, such as the Golden Goose Hotel (1909–1910), with its gables supported by altas figures; the Adam Pharmacy (1911–1913), whose decorative elements combined the archaism of Greek Antiquity with the luxurious elegance of modern materials, and the massive-looking Šupich department store (1913–1916), with its Assyrian-style masks emphasizing the vertical articulation of the wall. Antonín Pfeiffer's project for the Koruna Building (1912–1914), selected in preference to the one submitted by his teacher, Kotěra, developed a more lyrical conception and was set within a block of other buildings on the same square.

The decorative geometrical style was characterized by relationships developed on two different levels: first, between the basic form and its decoration, and second, between the building's rational and modern functionality – including comfort and sanitation – and its symbolic decor. Decorative references could range anywhere from reminiscences of the Empire and the Biedermeier styles (an apartment building by František Weyr and Richard Klenka z Vlastimilu in Prague-Josefov in 1911), to the uncompromising exoticism of the Šupich department store.

It appears, however, that this dualism was no longer acceptable to the young avant-garde architects, who were already searching in their pre-cubist work for a more unifying concept. Pavel Janák, for example, resolved the body of the construction of his Hlávka bridge (1909–1912) into a powerful, dominant curve. For his part, Josef Gočár appalled the judges of a competition for the Old Town Hall annex with his project for a pyramid so high that it would have loomed above all the towers in the historic neighbourhoods of Prague, drastically changing the city's look.

Cubism in architecture represented more than just the cohabitation of function and art, which had finally turned into a solid Classicism. Art was given priority, even if this meant going to extremes. Nonetheless, this did not eliminate respect for cultural traditions. Baroque Gothic, which was spectacularly represented in eighteenth-century Bohemia by J. B. Santini (whose work was being studied by art historians at the time), interested the young Cubists as a model of creative

The "Black Virgin" building, entrance door, 1911–1912. Prague Old Town (Ovocný trh 19). Arch.: Josef Gočár.

stylistic evolution in architecture, just like El Greco in painting. Similarly, Gothic architecture was a source of inspiration for Hofman's only partly finished entrance pavilions to the Prague-Ďáblice Cemetery (1912), as well as for Josef Chochol's apartment house in Prague-Vyšehrad (1912–1913), perhaps the most unadulteratedly cubist building in Prague. The "Black Virgin" building (1911–1912) built by Josef Gočár in the Old Town showed traces of a Classical Empire style. References like these were not, however, throwbacks to historicism: Prague Cubism was perfectly original, and had its own viewpoint on the past.

The Cubists' ambition was to create a new style; their interest went beyond the general composition of the facades, encompassing details and the interior decoration of their buildings. Their models were the group's exhibition decors, based on the crystal form. The furnishings and accessories were made by the Prague Art Workshops, set up in 1912.

Despite limited production possibilities, the cubist furniture designed by Janák, Hofman, and especially Gočár demonstrated the importance these young archi-

tects attached to style. Some magnificent pieces – such as Gočár's display cabinet and sideboard – were shown at the Werkbund exhibition in Cologne in 1914. Their avant-garde forms featured a striking central recessed effect, but the most impressive thing about them was their size. To better understand this conception, it is helpful to examine an architectural detail on the facade of the "Black Virgin" building. The facade, which creates the effect of an imposing mass thanks to the mansard roof, is in fact inverted – in other words, the facade is designed on the basis of a central tension. The interior/exterior relationship is handled in such a way that one seems to be inside a great, artistically designed

ABOVE: Facade detail, c. 1910. Vinohrady (Chopinova 6). Arch.: Bohumil Waigant.

LEFT: Ornamental metalwork, Adam Pharmacy.

FACING PAGE: Koruna building, 1912–1914. Prague New Town (Wenceslas Square 1–3). Arch.: Antonín Pfeiffer.

crystal. The essential element is the visual effect of the shape, which is conceived as a mass unfolding in space and as a concrete expression of the spiritual abstraction of the mass.

In 1913, *Styl* published an article by Hofman entitled "On the Secession", which summarized the evolution of modern architecture from the young generation's point of view. Hofman spoke of the Secession as a "vision of a time now past", yet also emphasized its modern aspects. The Secession had represented "the spontaneous application of the potential of current forms". The path it followed in pursuit of new formal concepts took it through the free world of nature, toward mobile, consistently functional forms. In plant shapes it found the means of expressing its intuition of the importance of construction, although in a different manner from Otto Wagner's approach to the technical structure of matter. Ornamental elements acquired a strange, mysterious quality that was felt by the group as a whole. The Secession was not merely a matter of taste; it gave expression to its own milieu; it was democratic, and took account of folk traditions as well as prehistoric and "primitive" and tribal art. Essentially it held that a kind of synthesis, or a reciprocal link, existed between things, as though sap-filled substances that expressed themselves through the form of the unifying line ultimately grew together. This was completely different from the ancient Greek systems based on the right-angled intersection of vertical and horizontal lines.

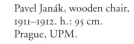

Pavel Janák, wooden chair, 1911–1912. h.: 95 cm. Prague, UPM.

Alongside this notion of pure Secession, Hofman also discussed Viennese "modern art", which had become increasingly concerned with space and the cubic surface of physical objects. However, he criticized the Viennese modernists' return to the Empire tradition and the bourgeois Biedermeier style. In his view, the new architectonic concept could "once again acknowledge pure Secession, in which the potential expansion of sculpture and space is inherent, whereas Viennese modern art is static and impassive". For similar reasons, Hofman defended the Secession against the new Classicism. "Classicists" were characterized by a taste for traditional, calm beauty and a sense of harmony that found the contemporary environment intolerable. They attempted to escape by turning to "the eternal forms of tradition". Modern "evolutive artists", on the other hand, felt close to the throb of contemporary life, to its sensibilities and intensity, which led them toward the discovery of new forms. Their architecture tended to grow out of "visions born of their conception of the movement of matter and its internal organization. Antiquity appropriated material very slowly, piling it up like boxes and planks; to the modern sensibility, this way of doing things is lifeless." Classical design should be broken down along the lines of modern architectonic thinking, "into slanted, uneven surfaces with a non-static look, mobile, sharp and acute-angled, rather than calm (triangular arrangements are indeed the most logical way of constructing materials), so that the result is as organized and controlled as a natural phenomenon. The Secession also tried to achieve something similar with its plastic principle; nowadays, however, a different treatment and a different architectural structure are needed."[11]

Hofman's text shows that the debate over the new style that was so fundamental to the emerging new Czech culture had given rise to two principal lines of action. These differed in the importance of the role they attributed to art itself. The Synthetism advocated by Šalda emphasized the "heroic view" and the artist's creative act, which he saw as an irreplaceable "service rendered to life" on the emotional plane. This conception was contrary to that of the Decadents, who saw an unavoidable antagonism between art and "natural" life; nonetheless, the two approaches managed to coexist peaceably enough among the young artists. Šalda's programme tended to lead to the Primitivist and then Neo-

There is an important difference here, however. Slavíček's Pantheist vision was relentlessly swept away by time, and his Impressionism lasted but a brief moment; whereas by arresting the psychic current, Gutfreund made it "eternal", embodied it in a geometrical form, and so transformed its natural energy into a spiritual force.

LEFT: Josef Gočár, sideboard, 1912–1913. Stained oak, 200 x 148 x 58 cm. Prague, UPM.

RIGHT: Antonín Slavíček, *View over Trója*, 1908. Oil, 144 x 193 cm. Prague, National Gallery.

Classical Utopia of the golden age of humanity. Cubism had the same faith in the absolute power of art, even if it construed the latter in a dynamic sense, as the expression of creative will.

In 1908, Antonín Slavíček painted one of his finest works, *View over Trója*. The picture depicts a river full of drifting ice in an early spring landscape. Its lyrical Impressionism transforms line into a representation of the very process of living growth. The artist's active participation in the dramatic events on nature's stage generates a spiritual energy whereby the entire universe is perceived emotionally. In an article written in 1912 entitled "Surface and Volume", Otto Gutfreund's description of a piece of sculpture could almost paraphrase Slavíček's painting: "incessantly rippling surfaces, an illusion of volumes, undulations and faith that reveal the depths underlying the surface, rippling waves whose ever-moving currents reflect fragments of reality".[12]

Epilogue

The First World War broke out after the Sarajevo assassination in the summer of 1914. At first everyone thought it would end quickly, but it lasted four long, bloody years that brought the chapter of cultural and artistic renewal to a close. For Bohemia, the war meant immense suffering and bitter sacrifice on behalf of an Austro-Hungarian monarchy whose authority had long been challenged.

The psychological impact of the war on artists is poignantly reflected in *Hanged Man,* a painting Kubišta produced in Pula, where he was serving as an artillery officer. Kubišta had been obliged to sink a French submarine that had entered the port, for which he was severely criticized in Prague. The painting was probably a reaction to this event as well as to his being forcefully dragged away from the creative work that was the sole purpose of his existence.[1] At that time, Kubišta had explicitly rejected Cubism, which in his opinion remained on the surface of things; he sought instead to penetrate "into the spiritual domain". *Hanged Man* was a more universal reflection on life and death, symbolized by combinations of triangles. The painting's pessimism was accentuated by the harsh reality of the rope and its powerful chiaroscuro, but its geometric structure nonetheless gave it another dimension: the idea behind the painting was probably that of an end to existence in the material world, an initiatory death as a necessary stage on the path to transsubstantiation. This explains the light colour of the inverted triangle, as well as the three-sided pyramid above the hanged man's head, with its summit pointing toward the viewer.

When the war ended, Kubišta returned to Prague full of new projects, but he suffered a relapse after an attack of Spanish influenza and died in a military hospital. The posthumous exhibition of his work organized in 1920 by Jan Zrzavý was addressed to the new postwar generation. Since then, Kubišta has been considered one of the pillars of Czech modern art: his lonely struggle was not in vain. His tombstone, which was created by František Bílek, bears the inscription "Master life with strong artistry".

František Kupka, *Cosmic Spring*, 1911–1920. Oil on canvas, 111 x 125 cm. Prague, National Gallery.

Kubišta's austere work resounds with the ardent, mystical, ascetic side of Czech Symbolism, which is closely related to modern Primitivism and Existentialism. Jan Zrzavý then picked up its more lyrical and erotic elements. He too painted subjects inspired by the war, including *The Good Samaritan, Affliction* and *The Widow,* whose subjects are purified by colour. Zrzavý later wrote a text explaining his basic concept of colour: it partook of vision and hence had no tactile meaning; it was an attribute of matter that paradoxically enabled the artist to give immaterial expression to the universe's materiality. To do so, however, the artist had to replace the light and shade of actual objects with his own colours – in other words, by the polarity of black and white encompassing the range of contrasts of all other hues. With sensitive handling of colour, the painter could express every human feeling, because in nature and life all things were connected, everything was born of the tension between the two basic poles of activity and passivity.[2] Zrzavý's system enabled him to give his paintings – which consisted mainly of primitive symbolic signs – a mysterious unity, expressed in a luminous radiation of colour. In his *Portrait of Mrs. D.* (1917), the figure is reflected in a symphony of blues and reds, between the sleeping lunar landscape and nature's esoteric, secret flame in man. The red, white and blue astral flowers in the backgound represent the synthesis of psychic and cosmic forces. With this picture, emanating its mysterious force, Zrzavý already paved the way for postwar poetism.

Kubišta's virile severity and Zrzavý's feminine melancholy were both manifestations of the inner polarity that had been present in Czech culture since the turn of the century, and that was in large measure responsible for its vitality. This polarity was not simply a matter of differences among individual creators. It was a far deeper and broader phenomenon that affected the very fundamentals of the new Czech culture. One essential, recurring issue was the relationship between art and nature. This was actually the title of a dialogue written by Šalda in 1912, in which two friends, a painter and a poet, are walking in the abandoned gardens of a castle. The setting inspires a reflective exchange, but the friends' conclusions differ.[3] The painter upholds nature's importance to art, and describes the ecstasy he feels, far from the city in the solitude of the forest and the mountains. He has the impression of going back to

a world that is "younger, darker and more sensual", where he becomes the instrument of a higher, nameless force that eventually exhausts him, leaving him sick and melancholy. The poet retorts that what he finds intoxicating is a cultural, refined, reflective state that gives rise to a style that goes against the grain, and which is possible only in the great cities. Only there has history created a sufficient accumulation of wealth and a cultural base to make this possible. He views nature itself as something negative, a misconception, death in disguise, chaos and ruin, against which art provides a bulwark. In art, all that counts is nature that has become human and cultivated, "living off these few centimetres of fertile humus that contain the decomposed bones of all our ancestors on this planet".

Šalda's dialogue illustrates the dilemma of a turn-of-the-century generation of artists who rejected the ideologically official "national art" inherited from nineteenth-century cultural policy, and was trying to find a new framework for expressing its own sensibilities. Šalda certainly opposed excessive sentiment in the relationship with nature, which had been a principle of the lyrical Impressionism he had once defended in his emotive analysis of Rodin's work. He no longer respected impressionist theories, which he considered pseudo-scientific. The Impressionist page had been turned. Furthermore, the greatest of the Czech Impressionists were dead and gone: Antonín Slavíček committed suicide in 1910, when he realized that the paralysis he suffered as a result of a stroke meant that he would never paint again, and Miloš Jiránek died the following year. However, alongside the few imitators of Impressionism appeared a young painter whose work combined the lyrical heritage of Impressionism, the new concept of colour of Fauvism and the content of Expressionism. This painter was Jindřich Prucha. In his different versions of *The Beech Forest* – a recurrent theme throughout his work – Prucha expressed a state of emotion before nature as pure as the painter's in Šalda's dialogue, pushing the cult of visual union with nature to its limits. Unfortunately, Prucha disappeared prematurely, swept up in the deadly maelstrom of the First World War.

The concept of Synthetism and the new style propounded by Šalda since the 1890s, which found a favourable echo among leading Czech artists, saw nature as the basis for regenerating the new art. This view also stimulated the interest in landscape painting and fostered the success of naturalistic decorativism. Nevertheless, from the outset the emphasis was on the artist's creativity, the development of his individuality and artistic nature, and his creative will. The demands of a new artistic ethos thus made themselves felt: although art was no longer regimented, there was an increasing conviction that its true strength lay in its ability to give a determined form and meaning to nature, instinct and chance. Hence the view that naturalism was "suicidal", while in mature Synthetism, imagination became divorced from the fantastical and was considered "a great theoretical force of spirituality", with its own laws leading toward formal purity. The inherent originality of such imagination invariably went hand in hand with a positive, lively attitude to tradition. In this sense, Šalda, who admired Neo-Classicism's form and its attempts to express "human grandeur", attempted its revival. At the same time, however, he drew attention to the danger of form being convertd into formula, and to the risk that a new dogmatism might hamper the rational search for the living essence of art.[4]

This evolution in Synthetism's doctrine brought figurative art and architecture back to the fore. In sculpture, this meant moving away from Rodin's dramatic, ultimately naturalist conception and toward the stylization and "architectonic" composition inherent in the new archaism and Neo-Classicism. Even sculptors belonging to the "Rodin generation" took part in this evolution. Josef Mařatka created *Perseverance and Strength,* a group of larger-than-life Neo-Classical sculptures for the facade of the new Town Hall built by Polívka in 1911. But Jan Štursa remained the major figure in this trend. For all their stylization, the older sculptors still continued to see sculpture as an imitation of the body in its natural unity. On the other hand, Štursa, who had learned from Gauguin's Synthetism and Derain's Primitivism, treated the body as an ensemble of elementary volumes in a lively, classically balanced relationship. A good example of Štursa's approach is his *Dancer at Rest,* sculpted in 1913, in which he achieved a perfect balance between formal restraint and the subject's rich sensual and emotional content. In Štursa's case, this new style was grounded in extensive collaboration with architects and wide experience in decorative sculpture. In the latter field, he introduced a new monumentalism in, for example, the

Jan Štursa, *Dancer at Rest*, 1913. Bronze, 118 cm. Prague, National Gallery.

group of sculptures *Work* and *Humanity* (1912–1913) for the pylons of Hlávka bridge. There, he created a lively array of athletic "Greek" male and female figures in standing and kneeling positions. Štursa's almost instinctive avoidance of the pitfalls of abstract stylization and dogmatic formulae that Šalda had warned against made him a leading figure in the resurgence of Czech Classicism.

Štursa's ready involvement in architectural projects emerged straight from this sense of the living tectonic qualities of form. Jan Kotěra noticed him at a very early

Jindřich Prucha, *The Beech Forest,* 1911. Oil on canvas, 84 x 95.5 cm. Prague, National Gallery.

stage, and invited the sculptor to work with him on several projects. These included the Villa Bianca in Prague-Bubeneč (1910–1913) – for which Štursa created two sculptures, *Day* and *Night,* that bear traces of Bourdelle and the Czech Baroque – and the house built for the composer Urbanek in Prague New Town (1912–1913), where *Orpheus* and *Eurydice* appear on the consoles.

Like most architects at the time, Kotěra exchanged his pencil for the compass. His project for the facade of the University building (1913–1914) was no less complex than the geometrical creations of the young Cubist architects. The difference lay in Kotěra's rigorously symmetrical circular composition, with its sure-handed balance of materials, as opposed to the young architects' radical geometry. Kotěra's geometrical triangulation can be considered classic, and was an example of the sense of tradition and rationalism that signalled a new style toward the end of Synthetism. Fortunately, however, Kotěra avoided the temptation of comfortable traditionalism, as was demonstrated by his building for the General Pensions Bureau in Prague New Town (1912–1913), for which Josef Zasche designed the interiors. This work proved that Synthetism could also be appropriately applied to a large public building, and that Kotěra was perfectly capable of combining the

Jan Zrzavý, *Portrait of Mrs. D.*, 1917. Oil on canvas, 45 x 43 cm. Prague, Private Collection.

functional and the decorative to obtain a solemnity suitable to the pension bureau's humanitarian mission. Kotěra's projects for university buildings in front of the Čech bridge were equally complicated. He began work on these in 1906, and they were completed, with certain modifications, after his death. As far as the main elements were concerned, Kotěra abandoned both the structural dome-and-pillar combination characteristic of the Otto Wagner school, as well as the earlier monumental model of modern decorative style. He used instead a structure dominated by triangular gables, which gave vitality to the body of the building, and which apparently grew out of a controversy over the romanticism of Czech Cubism in architecture. This did not constitute a rejection of Cubism, however, but rather an effort to make it more realistic. Before the war, Kotěra participated in a number of competitions for major public buildings; his architecture, which had paradoxically sprung out of decorative sources, was at its best in some of the tombs he built in Prague's cemeteries.

Of special interest in the later period of Kotěra's Synthetism, which also included Neo-Classical tendencies, is the sense of balance that existed between functional and decorative elements and also between the personal and the official, in contrast to the somewhat uncompromising Cubism and Cubo-Expressionism and their spiritualization of art at all costs, which tended to overwhelm the viewer. Yet it must be said that young avant-garde radicalism was expressed in many different ways. During the years prior to World War I, there was a surge of critical analysis not only of politics and social institutions, but also of art and its achievements. This criticism went far beyond everyday polemics and took on new, sweeping forms in which the absurdities of modern life were represented by stingingly provocative, often blasphemous, pseudo-artistic creations.

Literature, in particular, was affected by a cult of banality, and witnessed an interest in minor genres that was a deliberate provocation to "serious art", and which used glosses, short stories and even newspaper reports and cabaret songs to expose society's new cultural conventions. Among those associated with this trend were poets, including František Gellner and the satirical writer Jaroslav Hašek, who later became famous for

Statues by Stanislav Sucharda and Josef Mařatka on the facade of the new Town Hall, 1910–1911, stone.
Prague Old Town (Marianské náměstí).

The Good Soldier Švejk, but also the "rabid reporter" Egon Ervín Kisch and a number of other writers who, because of their popular leanings, were determined to situate themselves on the marginal literary fringe.[5] The former anarchist and Satanist Stanislav Kostka Neumann, who was apparently equally inspired by Karl Kraus's Viennese periodical Die Fackel (The Torch) and the Futurist manifestoes, lent considerable weight to this tendency. In Lidové noviny (The People's Journal), he defended the very avant-garde Almanac of the Year 1914. He condemned aestheticism, Decadence, Symbolism, Impressionism, the exaltation of folklore and all "single-stringed artists", and lauded "the liberated word", current modern trends, the culture of exploration and discovery, and "modern art, life that goes by, and everyday art".[6]

This programme became an important component of modern Czech culture at the point when Czech society was withdrawing from the Austro-Hungarian Empire, rejecting its structures and mentality, and opening up to the radically new horizon of the independent Republic of Czechoslovakia. Although it superseded Šalda's Synthetism, it too attempted to link art to life, but it did so by rejecting all preconceived notions as to the educational function of art. Its source of inspiration was no longer nature, but the urban universe and the aesthetics of the machine. After the war, the cult of the machine led directly to the definitive rejection of the turn-of-the-century decorative style and its love of nature, and its whole conception, which was by then considered totally outmoded, became material for caricature.

In the arts, this new mentality was reflected in an evolution of Cubism. Differences of opinion led to systematic criticism and thus to pluralism. The technique of collage doomed the concept of the organic unity of a work of art, and set off a process of artistic re-evaluation of commonplace materials. Structure took on a dynamism very different from the serene equilibrium of the synthetic decorative style, as can be seen in some of the sculptures made by Otto Gutfreund during his unfortunate internment in a prisoner of war camp in southern France. (He was detained there in error, after having fought gallantly with the French in the Somme, Artois and Champagne in 1915 as a non-commissioned officer in the Czech unit of the Foreign Legion.) It seems that the salvaged wood he used was not simply the only material available, but also provided the means of a "civil" expression that, paradoxically, completed the unusual constructivism of the works.

Similarly, certain sketches by the architect Josef Chochol, although restrained, were very characteristic of this evolution. These drawings dated from the period when Vlastislav Hofman had designed a large complex of residential and public buildings, embodying Cubo-Expressionism's grand ambitions in urban architecture, to be established on the land around the Baroque fortress of Vyšehrad, overlooking the Vltava River. Chochol, who at the time had been distancing himself in his writings from the subjective and pictorial elements in Czech cubist architecture, proposed pure, smooth white facades devoid of ornamentation, with wholly geometrical rhythms; his projects already anticipated post-war architecture.

Looking at these new secret weapons, which were not actually put to immediate use, the art of the 1890s might seem to be a relic of bygone days. That generation itself also vanished prematurely, as though its mission had been accomplished. Slavíček and Jiránek, who went to their graves in 1916, were followed by the sculptor Stanislav Sucharda and then, at the end of the war, by the painter Jan Preisler, who died of complications from pneumonia. Preisler's last sketches were studies for *The Temptation,* a large, privately commissioned painting on a subject that was constantly present in his work, which Preisler must have gone back to during the war with a touch of melancholy. Near a wood in which an allegorical female figure is plucking ripe fruit from a tree, the hero is surrounded by fairies, who possibly represent the senses, trying to catch his attention. He does not seem to be paying attention to these voices from life, nor does he attempt to protect himself behind a shiny shield, as would a knight of old. The hero appears in three different forms: usually as a peasant boy, but also as a nude young man covered with drapery or a rider on a white horse. He is, therefore, a poet. His dreamy appearance and vacant, staring eyes seem to be looking at another image that is reflected emotionally in the warm colour, the fairies' vivacity and the serenity of autumn.

Preisler condensed all his experience as a painter and as a poet into these little sketches. This ability to define and express the very heart of his artistic concerns made him the ideal representative of an epoch. Although art of the period had extremely high aims, it raised first and foremost the issue of individualism and the artist's own personality, as if to mete out a kind of metaphysical punishment to any artist who dared stray from the comfortable path of nationalism and social conventions. Artists working at the turn of the century did not drift into the Utopia of a collective solution to this issue. Rather, they intuitively recognized the need to transcend egoism and create a coherent system based on new, truly universal fundamentals. Hence their new style, and their effort to create the total work, an organic unity, with a harmony of colour, a correlation between lines and surfaces, and a unity of form. This solution soon became common, but was later rejected as being purely decorative: the work of art was now conceived as an object, with its own intrinsic meaning. In fact, this showed a failure to understand the initial decorative style. Originally, the symbolist picture was only intended to be the mirror in which the modern Narcissus observed himself – not to further his self-admiration, but in order to understand the painting as an organic entity, an integral part of the natural order, which was symbolically present in the painting's microcosm.

This failure explains why Šalda criticized the young Cubists and their abstractions for their lack of the "deep, warm flow of creative intuition". He also affirmed that the source of art lay in "the deepest mysteries of a noble personality", and that dogma would never replace the "cosmic theatre" of the battle between that personality and objective, external conditions.[7]

Šalda's "noble personality" was of course the true artist, to whom painting was not an end in itself but a source of self-confidence and the means to express his values and his abilities. The artist's need for intuition is his need to be linked to the higher entity. This cosmological perspective was subsequently developed by other artists, including Jan Preisler's students, especially Josef Šíma, who rediscovered these verities and confirmed them in his post-war work. They also included veterans of the preceding generation, who were not directly exposed to the stricture of this programme.

During the 1920s, František Kupka painted a series of canvases called *Cosmic Spring,* which is a hymn to the miracle of the vital circuit of cosmic energies, crystallizing into magical, enchanting organic and inorganic forms. In these works, identification of the flower (the

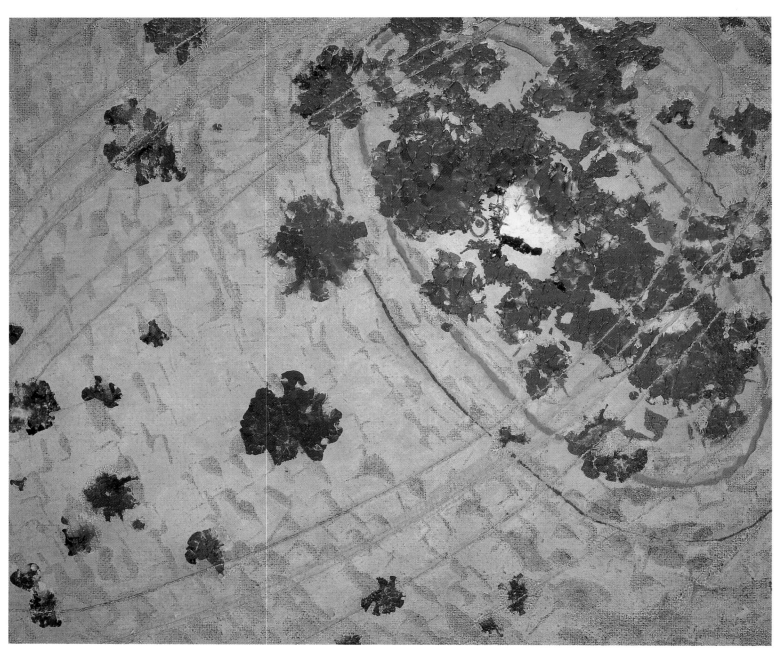

Vojtěch Preissig, *The Earth Is Born,* 1936. Mixed technique, 60.5 x 72 cm. Prague, National Gallery.

symbol of art) with the universe is transformed into a symphonic orchestration of the painter's ideas. Kupka's close binding of the plenitude of the senses and emotions with a cosmic conception could only be hinted at by the decorative forms of Art Nouveau. Nonetheless, the enthusiastic, vitalistic attitude of *Cosmic Spring* did not prevent the emergence of an abstract mode of

thought that found its counterpart in objectivation. Kupka too had to follow in the current of machine aesthetics before the universalist content of the earlier ornamentalism could be transposed onto a new, concrete basis.

Vojtěch Preissig drew inspiration from Kupka in 1920, and he later went far beyond his early specialization in graphic work. After his return to Bohemia in the 1930s, he created a set of pictures that summarized his technical investigations and also culminated his work on an ideological level. At first sight, the work appears heterogeneous, and lacking in what might be called "unity of style". Its forms are a mixture of linear, geometrical elements and very free pictorial content, and the effect is a kaleidoscopic vision in which organic and geometric principles are imaginatively combined. And yet in Preissig's series there is no lack of unity, however infrequently it may appear. This is because Preissig's is a completely new style, which, while it does not correspond to any particular morphological constants or modes, respects the structural variety of nature. Thus it is a respect for the diversity of the real, expressed in its totality by the imaginary. What is involved here is not imitation of the phenomena considered, but the expression of the correlation between general events and processes through plastic symbols that assume a variety of forms. Beside Kupka and his monumental demonstration, Preissig appears more lyrical and more intimate, but in no way less penetrating.

The Earth Is Born (1936) was the final link in the chain in the pursuit of the universal pictorial symbol. The superimposition of bright splashes streaked by two ellipses held together by the creative gesture of the artist expresses the eternal dynamism of the universe. Interestingly, there is a second version of this painting, which is completely reversed, like a mirror-image of the first. Preissig's series also included other mirror-pictures, which might be explained by his experience with typography and printing techniques. The works were not completely identical, though, nor were they merely mechanical copies. One of the two was invariably darker, hinting at some story behind it. This was not the Genesis cycle, for which Mucha was then making sketches of a series of seven pictures showing a progression from formlessness to the eventual birth of Man/ Prometheus. Preissig preferred to create binary compositions, as shown by the titles of his other pictures: *Equilibrium-Disharmony, Concentration-Restlessness,* and *Harmony-Contrasts.* Furthermore, *The Earth Is Born* is marked by Preissig's concern for identical handling of its mirror counterpart.[8] If the identity of the pairs of paintings was intended to express the reflections of the macrocosm and the microcosm, then their synthesis – in other words, the universe – has to be sought

in the mind of the viewer or of the creator who made them.

Among the many artistic projects that materialized in Czech culture at the turn of the century, the most viable of all was this cosmological conception, which had been engendered by Symbolism and had absorbed a great deal from decorative ornamentalism and the strong sensuality of lyrical Impressionism. This synthesis had greatly stimulated the process of creation that led to a conception of the pictorial work as a symbol that embraced reality.

All of this became a part of the way in which people created their environment. Despite the destruction in recent years, Prague can still be admired today as a living organism composed of a remarkable blend of ancient history and modern times. The credit for this is largely due to the cultural offensive launched at the turn of the century, which established solid foundations in this city for an approach to modern life that has universal value.

Otto Gutfreund, *Seated Woman,* 1917. Wood, 30 cm. Prague, National Gallery.

Notes

Introduction

1. The political history of Czech society during the period of transition from the nineteenth to the twentieth century, as well as matters concerning the relationship between Czech political representation and the central Austro-Hungarian authorities, are dealt with in detail in Otto Urban's book *Ceská spolecnost* (Czech Society 1848–1918), Prague, 1982.

2. F. X. Šalda, "Težká kniha" (The weighty book), *Rozhledy*, 4, no. 11, August 1895, pp. 641–650, and no. 12, September 1895, pp. 709–721. Reproduced in F. X. Šalda: "Kritiké projevy II (1894–1895)," *Critical Articles II*, Prague, 1950, pp. 267–301. "Decisions must be taken. Choices have to be made. Good must be clung to and bad rejected. We must throw off uncertainty, vacillation, condescendence and indifference. Let us discard the deceptive liberalism that seeks to make bedfellows of the most disparate ideas; let us discard this liberalism of compromise, which in fact is lack of faith, scepticism, indecision and absence of cohesion that poisons the conscience and infects the mind. Let us free ourselves of the soporific potion of dilettantism, that bourgeois epicurean salon philosophy, which seems to me no more than a form of historical empiricism, defined by its virtuoso exponents Bourget and Lemaître as a cast of mind characterized by finesse and sensuality. For this attitude leads us to contemplate all modes of existence, understanding each but choosing none, because with the passion and precision of an antiquary, we take up the most diverse epochs and cultural and moral attitudes, but commit ourselves to none. Let us divest ourselves of what is after all the luxury constituted by unbridled consumption, obsessive collection of antiques, pursuit of period objects, boxes of historical costumes, museums representing every possible cut and fashion – no amount of this will ever give birth to a new style. And this is precisely what is needed: a new style, of a new order altogether, a univocal style that emanates from the soul, engendered from within and projected outward, reflecting its desires and needs: a way of life and a reason for living and dying. This is the real issue."

3. "Česká moderna" (Czech modernism), *Rozhledy*, 5, no. 1, October 1895.

4. *Lumír*, 10 June 1893.

5. *Almanach secese*, Prague, 1896.

6. F. X. Šalda, "Kotárce dekadence" (On the question of decadence), *Rozhledy*, 4, no. 7, April 1895, pp. 385–389, and no. 8, May 1895, pp. 449–455.

7. Ibid. "Through an exaggeratedly developed sensibility, through communication on an exclusively emotive level, through the magnetic somnolence that closes the reader's eyes as though the lids were weighted with lead, through the depressing languor, through an influence that enslaves, binds and crushes down, that seeps into the heavy, suffocating air, gripping the temples in a dizzying vice and befuddling the mind with drunken exhilaration. . . ."

8. K. Hlaváček, *Pozdě k ránu* (Late in the early hours), Prague, 1896. In the introduction to *Late in the early hours*, a selection of his writings published in *Moderní revue* in 1896, he wrote: "I have mixed the most delicate colours and drawn the subtlest lines; I have tried out harmonies in the deepest minor chords and composed in the most daring keys and tonalities before beginning to materialize my visions. Capturing all that is sublime, mysterious, pallid and fearful within a web of delicate mystification, irony and warm intimacy, creating in a few sister-souls the blaze of a brief magical incantation, a mysterious, enchanted rare atmosphere evoked by these few words: late in the early hours – that is my role, my *raison d'être*."

9. F. X. Šalda, *Jan Voborník*, "o poesii Julia Zeyera" (On the poetry of Julius Zeyer), *Literarni listy*, XVIII, no. 22, September 1897, Prague, 1949, pp. 11–54.

10. F. X. Šalda, "Synthetism v novém umění" (Synthetism in the new art), *Literarni listy*, XIII, nos. 1–8, December 1891–April 1892. Reproduced in F. X. Šalda, *Critical Articles I* (1892–1893), Prague, 1949, pp. 11–54.

11. See O. Březina's letter to A. Pammrová on 15 November 1896. Quoted by E. Chalupný in his article "Tvorba a ohlas doma" (Creation and its echo in the country), *Stavitel chrámu, Památník básníka a myslitele Otokara Březiny*, Prague, 1941, pp. 155–197.

12. Ibid. Letter from O. Březina to F. X. Šalda. Březina's oddity did not mean that he was in any way an outcast. The critics considered him a serious poet but found Machar's irony and Sova's psychologism and lyrical exaltation more easily accessible, and Březina was accepted only gradually. Šalda himself had the same reaction, despite the fact that Březina had enthusiastically welcomed his programme and told him that he wanted to "build, and finally prepare the synthesis of all syntheses".

13. Letter no. 14 in Franz Kafka, *Briefe 1902–1924, Gesammelte Werke*, Frankfurt am Main, 1950.

The 1890s
On the threshold to modernity

1. *Jubilejní výstava zemská království Českého v Praze 1891* (The 1891 Prague Jubilee Exhibition of the countries of the Kingdom of Bohemia), Prague, 1894, p. 147. Münzberger (who was related to Ignác Ullman, the first Czech architect to work in the Neo-Renaissance style) had earlier built the town hall in the Karlín suburb of Prague during the 1880s, and was also the creator of the prestigious Palacký bridge.

2. Ibid., p. 154.

3. Ibid.

4. *The Works of Hubert Gordon Schauer*, Prague, 1917. The building remained permanently in the Prague Exhibitions Park and was later used to house other major events, including the 1895 Ethnographic Exhibition and the 1898 Architecture and Engineering Exhibition, both of which had a marked influence on the younger generation.

5. M. Jiránek, *Hanuš Schwaiger*, Prague, 1912, p. 30.

6. *Jubilehní výstava*, op. cit., p 1.

7. See M. Mzyková, *Vojtěch Hynais*, Prague, 1990, p. 103.

8. J. V. Myslbek, *Korespondence* (Correspondence), catalogued by A. Lodr, Prague, 1960, p. 187.

9. Vrchlický considered this statue an outstanding piece in Myslbek's work, and referred to it in one of the very beautiful sonnets from the *Posledni sonety samotar* (Last sonnets of a solitary man), published in 1896:

The swansong. – You will not hear it
From your own springs a new song of life
Slumbering, all whole, in the palm
Of your mighty hand.

10. *Volné směry,* VI, 1902, p. 89. After the completion of *Ctirad and Šárka,* conflict broke out between the somewhat paternalistic Myslbek and his pupil Quido Kocian, whose sculpture of *Šárka* depicting an isolated figure seemingly plunged in tragic solitude, met with greater appreciation from the critics. This was followed by a succession of confrontations with the young modernists.

11. Z. Wirth and A. Matějček, *Česká architektura XIX století, 1800–1920* (Nineteenth-century Czech architecture), Prague, 1922, p. 67.

12. In 1899 H. Wölfflin finished his *Classic Art,* the premise of his major work, *Principles of Art History* (1915).

13. *Volné směry,* II, 1898, p. 523. "If I am not mistaken about the quality of upcoming young talent, and if Jan Kotěra settles in Prague, then the present squabbling and conflicts are going to blow up into a great battle from which modernity will emerge victorious – and of that you can be sure. One question remains: will it still look the way we know it here today, or will it find even more highly original forms of expression? It will be flanked by formidable allies: fine talent and the freshness of youth. And in the rearguard of the combat, like one of the *tableaux vivants* so greatly appreciated here, there will be a didactic group pontificating on this lesson of History."

Decadence and symbolism

1. M. Jiránek, "Výstava Jednoty umělců výtvarných" (The Group of Plastic Artists' exhibition), *Radikální listy,* 1899, p. 814.

2. J. P. Guillerm, *Tombeau de Léonard de Vinci,* Lille, 1981, p. 103.

3. Z. Braunerová, "Úvod k Bílkovým 'Modlitbám'" (Introduction to Bílek's "Prayers"), *Básník a Sochař. Dopisy Julia Zeyera a Františka Bílka z let 1896–1901,* Prague, 1948, p. 200.

4. In the 1890s, Bílek tried to take an active part in the Modern Catholics movement, in whose magazine, *Nový život,* he published an enthusiastic appeal entitled "Konfiteor

umělce" (The artist's confiteor). He also spoke at the movement's congress, and published his speech as a pamphlet. It is nevertheless significant that his opinions were incomprehensible to most of the participants, and were later judged to be erroneous – a mere manifestation of pride – and censured. Bílek was never again able to accept the teachings of a church.

5. Bílek had made Zeyer's acquaintance through his benefactress, Zdenka Braunerová, who had already taken him under her wing in Paris. This meeting with Zeyer, who was overwhelmed by Bílek's inner fortitude, was probably of crucial importance to the young artist.

6. *Básník a Sochař,* p. 208.

7. A. Procházka, *Rozhovory s knihami, obrazy a lidmi* (Conversations with books, pictures and people), Prague, 1916, p. 40. Without denying its decorative value, he claimed to be bothered by its stiffness and rather frozen look, which was more characteristic of the old Nazarenes than of modern painting. In support of his criticism he compared the painter to the younger Bílek: "Besides proposing new forms, Bílek has succeeded in transmitting a new flame to the embers of old abstractions through his white-hot religious fervour, and despite (or indeed thanks to) his religiosity, he has elevated them to the vertiginous heights of the symbol of infinite, immutable universal suffering. Perhaps in spite of himself, he has drawn from them cosmic visions that transcend the limits of all religion. Jenewein lacks such scope, such spiritual momentum. He does not appear to be particularly religious, nor even to have any mystical tendencies, and keeps to ground-level tradition. He composes attractive, decorative pieces, but fails to infuse them with a living spirit."

8. Letter from Karel Hlaváček, *Moderní revue,* XI, 1900, pp. 240–241.

9. See I. Schuster-Schirmer, *Traumbilder von 1770 his 1900,* Bremen, 1975, p. 34.

10. "Listy et Palety," *Moderní revue,* I, vol. I, January 1895, p. 91.

11. K. Hlaváček, *Tragedie ženy, cyklus obrazů Anny Constenoble (The Tragedy of Woman,* a series of paintings by Anne Constenoble), *Moderní revue,* III, vol. V, December 1896, pp. 77–79. The first exhibition organized by

the Mánes Union brought an initial disappointment: even though the members of the group invited their teachers to take part, the School of Fine Arts forbade its pupils to do so, whereas it allowed them to exhibit at the Rudolfinum. To make matters worse, in April of the same year the teachers founded their own association, the Union of Plastic Artists, in competition with the Mánes Union. Then the exhibition of Anne Constenoble's series of picture, *The Tragedy of Woman* provoked a dispute between the Mánes Union and the *Moderní revue,* with its demands for modernity. The Mánes Union's criticism of the series' pictorial weakness annoyed Hlaváček so much that he promptly retorted in *Moderní revue:* "Even those who call themselves the young artists have failed to show an iota of understanding. Bravo, gentlemen, you have finally revealed your true nature. With your opinions on art you give a helping hand to the most narrow-minded of feature-writers, and yet at the same time you reproduce the work of your kind, inoffensive teachers. Just try and talk to us about *young* art from now on!"

12. *Volné směry,* II, 1898, p. 231.

13. Ibid.

14. From Mánes, "Mikoláš Aleš," *Radikálni listy,* III, 1896, pp. 112–113.

15. F. Kaván, "Julius Mařak ve vzpomínce žákově" (Julius Mařak as remembered by his pupil), *Volné směry,* III, 1899, pp. 414–424.

16. F. X. Šalda, "Maurice Maeterlinck, Aglavena a Selysetia" (Maurice Maeterlinck, *Aglavaine et Sélysette*), *Literární listy,* XVIII, 1897, pp. 348–351.

17. K. B. Mádl, *Umění včera a dnes, Pětadvacet výstav "Mánesa"* (Art yesterday and today, twenty-five exhibitions of the Mánes Union of Artists, chronicle of the years 1898 to 1908), Prague, 1908, p. 52.

Toward a new style

1. K. Chytil, "O nejnovějších směrech vkusu v uměleckém průmyslu" (New trends in the decorative arts), *Věstník obchodní a živnostenské komory* for the year 1894, Prague.

2. See A. Matějček, *Jan Preisler,* Prague, 1950, p. 38.

3. K. Hlaváček, "Pařížká naroží" (Street-comers in Paris), *Moderní revue* IV, vol. VII, November 1897, pp. 49–53.
4. The School of Applied Arts' interior design was reproduced in the monographic issue no. 4 of the fifth year of *Volné směry* (1901), and that of the Chamber of Commerce and Crafts in the first year of the magazine *Dílo* (1903). The most important objects in the two exhibitions have been on display at the Prague Museum of Decorative Arts since 1900.
5. The model for these visions can be seen in a vase by Gauguin, which is decorated with a portrait of the artist with closed eyes. In *The Urn*, a lithograph made in 1896, Munch also developed this concept in the form of a lethal erotic symbol.
6. C. G. Jung, *Traumsymbole des Individuationsprozesses*, Erano-Jahrbuch, 1935, p. 13.
7. *Lötz, Böhmisches Glas, 1880–1940*, Werkmonographie I–II, edited by H. Ricke, T. Vlcek, A. Adlerová, E. Ploil, Munich, 1989.
8. S. K. Neumann, "Neřolik modernich představitelů aplikovaného umění" (Modern representatives of the applied arts). I. Louis C. Tiffany, *Moderní revue,* VI, vol. Xl, October 1899, pp. 26–28.
9. J. Kotěra, "O novém umění" (On Art Nouveau), *Volné směry*, IV, 1900, p. 189.
10. F. X. Harlas, "Moderna v pražských ulicích" (Modern art in the streets of Prague), *Architektonicky obzor*, III, 1904, p. 33.
11. R. Posva, "Plastika a mozaika v průčelích Osvalda Polívky" (Sculpture and mosaics on facades by Osvald Polívka), *Umění,* XXXV, 1987, pp. 449–459.
12. A. Engel, "Veřejné budovy pražké" (Public buildings in Prague), *Styl*, IV, 1911–1912, p. 30.
13. F. X. Šalda, "Ethika dnešni obrody aplikovaného umění (1903)" (The ethics of the present renascence of the applied arts), *Boje o zítřek, Meditace a rapsodie*, Prague, 1948, pp. 111–114.

THE EMOTIVE STYLE
The enigma of life

1. Letter from Kupka to Machar, quoted by L. Vachtová, *František Kupka*, Prague, 1968, p. 39.

2. M. Rowell, "František Kupka. The Metaphysics of Abstraction," *Frank Kupka, 1871–1957. A Retrospective*, The Solomon R. Guggenheim Museum, New York, 1975, pp. 47–80.
3. M. Jiránek, "Listy z Paříže I, II" (Letters from Paris I, II), *Volné směry*, V, 1901, pp. 13–22 and 36–42.
4. K. B. Mádl, "Luděk Marold", *Volné směry*, Ill, 1899, p. 180.
5. F. X. Šalda, "Hrdinný zrak" (The heroic view), *Volné směry*, VI, 1901, p. 73.
6. K. B. Mádl, "Moderni francouzké umění" (Modern French art), reproduced in *Umění včera a dnes*, II, Prague, 1908, pp. 85–103.
7. M. Jiránek, "Francouzšti impresioniste" (The French Impressionists), *Volné směry*, XII, 1908, pp. 7–10. "… It seems to me that in the beginning what we appreciated in the Impressionists was their more external, and therefore more striking qualities: we took the content of Impressionism to be the effects of light, momentary fleeting impressions. The great words 'plein air', the technical innovations, and consequently the masters too, compelled us to do so. They handled the new techniques with bravura and brilliance, and seemed to us to put the fighter- pioneers in the shade."
8. F. X. Šalda, "Experimenty" (Experiments), *Lumír*, XXVII, 1898, pp. 8–11.
9. F. X. Šalda, "Nová Krása: její genese a charakter" (The new beauty: its nature and origins), *Volné směery*, VI, 1903, pp. 169 and 181. "For this reason the new concepts of art and beauty are passionately attached to the present. More than this: they are the only present, they are the richest, the truest, they are reality that is. … For this is where man the artist differs from man the reproducer, and is distinct from average, mediocre man: ordinary human beings plod through life thinking about the past; unsatisfied, they button up, patch, adjust and stitch life laboriously together, obeying the external criteria of memory and logic. What they construct out of alien formulae are not even their own impressions, but echoes of other people's. On the other hand, the creative mind is unique and independent, lives an intense existence that is full and real, without help from logic, memory and abstrac-

tion. It is a life that multiplies and grows by degrees, experienced fully and directly solely through the perception of the senses."
10. "Style articulates and fuses, never imitates, it always abridges, interprets, makes more dense and synthesizes. *It judges and evaluates life,* extirpates what is petty, emphasizes what is great, highlights the essence, the law and the meaning of matter; it is the spiritual unity of life and the world, a parable of cosmic affinity and union. Style gives culture power and strength and makes it the organizer, the judge, the means by which life is re-evaluated; by serving life, art rules it and stimulates it for the furtherance of its own purposes; art becomes life, and life becomes art."
11. *Vybrané listy Antonína Slavíčka* (Selected letters from Antonín Slavíček), Prague, 1930, p. 95.
12. Ibid., p. 57.

The sources of intuition

1. S. Sucharda, "Sochat Rodin" (Rodin the sculptor), *Volné směry*, V, 1901, pp. 143–147.
2. J. Mařatka, *Vzpomínky a záznamy* (Memories and notes), Prague, 1987.
3. J. Peřirka, *Josef Mařatka*, Prague, 1942.
4. F. X. Šalda, "Géniova materstinda" (The mother tongue of genius), catalogue of the Prague exhibition of works by the sculptor A. Rodin, 4th Exhibition of the Mánes Union, Kinsky Gardens, 10 May–15 July 1902. "In his sculpture, more than in any other work of art of modern times, resounds the voice of the forces of life and destiny, of the most ancient and profound elements, the most deeply fundamental subtleties that create movement and its rhythms … We hear in it everything that is essential, eternal and demented in life and death, and it is all said by a line that is intoxicating, that sears like pain and pleasure, that is sensitive, vibrant, as responsive as nervous fluid, vast and triumphant as the law of being, creation and death."
5. *Volné směry*, IX, 1905, p. 185.
6. Ibid., p. 31.
7. D. L. Silverman, *Art Nouveau in Fin-desiecle France. Politics, Psychology and Style*, Berkeley and Los Angeles, California, 1989, pp. 229–269.

8. L. Šaloun, "Dílo" (Works), *Dílo*, XV, 1920, p. 10; "Z duševni dílny umělcovy" (From the artist's spiritual workshop), *Dílo*, XV, 1920, p. 83; "Jak hledím na umění" (My view of art), *Dílo*, XXV, 1933–1934, p. 117.

9. F. Šmejkal, "Secesně-symbolistní tvorba Ladislava Šalouna. Drobná plastika a Kresba" (Secession and Symbolist creation in Ladislav Šaloun. Small sculptures and drawings), *Umění*, XXVIII, 1980, p. 469.

10. P. Wittlich, "Edvard Munch a české umění (Edvard Munch and Czech art), *Umění*, XXX, 1982, pp. 422–447.

11. S. Przybyszewski, "Edvard Munch", *Moderní revue*, III, vol. V, January 1897, pp. 99–104.

12. K. B. Mádl, "Edvard Munch", *Národní listy*, 12 February 1905.

13. M. Jiránek, "Edvard Munch", *Nová česhá revue*, II, 1905, p. 336. Miloš Jiránek points out that contrary to the views of some of the country's critics, Munch was not isolated in modern painting. He mentions Vincent Van Gogh and Paul Cézanne as two comparable painters. Jiránek particularly admired Munch's courage: "His new greatness resides in the fact that he is broadening the content of art today to encompass the pain and sorrows of contemporary life. These melancholy gifts touch us because they are the pain and the sorrows of all who belong to modern times." Jiránek preferred Munch's portraits and appreciated his art as proof of the evolution of modern individualism. This is why he considered Munch's contemporary paintings superior to his "decadent" work from the 1890s. He saw in them "life that has been healed".

14. F. X. Šalda, "Násilník snu. Několik glos k dílu E. Munchovu" (The violator of dreams. Glosses on the work of E. Munch), *Volné směry*, IX, 1905, p. 103. Šalda unhesitatingly pointed out that the Munch affair had revealed Czech critics in their true light, and shown up those whose judgment was "bankrupt". Munch himself was someone "capable of being a painter with absolute plastic power, and with a pure sense of the picturesque". His only problem lay in his strangeness, for he was more of "a force of nature, an eruption from the dark depths of the race, than the representative of a 'nice' cultural universe and a man in the lime-light". Munch possessed a musical sense of colour, and in his finest paintings he achieved "something that may be barbaric, but is fine and strong in its own way. Something that is also a personal path toward style and rhythm". Nevertheless, he was a "violator of dreams". As a painter, Šalda saw Munch as the absolute opposite of Velázquez, whose gaze rested "silently and cleanly" on things, and who was a poet of the mystery of reality. Velázquez painted only atmosphere, the silvery shimmer of space seen through light. Unlike Munch, Velázquez's work, although it had been neglected for a long time, could be methodically developed by modern painters and enable them to evolve. Šalda too, therefore, felt that Munch was not an example to be followed by Czech painters.

15. M. Marten, *Edvard Munch*, Prague, 1905.

16. E. Filla, "O ctnosti novoprimitivismu" (On the virtue of Neo-Primitivism), *Volné směry*, XV, 1911, pp. 69–70.

17. F. X. Šalda, "Umělecká výstava v Obecním dome u Prasné brány" (The art exhibition at the Town Hall near the Powder Tower), *Novina*, V, 1912, p. 247.

18. Catalogue of the Josef Váchal Exhibition, *Dílo*, Roudnice nad Labem, 1984, p. 51.

The national myth

1. J. Mucha, *Alfons Mucha*, Prague, 1982.

2. V. Loers, "Alfons Mucha gnostische Botschaft", catalogue of the exhibition *Mucha, Meditation und Botschaft,* Museum Fridericianum, Kassel, 1989.

3. Illustrations by Alfons Mucha for "Adamitum" (The Adamites), *Moderní revue,* II, vol. V, November 1896, p. 63.

4. M. Jiránek, "Výstava Jednoty umělců výtarných" (Exhibition of the Group of Plastic Artists), *Radikální listy,* VI, no. 126, November 4, 1899, p. 806, and no. 127, November 7, 1899, p. 814.

5. M. Jiránek, "O mrtvém materiálu" (On inert matter), *Styl,* I, 1909, p. 81.

6. K. Hlaváček, "Souborná výstava Joži Úprky" (Retrospective exhibition of the work of Joža Úprka), *Moderní revue,* III, vol. V, March 1897, p. 188.

7. K. Hlaváček, "Souborná výstava Vítězslava Maška" (Retrospective exhibition of the work of Vítězslav Mašek), *Moderní revue,* III, vol. V, February 1897, p. 155.

8. J. Mařatka, *Vzpomínky a záznamy* (Memories and notes), Prague, 1897, p. 137.

9. F. X. Šalda, "Ležela země přede mnou, vodova po duchu, který odešel" (There she stood before me, the widow of the departed spirit), *Volné směry,* IX, 1903–1904, pp. 3–11.

10. K. B. Mádl, *Umění včera a dnes* (Art yesterday and today, II), Prague, 1908, p. 185.

11. M. Marten, "Souborná výstava J. Úprky" (Retrospective exhibition of the work of J. Úprka), *Moderní revue,* X, vol. XV, February 1904, p. 239.

12. M. Jiránek, "Bildende Kunst" (Frühjahrsübersicht 1910), *Tchechische Revue,* III, 1910, pp. 357–359; F. X. Šalda, "Mistr Mucha v Praze" (Master Mucha in Prague), *Novina,* III, 1909, p. 63.

13. S. Sucharda, *Historie pomníku Františka Palackého v Praze* (History of the František Palacký Monument in Prague), Prague, 1912.

14. L. Šaloun, "Husův pomník" (The Hus monument), *Dílo*, XIII, 1918, p. 19.

MODERNISM
The synthetist programme

1. G. Rodenbach, "Puvis de Chavannes," *Volné směry,* IV, 1900, pp. 144–147.

2. F. X. Šalda, "Úvodni slovo" (A word of introduction), *Katalog V. výstavy Spolku výtvarných umělců "Mánes" v Praze, Moderní francouzske umění, Kinskéoho zahrada od. 30. srpna do. 2. listopadu 1902* (pages unnumbered).

3. "Preislerův dopis S. Suchardovi" (Letter from Preisler to S. Sucharda), *Výtvarne umění,* VI, 1956, p. 228.

4. J. J. Winckelmann, *Dějiny umění starověku* (History of classical art), Prague, 1986, p. 342. Originally published in Dresden, 1764.

5. C. Mauclair, "Klasicism a akademism" (Classicism and Academicism), *Volné směry,* IX, 1904–1905, p. 47.

6. F. X. Šalda, "Boj o uměleckou kulturu" (The struggle for an artistic culture), *Volné směry*, IX, 1905, pp. 291–306.

7. P. Wittlich, "Medardo Rosso a české

sochařství" (Medardo Rosso and Czech sculpture), *Umění*, XXXI, 1983, pp. 473–485.

8. M. Marten, "O lirickém impresionismu" (On lyrical Impressionism), *Moderní revue*, XII, 1906–1907, pp. 9–24.

9. F. X. Šalda, "Impresionism: jeho rozvoj, rezultátyi dědicové" (Impressionism, its development, its results and its heirs), *Pokroková revue*, IV, 1907, pp. 70 and 159.

10. F. X. Šalda, "Nicolas Constantinovich Roerich", *Volné směry*, X, 1906, pp. 83–86.

11. B. Kubišta, "Émile Bernard", *Volné směry*, XIII, 1909, p. 80.

12. P. Wittlich, "E. A. Bourdelle a jeho výstava r. 1909 v Praze" (E. A. Bourdelle and his exhibition in Prague, 1909), *Umění*, IX, 1961, p. 476.

13. Z. Lukeš, J. Svoboda, "Josef Zasche", *Umění*, XXXVII, 1990, pp. 534–543.

14. P. Janák, "Otto Wagner", *Styl*, I, 1908–1909, pp. 41–48.

15. A. Engel, "Dům nájemný" (Apartment buildings), *Styl*, III, 1911, p. 189.

16. M. Lamač, *Osma a Skupina výtvarných umělců 1907–1917* (The Eight and the Group of Plastic Artists), Prague, 1988, p. 136.

17. F. X. Šalda, "Novoklasicism" (Neo-Classicism), *Národní listy*, 1912, January 5 issue, p. 2; January 12 issue, pp. 2–3; January 19 issue, p. 2.

18. E. Filla, "O ctnosti novoprimitivismu" (On the virtue of Neo-Primitivism), *Volné směry*, XV, 1911, p. 62.

The second wave of symbolism

1. "A burning wave of mystical desire for the universe mounts like a column of fire in the darkness of life, then hurls itself into the precipice of Sin, Pain and Evil: man, wounded by the intuition of the eternal, wanders blindly in search of the spring that can appease his thirst."

2. *Novina*, II, 1909, pp. 640 and 671.

3. A. Procházka, *Odilon Redon*, Prague, 1904, pp. 29–30.

4. J. A. Stuart, *L'Art plus que nous … Correspondance d'Émile Bernard avec Miloš Marten, 1908–1914*, (Art more than we …

Correspondence between Émile Bernard and Miloš Marten, 1901–1914), Grenoble, 1975.

5. *Moderní revue*, XXI, 1909, pp. 445–458.

6. J. A. Stuart, op. cit., pp. 30–31.

7. M. Marten, *Nad městem* (Above the city), Prague, 1917.

8. F. Kobliha, "Odilon Redon", *Hollar*, IV, 1927–1928, p. 86.

9. A. Procházka, "Kouzlo Prahy" (The enchantment of Prague), *Rozhovory s Knihami, obrazy i lidmi*, Prague, 1916, pp. 96–101.

10. K. Kerényi, *Labyrinth Studien*, Amsterdam – Leipzig, 1941.

11. F. Šmejkal, *Sursum*, 1910–1912, Hradec Králové, 1976.

12. B. Kubišta, "O předpokladech slohu" (On the premises of style), *Prehled*, X, 1911, p. 37.

13. M. Neslehová, *Bohumil Kubišta*, Prague, 1984, p. 142.

Decorative and geometric style

1. P. Janák, "Od moderní architektury k architektuře" (From modern architecture to architecture), *Styl*, II, 1909–1910, p. 105.

2. P. Janák, "Hranol a pyramida" (The prism and the pyramid), *Umělecký měsíčník*, I, 1911–1912, pp. 162–170.

3. P. Janák, "O nábytku a jiném" (On furniture and other things), *Umělecký měsíčník*, II, 1912–1913, pp. 21–29.

4. B. Kubišta, *Korespondcnce a úvahy* (Correspondence and reflections), Prague, 1960, p. 124.

5. O. Gutfreund, *Zázemi tvorby* (The premises of creation), Prague, ed. J. Setlík, 1989, p. 18.

6. B. Kubišta, "Druhá výstava Skupiny výtvarných umělců v Obecním domě" (Second exhibition of the Group of Plastic Artists in the Municipal building), *Česká kultura*, I, no. 2, October 18 1912, pp. 58–60.

7. M. Lamač, *Osma a Skupina výtvarných umělců 1907–1917* (The Eight and the Group of Plastic Artists, 1907–1917), Prague, 1989, p. 270.

8. P. Janák. "o nabytku a jinem" (On furniture and other things), op. cit.

9. Notes by Otto Gutfreund, *Volné směry*, XXV, 1927–1928, pp. 156–163.

10. F. X. Šalda, "Umělecká výstava v Obecním domě u Prašné brány" (Art exhibition at the Municipal building near the Powder Tower), *Novina*, V, 1912, pp. 247–248.

11. V. Hofman, "O secesi" (On the Secession), *Styl*, V, 1913, p. 118.

12. O. Gutfreund, "Plocha a prostor" (Surface and volume), *Umělecký měsíčník*, II, 1912–1913, pp. 240–243.

Epilogue

1. B. Kubišta, *Korespondence a úvahy* (Correspondence and reflections), Prague, 1960, p. 163. In a letter to Jan Zrzavý at the time, he complains that he had never met anyone who understood that his achievement as an artist had been "won at the terrible cost of a struggle against everybody else. … No-one gave me any help, and I suffered pain and sadness beyond anyone's imagination."

2. J. Zrzavý, "Barva" (Colour), *Svět Jana Zrzavého*, Prague, 1963, n. p.

3. F. X. Šalda, "Umění a přioroda. Dialog" (Art and nature. Dialogue), *Česká kultura*, I, 1912, pp. 47–52.

4. F. X. Šalda, "Novoklasicism" (Neo-Classicism), *Národní listy*, 1912.

5. T. Vlček, *Praha 1900* (Prague 1900), Prague, 1986, pp. 286–289.

6. S. K. Neumann, "At žije život!" (Long live life!), *Lidové noviny*, 1914.

7. F. X. Šalda, "Umělecká výstava v Obecním domě u Prašné brány" (Art exhibition at the Municipal building near the Powder Tower) *Novina*, V, 1912, pp. 247–248.

8. Catalogue for Voijtěch Preissig's exhibition *Grafika a malba, 1932–1938* (Engravings and paintings, 1931–1938), mounted by T. Vlček, Galerie výtvarného umění, Roudnici nad Labem, 1983, p. 34.

BIOGRAPHIES

Rudolf ADÁMEK
(1882–1953)
Engraver and painter. An active member of
the Sursum group.

Mikoláš ALEŠ
(1852–1913)
Painter and illustrator. Studied at the
Prague Academy and took part in the competition for the decoration of the Prague
National Theatre. Became popular for his
illustrations on national themes. First honorary president of the Mánes Union of
Artists.

Vilím AMORT
(1864–1913)
Sculptor and stucco artist, whose work
appears on a great many buildings in
Prague.

Franta ANYŽ
(1876–1934)
Studied under C. Klouček at the Prague
School of Applied Arts. Became the owner
of a well-known firm manufacturing
period objects in metal.

Antonín BALŠÁNEK
(1865–1921)
Architect. Designed buildings in late
historicist style (City of Prague Museum,
1899–1902) and Art Nouveau (co-
architect of the Prague Municipal building,
1904–1912). Designer of urban planning
projects for Prague and for the new bridge
near the National Theatre (1901).

Adolf BECKERT
(1884–1929)
Glassmaker. Designer at the Widow of Jan
Lötz Glassworks at Klášterský Mlýn
between 1909 and 1911. Taught at the
Kamenický Šenov Professional School of
Glassmaking from 1911.

Jaroslav BENDA
(1882–1970)
Engraver and typographer. Studied in
Prague at the School of Applied Arts and
the Academy. Member of the Mánes Union
and co-founder of the Artěl co-operative.

Bedřich BENDELMAYER
(1872–1932)
Architect. Studied under F. Ohmann at the
Prague School of Applied Arts. Collaborated on the design of the Central Hotel
(1899). Creator of the Archduke Štěpán
(now the Evropa) Hotel, (1903–1905) on
Wenceslas Square in Prague.

Vincenc BENEŠ
(1883–1979)
Painter. Member of the Group of Plastic
Artists.

František BÍLEK
(1872–1941)
Sculptor, engraver, designer. A student of
M. Pirner at the Prague Academy, he also
studied sculpture under Josef Mauder. In
1891–1892 he attended J. A. Injalbert's
classes at the Colarossi Academy in Paris.
His original work, which took a religious
and mystical direction, echoed the poetry
of J. Zeyer and O. Březina.

Matěj BLECHA
(1861–1919)
Architect, and owner of a construction
company in Prague.

Jaromír BORECKY
(1869–1951)
Poet, translator and journalist. One of the
first decadent Czech poets (Rosa mystica
anthology, 1892).

Anna BOUDOVÁ-SUCHARDOVÁ
(1870–1940)
Ceramic artist, textile designer. Studied at
the Prague School of Applied Arts.

Zdenka BRAUNEROVÁ
(1858–1934)
Engraver and painter. Played an important
role in establishing Franco-Czech cultural
ties.

Otakar BŘEZINA (real name Václav
Jebavý)
(1868–1929)
Poet and essayist. The most remarkable
representative of Czech literary Symbolism.

Vratislav Hugo BRUNNER
(1886–1928)
Engraver and painter. Co-founder of the
Artěl co-operative.

Josef ČAPEK
(1887–1945)
Painter, engraver and writer. Studied at the
School of Applied Arts in Prague. One of
the major representatives of the pre-First
World War avant-garde.

Karel Matěj ČAPEK-CHOD
(1860–1927)
Writer and journalist. Representative of a
naturalism with a social and grotesque bent.

Svatopluk ČECH
(1846–1908)
Poet, prose-writer. Famous for his poetry
committed to the Czech national cause
(Pisně otroka [Songs of the Slave], 1895).

Alois Jan CENSKY
(1868–1954)
Architect. Combined historicism and mod-
ern decorative style (Theatre, Prague-
Vinohrady, 1909, National Building,
Prague-Smíchov, 1916).

Antonín CHITTUSSI
(1847–1891)
Painter. Studied at the Academics of Prague,
Munich and Vienna. Lived in France
between 1879 and 1886. Landscape painter
influenced by the Barbizon School.

Josef CHOCHOL
(1880–1956)
Architect. Studied at the Institute of
Advanced Technical Studies in Prague, and
under O. Wagner at the Vienna Academy.
Cubist and purist (house at Prague-
Vysehrad, 1911–1914).

Karel CHYTIL
(1857–1934)
Art historian. Director of the Prague
Museum of Decorative Arts (1885–1916).

Jakub DEML
(1878–1961)
Catholic poet, prose-writer and essayist
(Hrad smrti [Castle of death], 1912).

Emanuel DÍTĚ
(1862–1944)
Painter, professor at the Prague School of Applied Arts.

František DRTIKOL
(1878–1961)
The most famous Czech photographer.

Alois DRYÁK
(1872–1932)
Architect. Studied under F. Ohmann at the Prague School of Applied Arts. Built the Garni (now the Evropa) Hotel, on Wenceslas Square, Prague (1903–1905).

Bohuslav DVORÁK
(1867–1951)
Painter. Studied at the Prague School of Fine Arts under J. Mařák. Landscape painter.

Antonín ENGEL
(1879–1958)
Architect. Also studied at the Vienna Academy under O. Wagner. Inclined toward Neo-Romanticism.

Ferdinand ENGELMÜLLER
(1867–1924)
Painter. Studied at the Prague Academy under J. Mařák. Landscape painter with a Neo-Romantic orientation.

Josef FANTA
(1856–1954)
Architect. Assistant to Professor Schulz, then professor at the Prague Institute of Advanced Technical Studies. Became an adept of Art Nouveau after 1900 (Main Station, 1900–1909).

Bedřich FEIGL
(1884–1965)
Painter. Member of The Eight (Osma).

Emíl FILLA
(1882–1953)
Painter, theorist. Leading representative of the pre-World War I avant-garde (The Eight and Group of Plastic Artists).

Jan GEBAUER
(1838–1907)
Philologist. Professor at Prague University.

František GELLNER
(1881–1914)
Writer, caricaturist, journalist. Writer of anarchist-leaning poetry (*Po nás a přijde potopa* [After us, come what may], 1901, *Radosti života* [The joys of life], 1903).

Josef GOCÁR
(1880–1945)
Architect. Studied at the Prague School of Applied Arts under J. Kotěra. Member of the Group of Plastic Artists (the "Black Virgin" building, Prague Old Town, 1911–1912).

Julius GRÉGR
(1831–1896)
Politician belonging to the Young Czech party.

Otto GUTFREUND
(1889–1927)
Sculptor. Studied at the school of ceramics in Bechyně, the School of Applied Arts in Prague, and in E. A. Bourdelle's workshop in Paris (1909–1910). Member of the Group of Plastic Artists. Cubist.

Jaroslav HAŠEK
(1883–1923)
Journalist, writer. Author of satirical stories and the famous *Dobrího voháka Švejka* [The adventures of the good soldier Švejk].

Kamil HILBERT
(1869–1933)
Architect. Studied at the Vienna Academy Finished St. Guy's Cathedral in Prague. Developed a personal Neo-Gothic version of Art Nouveau (church in Stěchovice, 1907–1908).

Karel HLAVÁČEK
(1874–1898)
Poet, illustrator, art critic. Representative of Czech Decadence. Wrote for *Moderní revue*.

Arnošt HOFBAUER
(1869–1944)
Painter and engraver. Studied under F. Ženíšek at the Prague School of Applied Arts and at the Academy under M. Pirner and V. Hynais. Member of the Mánes Union of Artists. Creator of elegant posters.

Vlastislav HOFMAN
(1884–1964)
Architect. Published theoretical articles in *Styl* and *Umělecky Měsíčník*.

Emil HOLÁREK
(1867–1919)
Creator of drawings, famous for his cycles of moralizing works.

Max HORB
(1882–1907)
Painter. Member of The Eight.

Jaroslav HOREJC
(1886–1983)
Sculptor, designer. Studied at the Prague School of Applied Arts. Created projects prefiguring Art Deco for the Artěl co-operative.

Bohumil HÜBSCHMANN
(1878–1961)
Architect. Studied at the Vienna Academy under O. Wagner. Prague city planner.

Antonín HUDEČEK
(1872–1941)
Painter. Studied at the Prague Academy under M. Pirner, and in Munich under A. Ažbé and Seitz. A remarkable landscape painter.

Vojtěch HYNAIS
(1854–1925)
Painter. Studied at the Vienna Academy under A. Feuerbach and in Paris under P. Baudry. Contributed brilliantly to the decoration of the Prague National Theatre. Professor at the Prague Academy (from 1893).

Pavel JANÁK
(1882–1956)
Architect. Studied at the Vienna Academy under O. Wagner. Co-founder of the Prague Art Workshops (1912). Theorist on modern architecture.

Hanuš JELÍNEK
(1878–1944)
Poet, journalist, translator. Particularly active in the development of Franco-Czech ties in the literary field.

Felix Jenewein
(1857–1905)
Painter. Studied at the Academies of Prague and Vienna. Professor at the Prague School of Applied Arts (until 1902). Creator of the cycle *Mor* [Plague] (1899–1900).

Miloš Jiránek
(1875–1911)
Painter, writer. Studied at the Prague Academy under M. Pirner and V. Hynais. Leading figure in the Mánes Union. Impressionist. Renowned art critic.

Dušan Jurkovič
(1868–1947)
Architect. Specialist in folk tradition (*Pustevně na hoře Radhošt* [Hermitage on Mount Radhošt], 1897–1899) and Modernist.

Bohumil Kafka
(1878–1942)
Sculptor. Studied at the Prague School of Applied Arts under J. V. Myslbek. Lived in Paris (1904–1908). Influenced by Rodin.

Josef Kaizl
(1854–1901)
Jurist and Young Czech political leader. Professor at the University of Prague, member of the Empire's Chamber of Deputies, and minister of Finance (1898–1899).

Jiří Karásek ze lvovic
(1871–1951)
Poet, translator, critic and collector. Co-founder of *Moderní revue* (1894). Representative of Czech Decadence (short story *Gotická duše* [The Gothic soul], 1900).

Jan Kastner
(1860–1912)
Sculptor, particularly in wood. Professor at the Prague School of Applied Arts.

František Kaván
(1866–1941)
Painter and poet. Studied at the Prague Academy under J. Mařák. Landscape painter who combined the principles of Realism, Symbolism and Impressionism.

Marie Louisa Kirschnerová
(1852–1931)
Painter and designer. Created glass objects for the Widow of Jan Lötz Glassworks at Klášterský Mlýn.

Egon Ervín Kisch
(1885–1948)
Journalist. Editor and reporter for the German paper *Bohemia* (from 1906).

Richard Klenka z vlastimilu
(1873–1954)
Architect. Professor at the Prague School of Applied Arts.

Celda Klouček
(1855–1935)
Sculptor, ceramic artist, professor at the Prague School of Applied Arts (1888–1916). Introduced Art Nouveau to Prague, particularly in the field of architectural decoration (Credit Bank, Prague Old Town, 1902).

František Kobliha
(1877–1962)
Engraver and painter. Studied at the Prague School of Applied Arts and at the Academy under F. Ženíšek. Representative of late Symbolism, associated with the *Moderní revue* circle. Member of the Sursum group.

Quido Kocian
(1874–1928)
Sculptor. Studied at the Prague School of Applied Arts, and at the Academy under J. V. Myslbek. Symbolist.

Jan Konůpek
(1883–1950)
Engraver and painter. Studied at the Prague Academy under M. Pirner. Member of the Sursum group. Symbolist.

Jan Kotěra
(1871–1923)
Architect. Studied at the Vienna Academy under O. Wagner (1894–1898). Professor at the School of Applied Arts in Prague (1898) and at the Prague Academy (1910). Founder of modern Czech architecture. Evolved from lyrical Art Nouveau (Peterka's house, Prague New Town, 1899) toward a more

purist and tectonic conception of architecture (Urbánek's house, Prague New Town, 1913).

Jan Koula
(1855–1919)
Architect and designer. Professor at the Prague Institute of Advanced Technical Studies (from 1897 onward). Combined historicism with an interest in folk tradition and Art Nouveau.

Otakar Kubín
(1883–1969)
Painter. Member of The Eight.

Bohumil Kubišta
(1884–1918)
Painter and art theorist. Outstanding figure in the pre-World War I Czech avant-garde. Member of The Eight. Expressionist and Cubist. Author of text/programmes and remarkable critical work.

František Kupka
(1871–1957)
Painter and engraver. Studied at the Prague Academy, followed by periods in Vienna then Paris (from 1895). Naturalist, Symbolist, and one of the earliest creators of abstract art. Author of the treatise *La Création dans les arts plastiques* (Creation in the plastic arts), which he wrote in French; the work was published in Czech in 1923 under the title *Tvoření v umění výtvarném* and in French in 1989.

Jaroslav Kvapil
(1868–1950)
Poet and playwright. Author of the libretto [for Antonín Dvořák's opera *Rusalka* (1901).

Hana Kvapilova
(1860–1907)
The greatest Czech dramatic actress around 1900.

František Kysela
(1881–1941)
Painter and engraver. Teacher at the Prague School of Applied Arts (from 1913). Member of the Group of Plastic Artists and Artěl. Famous for his posters.

Otakar LEBEDA
(1877–1901)
Painter. Studied at the Prague Academy
under J. Mařák and in Paris. Landscape
painter with impressionist sensibilities.

Josef Svatopluk MACHAR
(1864–1942)
Writer, poet and journalist. Representative
of trenchant criticism and political Realism
(*Tristium Vindobona*, 1893).

Václav MAŘAN
(1874–1962)
Sculptor, ceramic artist. Studied at the
Prague School of Applied Arts under C.
Klouček. Taught at the Bechyně School of
Ceramics.

Josef MAŘATKA
(1874–1937)
Sculptor. Studied at the Prague School of
Applied Arts under C. Klouček, and at the
Academy under J. V. Myslbek. Between
1900 and 1904 he worked in Paris, in Rodin's
workshop.

Luděk MAROLD
(1856–1898)
Painter and illustrator. Studied at the
Munich and Prague Academies. Worked in
Paris from 1889 to 1897. Famous for his illu-
sionistic illustrations.

Miloš MARTEN (real name Miloš Šebesta)
(1883–1917)
Writer, critic. Identified with the *Moderní
revue*. Symbolist and advocate of Classicism.

Tomáš Garrigue MASARYK
(1850–1937)
Sociologist, philosopher, political figure and
journalist. Professor at Prague University.
Representative of what was known as Political Realism. His political platform-writing
found a tremendous echo among Czech
intellectuals (*Česká otázka* [The Czech ques-
tion], 1895).

Karel Vítězslav MAŠEK
(1805–1927)
Painter, designer, architect. Studied at the
Academies of Prague and Munich, and at the
Julian Academy in Paris (1887). Professor at
the Prague School of Applied Arts (from
1898). His villa in Prague (1901) is an example
of a stylistic solution along Art Nouveau lines.

Josef MAUDER
(1854–1920)
Sculptor with a Neo-Romantic tendency.

Franz METZNER
(1879–1919)
Sculptor. Professor at the Vienna School of
Applied Arts (1903–1907).

Gustav MEYRINK
(1868–1932)
Writer. Co-founder of the Prague section of
the Theosophical Society. Author of the
novel *Golem* (1915).

Josef MOCKER
(1835–1899)
Architect and builder. Studied at the Institute
of Advanced Technical Studies and at the
Vienna Academy. Directed the completion of
St. Guy's Cathedral in Prague until 1898.

Alois MRŠTÍK
(1861–1925)
Writer in a naturalist vein and influenced by
folk tradition.

Vilem MRŠTÍK
(1863–1912)
Writer, playwright. Work based on realism
and naturalism (play *Maryša*, 1894, in collaboration with his brother, Alois). Author
of the pamphlet *Bestia triumfans* in protest
against the modernization of Prague Old
Town (1897).

Alfons MUCHA
(1860–1939)
Painter, engraver and photographer. Studied
at the Munich Academy and at the Julian
Academy in Paris (1888). He was one of the
creators of Art Nouveau in Paris during the
1890s. Until 1914, he divided his time
between Paris, the United States and Prague.
After his return to Bohemia he carried out
the extremely controversial decoration of the
Mayor's Room in the Prague Municipal
building (1911).

Bedřich MÜNZBERGER
(1846–1928)
Architect and builder. Introduced what was
called industrial architecture on a monumental scale with his Palace of Industry for
the Prague Jubilee Exhibition in 1891.

Josef Václav MYSLBEK
(1848–1922)
Sculptor. Professor at the Prague School of
Applied Arts (from 1885) and at the Prague
Academy (from 1896). Following his visit to
the Universal Exposition in Paris (1878), he
opened up Czech sculpture to French influence. Creator of the *Monument to St.
Wenceslas* in Prague.

Vratislav NECHLEBA
(1885–1965)
Painter. Studied at the Prague Academy
under M. Pirner. Portrait painter.

Otakar NEJEDLY
(1883–1957)
Landscape artist. Impressionist and Fauve
influences.

Josef Ladislav NĚMEC
(1871–1934)
Gold- and silversmith. Studied at the Prague
School of Applied Arts. Teacher at the Professional School of Goldsmiths (from 1896).

Stanislav Kostka NEUMANN
(1875–1947)
Writer, poet and journalist. Defendant in the
famous Omladina political trial. Adept of
satanism and anarchism. Editor of the journal *Nový kult* (New Cult, 1897–1905).
Defended the extremely avant-garde
Almanach na rok 1914 (Almanach for the
Year 1914).

Emanuel NOVÁK
(1866–1918)
Gold- and silversmith. Professor at the
Prague School of Applied Arts (from 1888).

Otakar NOVOTNY
(1880–1959)
Architect and architectural theorist. Studied
at the Prague School of Applied Arts under J.
Kotěra. Representative of decorative purism

(Stenc house, Prague Old Town, 1909). Contributed to the journals *Styl* and *Volné směry* (Free Tendencies).

Friedrich OHMANN
(1858–1927)
Architect. Professor at the Prague School of Applied Arts (1889–1898). Representative of late historicism, Neo-Baroque and the beginnings of Art Nouveau (Central Hotel, Prague New Town, 1898–1901).

Viktor OLIVA
(1861–1928)
Painter, engraver and illustrator.

Emil ORLIK
(1870–1932)
Painter and engraver. Representative of German culture in Prague. Professor at the Berlin School of Applied Arts from 1905.

Emil PACOVSKY
(1879–1948)
Painter and engraver. Member of the Sursum group.

Josef PEKÁREK
(1873–1930)
Sculptor. Studied at the Prague School of Applied Arts under C. Klouček, and at the Academy under J. V. Myslbek. Together with members of his workshop, he carried out a series of decorative works on Prague buildings (Municipal building).

Antonín PFEIFFER
(1879–1938)
Architect. Studied at the Prague School of Applied Arts under J. Kotěra, from whom he derived his decorative modernism (Koruna building, Prague New Town, 1911–1914).

Maxmilián PIRNER
(1854–1924)
Painter. Studied at the Academies of Prague and Vienna. Taught at the Prague Academy from 1887. Neo-Romantic and Symbolist.

Osvald POLÍVKA
(1859–1931)
Architect. Studied at the Prague Institute

of Advanced Technical Studies under J. Zítek. His wide activities in Prague ranged from late historicism and Neo-Baroque to a personal conception of Art Nouveau (Municipal building, in collaboration with A. Balšánek, 1903–1912).

Antonín POPP
(1850–1915)
Sculptor, stucco artist.

Jan PREISLER
(1872–1918)
Painter. Studied at the Prague School of Applied Arts under F. Ženíšek. Founder-member of the Mánes Union of Artists, and for many years a member of the editorial staff of *Volné směry*. Taught at the Prague School of Applied Arts (1908–1912). Professor at the Prague Academy (from 1913). Created a personal Czech version of Symbolism in his pictorial work, and was one of the precursors of Czech modern painting.

Vojtěch PREISSIG
(1873–1944)
Engraver, painter, specialist in book design and illustration. Studied at the Prague School of Applied Arts under F. Ohmann. Lived in Paris from 1898 to 1902. Founded the journal *Česká grafika* (Czech Engraving) in 1905. In his engraving work he achieved a synthetic personal version of Art Nouveau (the album *Coloured Etchings*, 1906).

Antonín PROCHÁZKA
(1882–1945)
Painter. Member of The Eight. Expressionist and Cubist.

Arnošt PROCHÁZKA
(1869–1925)
Poet, translator and journalist. Founder of the *Moderní revue* (1894). Apologist of individualism and Decadence.

Jindřich PRUCHA
(1886–1914)
Painter. Studied at the Munich Academy (1911–1912). Combined Impressionism and Expressionism.

Václav RADIMSKY
(1867–1946)
Painter. Studied at the Academies of Prague and Vienna. Lived in France from the early 1890s, where he followed in the footsteps of Claude Monet. Landscape painter, Impressionist.

František Ladislav RIEGER (Chevalier)
(1818–1903)
Jurist, Czech political leader belonging to the Old Czech party.

Rainer Maria RILKE
(1875–1926)
Poet. His Prague origins mainly influenced his earliest literary work, as can be seen in his collection of poems, *Larenopfer*, 1896.

Václav ROŠTLAPIL
(1856–1930)
Architect. Studied at the Prague Institute of Advanced Technical Studies, and in Vienna under T. Hansen. Contributed to introducing the Neo-Baroque style into Prague architecture, especially with works such as the Straka Academy (Prague, Malá Strana, 1892).

František ROUS
(1872–1936)
Sculptor. Carried out a series of decorative works on Prague buildings (Municipal building).

Josef SAKAŘ
(1856–1936)
Architect. Prepared the plan for the modernization of Prague (1902).

Artuš SCHEINER
(1863–1938)
Illustrator, caricaturist and decorator. Illustrated tales by Adolf Wenig and executed murals in the Prague Municipal building.

Jakub SCHIKANEDER
(1855–1924)
Painter. Studied at the Academies of Prague and Munich. Professor at the Prague School of Applied Arts (from 1890). Painted Intimist views of Prague.

Bohuslav SCHNIRCH
(1845–1901)
Sculptor. In addition to the decoration of
the Prague National Theatre, his studio also
executed a number of works on Prague
buildings.

Josef SCHULZ
(1840–1917)
Architect. Professor at the Czech Institute of
Advanced Technical Studies in Prague.
Designed the Prague National Museum
(1890).

Josef SCHUSSER
(1864–1940)
Painter. Studied at the Prague Academy,
under V. Hynais, whose Luminism he
applied in his work.

Hanuš SCHWAIGER
(1854–1912)
Painter, illustrator. Studied at the Academies
of Prague and Vienna. Professor at the
Prague Academy (from 1901). Neo-Romantic, also inspired by realism.

Antonín SLAVÍČEK
(1870–1910)
Painter. Studied at the Prague Academy
under J. Mařák. Ran his own school for a
short time. Prominent figure in the Mánes
Union. Impressionistic. His series of Czech
country landscapes of Kameničky, and his
renditions of Prague, are considered a typically Czech manifestation of modern art.

Antonín SOVA
(1864–1928)
Poet and prose writer whose symbolism had
a strong psychological and social orientation
(the compilation *Vybouřené smutky* [Out-
pourings of sadness], 1897).

Jiří STIBRAL
(1859–1939)
Architect. Professor and from 1897 director
of the Prague School of Applied Arts.

Stanislav SUCHARDA
(1866–1916)
Sculptor. Studied at the Prague School of
Applied Arts under J. V. Myslbek, and at the

Vienna Academy. Professor at the Prague
School of Applied Arts (from 1809) and at
the Prague Academy (from 1915). Leading
figure in the Mánes Union. Creator of the
Monument to František Palacký in Prague
(1912).

František Xaver ŠALDA
(1807–1937)
Literary theorist, critic and writer. Also interested in the plastic arts from a theoretical
standpoint. Editor of the review *Volné směry*
from 1902 to 1907. From the outset of the
1890s, Šalda emerged in the forefront of
Czech culture, and his programme of Synthetism followed by Neo-Classicism also
found a vast echo in the plastic arts (*Boje o
zítřek* [Struggle for tomorrow, 1905).

Ladislav ŠALOUN
(1870–1946)
Sculptor. Trained in the workshops of
T. Seidan and B. Schnirch. Particularly
noted for his decoration of modern buildings, which was often carried out in collaboration with the architect O. Polívka (Municipal building, Praha Insurance Company,
the New Prague Town Hall). His sensitive
naturalism was influenced by the work of
Rodin. Creator of the *Monument to Jan Hus*
in Prague (1915).

Otakar ŠPANIEL
(1881–1955)
Sculptor, medallist. Studied at the School of
Medal-Making in Vienna, at the Prague
Academy under J. V. Myslbek, and under
Charpentier in Paris (1905–1912). Initially an
Impressionist, he subsequently became an
adept of Classicism.

Karel ŠPILLAR
(1871–1939)
Painter. Studied at the Prague School of
Applied Arts under F. Ženíšek. Sojourned
several times in Paris. Carried out a series of
decorative works for modern buildings in
Prague (Central Hotel, Municipal building).

Jan ŠTURSA
(1880–1925)
Sculptor. Studied at the Prague Academy
under J. V. Myslbek, working as his assistant

from 1908. After impressionist and decadent
beginnings, he became noted for his Synthetism and Classicism. Also created decorative sculptures, particularly in collaboration
with the architect J. Kotěra (Urbánek's house,
Prague New Town, 1913).

Maxmilián ŠVABINSKÝ
(1873–1962)
Painter and engraver. Studied at the Prague
Academy under M. Pirner. As a professor, he
specialized in engraving at the Academy
(from 1910). Important member of the
Mánes Union. He became particularly
prominent as a painter of portraits of cultural
personalities.

Karel TOMAN (real name Antonín
Bernášek)
(1877–1946)
Poet, lyrical, influenced by Decadence and
Anarchism (*Pohádky krve* [Tales of blood],
1898).

Joža ÚPRKA
(1861–1940)
Painter and engraver. Studied at the Academies of Prague and Munich. Resided in
Paris in 1893. Impressionist. Representative
of Moravian regionalism, he drew the subjects for his paintings exclusively from humble life in Slovakian Moravia.

Josef VÁCHAL
(1884–1969)
Painter, engraver, sculptor and writer. Auto-
didact. Member of the Sursum group. Influenced by anarchism, he later became a Symbolist and an Expressionist. Developed the
modern form of the grotesque, and was
inspired by popular fantasy, the cult of
magic, and religious heresies. Produced some
remarkable graphics printed on a hand-
press.

Jaroslav VRCHLICKY (real name Emil
Frída)
(1853–1912)
Poet, playwright, translator, essayist. Professor at the University of Prague. Representative of Czech literature, whose ideas and
work stimulated discussions of fundamentals
in the early 1890s.

Antonín Waigant
(1880–1018)
Sculptor. Executed a series of decorative
works on Prague buildings, in late geometrical and Neo-Classical style.

Bohumil Waigant
(1886–1930)
Architect. Studied at the Prague School of
Applied Arts under J. Kotěra. Representative
of the late geometrical decorative style.

Franz Werfel
(1890–1945)
Poet and writer. Representative of German
literature in Prague.

Antonín Wiehl
(1846–1910)
Architect. Studied at the Prague Institute of
Advanced Technical Studies under J. Zuck.
President of the Association of Engineers
and Architects. His late historicism, dubbed
"Czech Renaissance", shows a picturesqueness characteristic of the 1890s in Prague
(the Wiehl house, Prague New Town, 1896).

Josef Zasche
(1871–1957)
Architect. Studied at the Vienna Academy
under Hasenauer. Adept of decorative Classicism (Union of Viennese Banks building,
Prague Old Town, 1906–1908).

Julius Zeyer
(1841–1901)
Poet, playwright, prose writer. Contributed
to the *Almanach secese* (1896). His Neo-
Romanticism led to close contacts with the
young generation through its interest in
Symbolism. His vivid and fertile imagination, essentially focused on the question of
modern individualism, also influenced the
young plastic artists (F. Bílek, J. Preisler,
J. Zrzavý).

Jan Zrzavý
(1890–1977)
Painter, engraver, illustrator. Studied at the
Prague School of Applied Arts under E. Dítě
and J. Preisler. Founder-member of the Sursum group. Member of the Mánes Union
from 1912 to 1917. Late Symbolist.

Vladimir Župansky
(1869–1928)
Painter and engraver. Studied at the Prague
Academy under M. Pirner and V. Hynais.
Member of the Mánes Union. Particularly
noted for his posters and book illustrations
(poster for the Rodin exhibition in Prague,
1902).

Bibliography

A

Alfons Mucha et son œuvre, Paris, 1897.
Antonín Slavíček, výbor z jeho díla (Antonín Slavíček, selected works), Prague, 1910.

B

BENEŠ, V., *Antonín Slavíček*, Prague, 1938.
BENEŠOVÁ, M., *Česká architektura v proměnách dvou století 1780–1980* (Transformations in Czech architecture over two centuries, 1780–1980), Prague, 1984.
– "Secese v Čechách" (The Secession in Bohemia), *Architektura CSR* no. 2, 1975.
BÍLEK, F., *Jak mi dřeva povídala* (What the wood told me), Prague, 1946.
BRABCOVÁ, J., *Luděk Marold*, Prague, 1988.
BROŽOVÁ, J., "Artěl, mezník ve vývoji českého užitého umění" (Artěl, a turning-point in the evolution of Czech applied art), *Umění a remesla*, 1967.
BRYNYCHOVÁ, M. A., *Antonín Hudeček*, Prague, 1942.
BURCKHARDT, F., LAMAROVÁ, M., HERBENOVÁ, O., and ŠETLÍK, J., *Cubismo cecoslovacco – architetture e interni*, Milan, 1982.
BURCKHARDT, F., "Appunti sul cubismo nell'architettura cecoslovacca" (Notes on Cubism in Czech architecture), *Lotus International* no. 20, 1978.

C

České secesn, sklo – Böhmisches Jugendstilglas – Bohemian Glass of the Art Nouveau Period, Prague, 1985.
CHALUPNÝ, E., "František Bílek, Tvůrce a člověk" (František Bílek, the creator and the man), *České Budějovice*, 1970.
CZAGAN, F., "Kubistische Architektur in Böhmen" (Cubist Architecture in Bohemen), *Werk*, 56, 1969.

D

Dílo Jana Zrzavého, 1906–1940 (The work of Jan Zrzavý, 1906–1940). Ed. K. Šourek, Prague, 1941.
DOLENSKÝ, A., *Moderní česká grafika* (Modern Czech engraving), Prague, 1912. DOSTAL, O., PECHAR, J., and PROCHÁZKA, V., *Moderní architchtura v Československhu* (Modern Architecture in Czechoslovakia), Prague, 1970.

F

FÉDIT, D., *L'œuvre de Kupka,* Paris, 1966.
FILLA, E., *Otázky a úvahy* (Questions and reflections), Prague, 1930.
– *o výtvarném umění* (On plastic art), Prague, 1948.

G

GRÉMILLY, L. A., *Frank Kupka*, Paris, 1922.
GUTFREUND, O., *Zázemi tvorby* (The premises of creation). Ed. J. Šetlík, Prague, 1989.

H

HARLAS, F. X., *Malířstvi* (Painting), Prague, 1908.
HEWESI, L., "Hans Schwaiger", *Ver Sacrum*, 1898.
HOFMAN, W., "Kupka a Vídeň" (Kupka and Vienna), *Výtvarné umění* XVIII, 1968.

J

JEŽ, S., *Joža Úprka*, Prague, 1944.
JIRÁNEK, M., *Hanuš Schwaiger*, Prague, 1908.
– *Literární dílo* (Literary works), Prague, 1936.
– *Literární dílo I. Dojmy a potulky a jiné práce.* (Literary works I. Impressions and meanderings and other works), introduction by J. Kotalík, Prague, 1959.
– *o českém malířství moderním* (Modern Czech painting), Prague, 1934.
Jubilejní výstava zemská kráilovství Českého v Praze 1891 (Jubilee Exhibition of the countries of the Kingdom of Bohemia, 1891), Prague, 1894.

K

KOBLIHA, F., "Karel Hlaváček", *Hollar* XV, 1939.
– *Sedm statí o výtvarném umění* (Seven essays on plastic art), Prague, 1929.
KONŮPEK, J., *Život v umění* (Life in art), Prague, 1947.
KOPA, J., *Čeští malíři impresionisté* (Czech Impressionist painters), Brno, 1934.
KOTALÍK, J., *Jan Preisler*, Prague, 1968.
– "Moderní československé malířství" (Modern Czech painting), *Československo* II, 1947.
– "o trech umělcích secese, Bílek – Kupka – Mucha" (Three Secession artists, Bílek –

Kupka – Mucha), *Výtvarné umění* XVII, 1967.
KOTĚRA, J., *Meine und meiner Schüler Arbeiten, 1898–1901* (My Own and my Pupil's Work, 1898–1901), Vienna, 1902.
KOULA, J. E., *Nová česká architektura a její vývoj ve xx. století* (The new Czech architecture and its evolution in the twentieth century), Prague, 1940.
KOVÁRNA, F., *Antonín Slavíček,* Prague, 1930.
– *České malířství, let devadesátých* (Czech painting in the 1890s), Prague, 1940.
– *Ludvík Kuba*, Prague, 1935.
– "Pokolen, let devadesátých" (The 1890s Generation), *Dílo* XXXV, 1947.
KUBIŠTA, B., *Předpokɪady slohu* (The premises of style), Prague, 1947.
KVĚT, J., *Má vlast. Česká krajina v d'le našich malířů* (My native land. Czech landscape in the work of our painters). Prague, 1943.

L

LAMAČ, M., Hanuš Schwaiger, Prague, 1957.
– "Symbol v obrazech Jana Zrzavého" (The symbol in the paintings of Jan Zrzavý), *Výtvarné Umění* XIII, 1963.
– *Moderne tschechische Malerei 1907–1917* (La peinture moderne tchèque 1907–1917), Prague, 1967.
– *Jan Zrzavý*, Prague, 1980.
– *František Kupka*, Prague, 1984.
– *Osma a Shupina výtvarných umělců 1907–1917* (The Eight and the Group of Plastic Artists 1907–1917), Prague, 1988.
– *Cubisme tchèque*, Éditions du Centre Pompidou, Paris and Flammarion, Paris, 1992.
LAMAROVÁ, M., "Cubismo cd espressionismo nell'architettura e nel design" (Cubism and Expressionism in Architecture and Design), *Lotus International* no. 20, 1978.
LUKEŠ, Z., and SVOBODA, J., "Architekt Emil Králíček, zapomenutý zjev české secese a kubismu" (The architect Emil Králíček, a forgotten phenomenon of the Czech Secession and Czech Cubism), *Umění* XXXII, 1984.
– "Josef Zasche", *Umění* XXXVIII, 1990.

M

MACKOVÁ, O., *Otakar Lebeda,* Prague, 1957.

MÁDL, K. B., *Bohumil Kafka. Jeho dílo od r. 1900 do r. 1918* (Bohumil Kafka. His work from 1900 to 1918), Prague, 1919.
– *Joža Úprka*, Prague, 1901.
– *Umění včera a dnes* I (Art yesterday and today), Prague, 1904.
– *Umění včera a dnes* II, Prague, 1908.
– *Výbor z kritických projevů a drobných spisů* (Selection of criticisms and minor writings), Prague, 1959.
MAREK, J. R. (ed.), *Básník a sochař. Dopisy J. Zeyera a F. Bílka z let 1896–1901* (The poet and the sculptor. Letters by J. Zeyer and F. Bílek, 1896–1901), Prague, 1948.
MARGOLIUS, I., *Cubism in Architecture and the Applied Arts: Bohemia and France 1910–1914*, Londres, 1979.
MASARYKOVÁ, A., *České sochařství XIX. a XX. století* (Nineteenth- and twentieth-century Czech sculpture), Prague, 1963.
–*Josef Mařatka*, Prague, 1958.
– "The Secession in Eastern Central Europe: Czechoslovakia", *Art Nouveau Architecture*, London, 1979.
MATĚJČEK A., *Antonín Slavíček*, Prague, 1921.
– *Hlasy světa a domova* (Voices from the world and from home), Prague, 1931.
– *Max Švabinský*, Prague, 1937.
– *Antonín Hudeček*, Prague, 1947.
– *Jan Preisler*, Prague, 1950.
– *Jan Štursa*, Prague, 1950.
MATĚJČEK A., and WIRTH, Z., *L'Art tchèque contemporain*, Prague, 1920.
MRÁZOVÁ-SCHUSTEROVÁ, M., "Duchovní umění Františka Bílka" (The Spiritual Art of František Bílek), *Výtvarné umění* XVI, 1966.
MRÁZOVI, B., and M., *Secese* (The Secession), Prague, 1971.
MUCHA, J., *Alfons Mucha, the Master of Art Nouveau*, Prague – London, 1966.
MUCHA, J., and HENDERSON, M., *The graphic Work of Alfons Mucha*, London, 1973.
MUCHA, J., HENDERSON, M., and SCHARF, A., *Alfons Mucha, Posters and Photographs*, Londres – New York, 1971.
MŽYKOVÁ, M., *Vojtěch Hynais*, Prague, 1990.

N

NEBESKÝ, V. M., *L'Art moderne tchécoslovaque*, Prague, 1937.

NEŠLEHOVÁ, M., *Bohumil Kubišta*, Prague, 1984.
NOVOTNÝ, K., *Jan Štursa*, Prague, 1940.
– *Miloš Jiránek*, Prague, 1936.
NOVOTNÝ, V., *Jan Kotěra a jeho doba* (Jan Kotěra and his times), Prague, 1958.
– *Národní Galerie IV* (National Gallery IV), Prague, 1957.

P

Padesát let statní Uměleckoprůmyslové školy v Praze, 1885–1935 (Fiftieth anniversary of the Prague School of Applied Arts, 1885–1935), Prague, 1935.
PÁLENÍČEK, L., Mladý *Švabinský* (The young Švabinský), Gottwaldov, 1958.
PECHAR, J., and ULRICH, P., *Programy české architektury* (Czech architectural programmes), Prague, 1981.
PEČÍRKA, J., *Jan Preisler*, Prague, 1940.
– *Josef Mařatka*, Prague, 1942.
PEŠINA, J., *Česká moderní grafika* (Modern Czech engraving), Prague, 1940.
PETROVÁ, S., and OLIVIÉ, J. L. (under the direction of), *Verres de Bohême, 1400–1989*. *Chefs-d'œuvre des musées de Tchécoslovaquie*, Musée des Arts décoratifs, Paris, et Flammarion, Paris, 1989.
POŠVA, R., "Plastika a mozaika v průčelích Osvalda Polívky" (Sculpture and mosaics on facades by Osvald Polívka), *Uměí* XXXV, 1987.
PROCHÁZKA, V., *Sbírka českého sochařství na zbraslavském zámku* (The Zbraslav Castle collection of Czech sculpture), Prague, 1961.

R

RICKE, H., (ed.) *Lötz, Böhmisches Glas 1880–1940* (Lötz, le verre de Bohême 1880–1940), I–II, Werkmonografie, Munich, 1989.

S

ŠALDA, F. X., *Boje o zitrek* (Struggle for the future), Prague, 1905.
SIBLÍK, E., *J. Mařatka*, Prague, 1935.
ŠLAPETA, V., *Praha 1900–1978. Průvodce po moderni architektuře* (Prague 1900–1978. A guide to modern architecture), Prague, 1978.
SLAVÍČEK, A., Dopisy (Letters), Prague, 1954.
ŠMEJKAL, F., "Básník noci. K rané tvorbě

Fr. Koblihy" (Poet of the night. The early work of Fr. Kobliha), *Umění* XXIl, 1974.
– "Česká symbolistní grafika" (Czech symbolist engraving), *Umění* XVI, 1968.
– "La grafica simbolista cecoslovacca" (Czech symbolist engraving), *Arte illustrata* no. 3, 1970.
– "Povaha a význam secese" (Nature and significance of the Secession), *Výtvarné umění* XII, 1962.
– *Sursum 1910–1912*, Hradec Králové, 1976.
de Solier, R., "Prostor a barva u Kupky" (Space and colour in the work of Kupka), *Výtvarné umění* XVIII, 1968.
ŠTECH, V. V., *Čteni o Antonínu Slavíčovi* (Readings on Antonín Slavíček), Prague, 1947.
– *Moderní český dřevoryt* (Modern Czech wood engraving), Prague, 1933.
– *Pod povrchem tvarů* (Under the appearance of forms), Prague, 1941.
– *Včera a dnes* (Yesterday and today), Prague, 1921.
ŠTURSA, J., *Svědectv, současníků a dopisy* (Testimonies from contemporaries and letters), Prague, 1962.
– *Dílo* (Work), Prague, 1926.
ŠVABINSKÁ, E., *Vzpomínky z mládí* (Memories of youth), Prague, 1960.
ŠVÁCHA, R., *Od moderny k funkcionalismu* (From modern to functionalism), Prague, 1985.
SVRČEK, J. B., *F. X. Šaldy boje a zápasy o výtvarné umění* (F. X. Šalda's fight for modern art), Prague, 1947.
– *Miloš Jiránek*, Prague, 1932.

T

TOMAN, P., *Nový slovník čsl. výtvarných umělců* (New dictionary of Czech artists), 3rd edition, vol. I, Prague, 1947; vol. II, Prague, 1950.
TOMAN, P. H., *Zdenka Braunerová*, Prague, 1963.
TOMEŠ, J., *Antonín Slavíček*, Prague, 1966.

U

UHLÍŘ, L., *Ladislav Šaloun a jeho dílo* (Ladislav Šaloun and his work), Prague, 1930.

V

VACHTOVÁ, L., *František Kupka*, Prague, 1968.

VANCL, K., *František Kávan*, Liberec, 1962.
VLČEK, T., "Der Baum im Schaffen Vojtěch Preissigs", *Jahrbuch der Hamburger Kunstsammlungen* XXI, 1976.
– *Jakub Schikaneder*, Prague, 1985.
– *Praha 1900, Studie k dějinám kultury a umění Prahy v letech 1890–1914* (Prague 1900, Studies for the history of culture and art in Prague between 1890 and 1914), Prague, 1986.
– "Velkà lyra českého symbolistního básníka, proletáře Karla Hlaváčka" (The great lyre of a Czech Symbolist poet, the proletarian Karel Hlaváček), *Umění* XXIII, 1975.
– "Vojtěch Preissig", *Výtvarné umění* XVIII, 1968.
VOLAVKA, V., *J. V. Myslbek*, Prague, 1942.
VOLAVKOVÁ, H., *Maxmilián Švabinský*, Prague, 1977.
VONDRÁČKOVÁ, S., "Artěl", *Tvar* III, 1968.
Vybrané listy Antonína Slavíčka (Selected letters by Antonín Slavíček), Prague, 1930.

W
WIRTH, Z., and MATĚJČEK, A., *Česká architektura XIX. století, 1800–1920* (Nineteenth-century Czech architecture), Prague, 1922.
WITTLICH, P., *Art Nouveau Drawings (Zeichungen aus der Epoque des Jugendstils, Art Nouveau)*, Prague, 1974.
– "Art Nouveau in Czechoslovakia", *Art Nouveau, Jugendstil Architecture in Europe*, Munich, 1988.
– *Art Nouveau*, Prague–Paris, 1984.
– *Česká secese* (The Czech Secession), Prague, 1982.
– *České sochařstvi ve XX. století* (Twentieth-century Czech sculpture), Prague, 1978.
– *Jan Preisler, Kresby* (Jan Preisler, drawings), Prague, 1988.
– "Mladý Bohumil Kafka" (The young Bohumil Kafka), *Výtvarné umění* XII, 1962.
– "Secesní Orfeus. Symbolika formy v českém secesním sochařství" (The Art Nouveau Orpheus. The symbolism of forms in Czech Art Nouveau sculpture), *Umění* XVI, 1968.

Z
ŽÁKAVEC, F., *O českých výtvarnících* (Czech plastic artists), Prague, 1920.

– *Dílo Dušana Jurkoviče* (The work of Dušan Jurkovič), Prague, 1929.
– *Max Švabmský I*, Prague, 1933.
– *Max Švabmský II*, Prague, 1936.

Exhibition Catalogues

Jan Preisler, 1872–1918. National Gallery, Prague, 1964.
Česká Secese. Umění 1900 (The Czech Secession. Art, 1900). Alšova jihočeská galerie, Hluboká nad Vltavou. Moravská Gallery, Brno, 1966.
100 secesních plakátů (100 Art Nouveau posters), Uměleckoprůmyslové museum (Museum of Decorative Arts), Prague, 1966.
Tschechoslowakische Plastik von 1900 bis zur Gegenwart. Folkwang Museum, Essen, 1966.
František Bílek. Hlavního města Prahy Gallery, Prague, 1966.
Paris/Prague 1906–1930. Musée National d'Art Moderne, Paris, 1966.
Josef Váchal, 1906–1954. Hlavního města Prahy Gallery, Prague, 1966.
F. X. Šalda a vytvarné umění (F. X. Šalda and plastic art). Liberec Gallery, National Gallery, Prague, 1967–1968.
František Kupka, 1871–1957. Kunstverein, Cologne; Lenbachhaus, Munich; Stedelijk Museum, Amsterdam. National Gallery, Prague, 1967–1968.
Sculpture tchécoslovaque de Myslbek à nos jours. Musée Rodin, Paris, 1968.
La grafica bœma nel periodo dell'Art Nouveau (Graphic art in Bohemia during the Art Nouveau period). Calcografia Nazionale di Roma, Rome, 1968.
Vojtěch Preissig. Špálova Gallery et Nová síň, Prague, 1968.
Josef Mařatka, kresby a plastiky (Josef Mařatka, drawings and sculptures). Hlavního města Prahy Gallery, Prague, 1969.
Grafica Simbolista Cecoslovacca (Czechoslovak Symbolist Graphic Art). Galleria Michelucci, Florence, 1970.
České malířstvi XX. století ze sbírek Národní Galerie v Praze, dil I. Generace let devadesátých (Twentieth-century Czech painting in the collections of the Prague Nationla Gallery, part I. The 1890s Generation). National Gallery, Prague, 1971.
Edvard Munch og den tsjekkiske Kunst (Edvard Munch and Czech art). Munch Museet, Oslo, 1971.

Česky plakát 1890–1914 (Czech posters, 1890–1914). Uměleckopršmyslové museum, Prague, 1971.

České malířstvi 1850–1918 (Czech painting, 1850–1918). Hlavního města Prahy Gallery, Prague, 1971.

Václav Špála. Neue Berliner Galerie, Berlin, 1971.

České malířstvi XX. století ze sbírek Národní Galerie v Praze, dil II. Generace Osmy, Tvrdošijných, Umělecké besedy (Twentieth-century Czech painting in the collections of the Prague Nationla Gallery, part II. The Generation of the Eight, the Obstinates and the Artists' Society). National Gallery, Prague, 1973.

František Kobliha, výběr z celoživotního dila (František Kobliha, selected works). Krajská Gallery, Hradec Králové, 1973.

Max Švabinský, 1873–1962. National Gallery, Prague, 1973.

Tjeckist avantgarde 1900–1939 (The Czech avant-garde, 1900–1939). Kunstmuseum, Stockholm, Göteborg, 1973.

La Médaille tchécoslovaque. Musée de la Monnaie de Paris, 1973–1974.

Il Cubismo. Galeria Nazionale d'Arte Moderna, Rome, 1973–1974.

Zdenka Braunerová. Městké muzeum, Roztoky u Prahy, 1974.

Quido Kocian. Krajská galerie, Hradec Králové, 1975.

Frank Kupka, 1871–1957, A retrospective. The S. R. Guggenheim Museum, New York, 1975.

Mikoláš Aleš, 1852–1913. Alšova jihočeská galerie, Hluboká nad Vltavou, 1976.

Český kubistický interiér (Czech Cubist interiors). Uměleckopršmyslové Museum, Prague, 1976.

Czeh grafika és kisplastika 1900. Magyar Nemzeti Galeria, Budapest, 1977.

Jaroslav Horejc, souborné dílo (Jaroslav Horejc: Complete works). Galerie hlavního města Prahy, Prague, 1977.

Otakar Lebeda. National Gallery, Prague, 1977.

Jakub Schikaneder, 1855–1924. Středočeská Gallery, Prague, 1977–1978.

Otto Gutfreund 1889–1927. Edinburgh, 1979.

Ladislav Šaloun. Krajská Gallery, Hradec Králové, 1980.

Kupka–Gutfreund. Venice Biennial, 1980.

Alfons Mucha 1860–1939. Mathildenhöhe, Darmstadt; Grand Palais, Paris; National Gallery, Prague, 1980.

Josef Čapek. National Gallery, Prague, 1980.

Jan Štursa, 1880–1925. National Gallery, Prague, 1980.

Česká secese. Užité umění (Czech Art Nouveau. Applied arts). Uměleckopršmyslové museum, Prague, 1981.

Czechoslovakia Glass 1350–1980. The Corning Museum of Glass, Corning, 1981.

Alfons Mucha – Tjeckist art nouveau (Alfons Mucha – Czech Art Nouveau). Malmö, 1981–1982.

Alfons Mucha i češká secesija (Alfons Mucha and the Czech Secession). Národní muzej, Zagreb, Belgrade, 1982.

Antonín Procházka. Dum umění, Brno, 1982.

E. Munch a českém umění (E. Munch and Czech art). National Gallery, Prague, 1982.

Světlo v českém malířství generace 80. a 90. let (Light in Czech painting by the generation of the 'Eighties' and 'Nineties'), Hlavního města Prahy Gallery, Prague, 1982.

Filla, Gutfreund, Kupka. Tjeckist Kubism 1907–1927 (Filla, Gutfreund, Kupka. Czech Cubism 1907–1927), Konsthall, Malmö, 1982–1983.

Alfons Mucha und die tschechische Graphik um 1900. Stadtmuseum, Linz, 1983.

Česká kniha z přelomu XIX. a XX. století (Czech books at the turn of the century). Uměleckopršmyslové museum, Prague, 1983.

Zdenka Braunerová. Středočeské muzeum, Roztoky u Prahy, 1983.

Secesní keramika ze sbírek Krajského muzea v Teplicích (Art Nouveau ceramics in the Teplice Regional Museum). Teplice. 1983.

Alfons Mucha. Tokyo, 1983.

Vojtěch Preissig. Galerie výtvarného umění Roudnice nad Labem, 1983.

Czech Sculpture 1867–1967. National Museum of Wales, Cardiff, 1983.

Secesní sklo z Klášterského mlýna (Kláštersky Mlýn Art Nouveau glass). Muzeum Šumavy, Kašperské hory, 1984.

Josef Váchal, 1884–1969. Oblastní galerie výtvarného umění, Roudnice nad Labem, 1984.

Pavel Janák, 1882–1956. Architektur und Kunstgewerbe. SemperDepot, Vienna, 1984.

Die tschechische Malerei des XIX. Jh. aus der National Galerie Prag. Österreichische Galerie, Vienna, 1984.

Tschechische Kunst 1878–1914. Auf dem Weg in die Moderne. Mathildenhöhe, Darmstadt, 1984–1985.

Maxmilián Pirner, 1854–1924. National Gallery, Prague, 1987.

František Kupka. Palazzo Massari, Ferrare,1987.

Il simbolismo cosmico di Jan Konůpek (1883–1950). Galleria Carlo Virgilio, Rome, 1987.

Arte a Praga, Arte a Parigi. Impressionismo simbolismo cubismo. Palazzo dei Conservatori di Roma, Milan, 1988.

Julius Zeyer a výtvarné umýní. Sochy obrazy a sny (Julius Zeyer and plastic art. Statues, paintings and dreams). Vodňany Gallery. Středočeské muzeum, Roztoky u Prahy, 1988.

Czech Modernism, 1900–1945. The Museum of Fine Arts, Houston, 1989.

Tschechischer Kubismus. Architektur und Design, 1910–1925. Vitra Design Museum, Weil am Rhein, 1991.

Alfons Mucha. Idee und Gestalt (Alfons Mucha. Concept and form). Museum Fridericianum, Kassel, 1991.

Index